Microsoft Power Apps Cookbook

Become a pro Power Apps maker by applying practical use cases to solve ever-evolving business challenges

Eickhel Mendoza

BIRMINGHAM—MUMBAI

Microsoft Power Apps Cookbook

Copyright © 2021 Packt Publishing

Group Product Manager: Aaron Lazar

Publishing Product Manager: Alok Dhuri

Senior Editor: Rohit Singh

Content Development Editor: Kinnari Chohan

Technical Editor: Rashmi Choudhari

Copy Editor: Safis Editing

Project Coordinator: Francy Puthiry

Proofreader: Safis Editing

Indexer: Pratik Shirodkar

Production Designer: Nilesh Mohite

First published: January 2021

Production reference: 2190321

Published by Packt Publishing Ltd.

Livery Place

35 Livery Street

Birmingham

B3 2PB, UK.

978-1-80056-955-3

www.packt.com

To my wife, Pili, the strongest woman who ever lived, and to my daughter, Amanda, the spark of my life.

Without their love and support, nothing would make sense.

– Eickhel Mendoza

Packt.com

Subscribe to our online digital library for full access to over 7,000 books and videos, as well as industry leading tools to help you plan your personal development and advance your career. For more information, please visit our website.

Why subscribe?

- Spend less time learning and more time coding with practical eBooks and Videos from over 4,000 industry professionals

- Improve your learning with Skill Plans built especially for you

- Get a free eBook or video every month

- Fully searchable for easy access to vital information

- Copy and paste, print, and bookmark content

Did you know that Packt offers eBook versions of every book published, with PDF and ePub files available? You can upgrade to the eBook version at packt.com and as a print book customer, you are entitled to a discount on the eBook copy. Get in touch with us at customercare@packtpub.com for more details.

At www.packt.com, you can also read a collection of free technical articles, sign up for a range of free newsletters, and receive exclusive discounts and offers on Packt books and eBooks.

Contributors

About the author

Eickhel Mendoza is a Microsoft Business Applications MVP with many years of experience from various roles in project management, Microsoft Azure development and operations, and, most recently, in Microsoft Power Platform technologies.

He is a team lead of the Business Apps department and oversees all projects related to Microsoft 365, Power Platform, and web development.

He has contributed to significant community events, such as the Power Platform World Tour, Global Azure Bootcamp, Microsoft 365 Developer Bootcamp, and Dynamics 365 Saturdays in recent years.

Eickhel also coordinates the TenerifeDev and Power Platform Canarias user groups with a group of like-minded developers eager to share their knowledge in different technologies.

I want to thank all the people who have helped shape my love of technology: my parents, my school teachers, and my co-workers, who always challenge me to create great things.

About the reviewer

Rebekka Aalbers-deJong started her career as a regular business but switched to work in IT over 10 years ago, first as an IT administrator, later as a technology consultant. She is an active contributor to the Microsoft Power Platform community as a speaker, blogger, and organizer of a local user group. She received the Microsoft MVP award for Business Applications for her contributions to the technical community in 2019.

Rebekka works as a technology consultant at Dutch Microsoft Partner Macaw, where she combines her experience as a non-IT business user, IT administrator, and software consultant to help companies implement Power Platform and build Power Platform solutions.

Rebekka lives in the Netherlands together with her husband and their two cats.

Packt is searching for authors like you

If you're interested in becoming an author for Packt, please visit authors. packtpub.com and apply today. We have worked with thousands of developers and tech professionals, just like you, to help them share their insight with the global tech community. You can make a general application, apply for a specific hot topic that we are recruiting an author for, or submit your own idea.

Table of Contents

Preface

1

Building pixel-perfect solutions with Canvas Power Apps

2

Building from data with model-driven apps

3

Choosing the right data source for your applications

4

Automating processes with Power Automate

5

Extending the Platform

8

Empowering your applications with no code Artificial Intelligence

9

Discovering the Power Platform admin center

10
Tips, Tricks, and Troubleshooting

11
Advanced Techniques with Power Apps Component Framework

Other Books You May Enjoy

Index

Preface

Power Apps is a low-code platform to build applications from Microsoft. With this platform, you can create solutions to solve your business needs while integrating with other components of the Power Platform, such as Power Automate or Power BI.

Quite different from the complete documentation that exists online, you will find that this is not your regular reference book. Instead, this book deals with real-world scenarios and experiences to help you get a headstart in your Power Apps projects.

Using a curated set of chapters, you will discover different aspects of Power Apps, from building canvas apps, designing model-driven solutions, extending with custom connectors, and integrating with other platforms to moving to the pro-developer side using Power Apps Component Framework.

Who this book is for

Since we are covering practical use cases, basic knowledge of building applications using Power Apps is required to take advantage of the solutions explored in this book. You will get a step-by-step tutorial on building the recipes crafted for each chapter.

What this book covers

Chapter 1, Building pixel-perfect Solutions with Canvas Power Apps, starts with the best practices for building canvas apps and continues with building solutions, including coverage of data source setup.

Chapter 2, Building from data with Model-Driven Apps, continues our journey by following a collection of recipes joined together to create an all-around help desk solution.

Chapter 3, Choosing the right Data Source for your applications, will help you to make a sound decision when determining the data source of your applications. This chapter also explains the importance of the licensing model on this platform.

Chapter 4, Automating Processes with Power Automate, focuses on several use cases to improve business processes using this component of the Power Platform.

Chapter 5, *Extending the Platform*, builds upon the concept of enhancing the application building process by using components. We will also learn how to extend the platform by creating custom connectors.

Chapter 6, *Improving User Experience*, looks at how to enrich your user interfaces to make your applications more appealing to end users. This chapter will also cover how to create a responsive application using the latest techniques available in Power Apps.

Chapter 7, *Power Apps Everywhere*, explains all the possible ways to use and integrate Power Apps on many platforms, from mobile device consumption to embedding scenarios on SharePoint and Power BI, without forgetting the latest on Microsoft Teams development, including Dataverse for Teams.

Chapter 8, *Empowering Your Applications with no code Artificial Intelligence*, focuses on using AI Builder solutions to improve our applications and processes by bringing artificial intelligence into the mix.

Chapter 9, *Discovering the Power Platform admin center*, is about learning how to manage the Power Platform using the tools and settings available in this admin center.

Chapter 10, *Tips, Tricks, and Troubleshooting*, offers a collection of hints from the application building experience in Power Apps with a set of topics that will help solve or improve a wide variety of scenarios.

Chapter 11, *Advanced Techniques with Power Apps Component Framework*, tackles the pro-developer side of things by building a Power Apps Component Framework component from scratch. We will look at setting up our development environment and deploying the component to an application.

To get the most out of this book

Before diving into building solutions with Power Apps, you are going to need a Microsoft 365 subscription. You might have one already from your work organization, but if you want to have a playground to build apps, I'm going to give you two suggestions.

Microsoft 365 Developer Program

This program allows you to have a Microsoft 365 subscription with many features available: 25 E5 user licenses, apps such as SharePoint and Microsoft Teams, learning resources, and more. It's the perfect sandbox environment to create your apps, not only to build Power Apps but also to learn other technologies from the whole Microsoft 365 ecosystem. This subscription renews automatically every 3 months as long as you are actively using it.

To get more information, please refer to `https://developer.microsoft.com/en-us/microsoft-365/dev-program`

Power Apps Community Plan

This option is the ideal choice if you want a more focused approach to the Power Platform. It offers a free environment for individual use with the same advantages of a paid plan, including premium connectors. However, there are some restrictions, such as app sharing, the need for a Microsoft organizational account, and the ability to use dataflows.

This subscription has no renewal process; it's perpetual. For more information, please visit `https://powerapps.microsoft.com/en-us/communityplan`.

Power Apps paid plans

The licensing model on this platform depends on the type of connector needed for your data sources. Standard connectors such as the one used for SharePoint don't require an additional license besides Microsoft 365, but premium or custom connectors do require a Power Apps license:

- **Per app**: Allows building and using two apps (canvas or model-driven) plus one Power Apps portal
- **Per user**: Allows building and using unlimited apps (within service limits)

To get more insight into the licensing model, please visit `https://powerapps.microsoft.com/en-us/pricing/`.

If you are using the digital version of this book, we advise you to type the code yourself or access the code via the GitHub repository (link available in the next section). Doing so will help you avoid any potential errors related to the copying and pasting of code.

Download the example code files

You can download the example code files for this book from GitHub at `https://github.com/PacktPublishing/Microsoft-Power-Apps-Cookbook`. In case there's an update to the code, it will be updated on the existing GitHub repository.

We also have other code bundles from our rich catalog of books and videos available at `https://github.com/PacktPublishing/`. Check them out!

Download the color images

We also provide a PDF file that has color images of the screenshots/diagrams used in this book. You can download it here: https://static.packt-cdn.com/downloads/9781800569553_ColorImages.pdf

Conventions used

There are a number of text conventions used throughout this book.

Code in text: Indicates code words in text, database table names, folder names, filenames, file extensions, pathnames, dummy URLs, user input, and Twitter handles. Here is an example: "Mount the downloaded WebStorm-10*.dmg disk image file as another disk in your system."

A block of code is set as follows:

```
html, body, #map {
  height: 100%;
  margin: 0;
  padding: 0
}
```

When we wish to draw your attention to a particular part of a code block, the relevant lines or items are set in bold:

```
[default]
exten => s,1,Dial(Zap/1|30)
exten => s,2,Voicemail(u100)
exten => s,102,Voicemail(b100)
exten => i,1,Voicemail(s0)
```

Any command-line input or output is written as follows:

```
$ mkdir css
$ cd css
```

Bold: Indicates a new term, an important word, or words that you see onscreen. For example, words in menus or dialog boxes appear in the text like this. Here is an example: "Select **System info** from the **Administration** panel."

> Tips or important notes
> Appear like this.

Get in touch

Feedback from our readers is always welcome.

General feedback: If you have questions about any aspect of this book, mention the book title in the subject of your message and email us at customercare@packtpub.com.

Errata: Although we have taken every care to ensure the accuracy of our content, mistakes do happen. If you have found a mistake in this book, we would be grateful if you would report this to us. Please visit www.packtpub.com/support/errata, selecting your book, clicking on the Errata Submission Form link, and entering the details.

Piracy: If you come across any illegal copies of our works in any form on the Internet, we would be grateful if you would provide us with the location address or website name. Please contact us at copyright@packt.com with a link to the material.

If you are interested in becoming an author: If there is a topic that you have expertise in and you are interested in either writing or contributing to a book, please visit authors.packtpub.com.

Reviews

Please leave a review. Once you have read and used this book, why not leave a review on the site that you purchased it from? Potential readers can then see and use your unbiased opinion to make purchase decisions, we at Packt can understand what you think about our products, and our authors can see your feedback on their book. Thank you!

For more information about Packt, please visit packt.com.

1
Building pixel-perfect solutions with Canvas Power Apps

Power Apps is the platform of choice for building business solutions using a low-code method. This approach enables the rise of the citizen developer, a being inside every organization who is keen on learning technology, which also brings the expertise of the business process to which this person belongs.

One of its versions, canvas Power Apps, allows the creation of pixel-perfect implementations of user interfaces. As its name suggests, it brings a variety of tools to build any imaginable design into your applications. Whether it's a critical business application or a mobile tracking system, canvas apps gives you all the tools required to design your app.

During this chapter, we will discover how to create a sample of real-life applications that will give you an insight into different approaches when building canvas applications: standalone and embedded Power Apps. We will also learn how to set up different types of data sources for our applications.

This chapter consists of the following recipes:

- Discovering best practices when building canvas apps
- Creating an incident tracking solution – Setting up the data source
- Creating an incident tracking solution – Building the user interface
- Embedding an expense tracking list with SharePoint list Power Apps
- Creating a Power App from existing data

Discovering best practices when building canvas apps

Setting up data sources, defining business process flows, creating user interfaces; all these tasks are pieces of an application building process. These pieces come together to accomplish the main goal: to build a solution that solves a specific need.

One of the things that you need to consider is the maintainability of your app. Whether you are in charge of fixing bugs or adding new features in the future, using best practices is always a good idea. No matter the technology you are using, well-documented code is easier to maintain.

Even though Power Apps is a low-code platform, you need to consider certain things before you start building applications. Like any other developer team, you need to establish code standards. These standards allow your team to be more productive by setting predefined patterns for variable naming, control usage, and coding methodology.

Variable naming

Proper naming gives your developers instant insight into the scope of your variables. For example, if a variable name prefix starts with lcl (short for local), it means it's value will only be available on the current screen. On the other hand, using gbl (short for global) means that this variable is accessible across the whole application.

These examples might seem trivial, but if another developer needs to maintain your app or if your app serves as a template for other apps in your organization, setting these patterns from the start can help the app building and maintaining process.

Control usage

One of the vital elements of an application's success is performance. If an application is slow to start or takes several seconds to perform a task, it hurts user adoption.

Here are a few examples of this:

- Having a great-looking app using many controls to build its user interface but hurting performance each time the screens get rendered.

- Displaying data to the user using a gallery inside a gallery. This approach might be tempting to present master-detail data, but this would be a significant slowdown in your application.

To avoid this, you need to learn the performance points of your platform. In Power Apps, one of the main recommendations for improving responsiveness is to reduce the number of controls.

Coding methodology

This concept describes a set of rules to regulate the application building process in a low-code team. Your solution infrastructure can also help you make an informed decision on how to build your application:

- If you have data that rarely changes, you can create collections on application start to avoid round-trips each time data is required. Even more, if you have data that never changes, you can import this as static data inside your app for speedier access.

- Taking advantage of the features available in your data source can significantly improve your application building process and even its performance. For example, when using Dataverse or a relational database, there is a significant difference when querying data if you use a data source view instead of building the actual query in your application logic, especially if it needs complex relationships. Using these views gives you cleaner code while also improving performance. This improvement relays on the data source engine as it is the one that executes the data processing instead of the Power App.

These are examples of practices you can coordinate with your team when building apps. For a detailed list of best practices, please refer to https://powerapps.microsoft.com/en-us/blog/powerapps-canvas-app-coding-standards-and-guidelines/

Creating an incident tracking solution – Setting up the data source

Tracking processes is always an accustomed request from customers everywhere. As in any development process, the first step is to gather all the requirements needed to fulfill the business need; this will then help us design the data structure to support our application.

This recipe will set up the required fields in a SharePoint list to be our data source. We will also apply some settings to this list to make it as performant as it should be.

Explanation and overview

For this recipe, we will use SharePoint as a data source, so we will start by creating a list. The actual list creation process is pretty straightforward, but that leaves us with plenty of time for planning.

SharePoint Online performance considerations

When working with SharePoint Online, you need to keep in mind that we are working on a web application with specific response and performance levels to provide the best user experience. To meet this, Microsoft has set a view threshold of 5,000 elements per list. Even though a list can hold up to 30 million items, querying data exceeding this limit will result in platform errors and will make the list unresponsive.

These are a few recommendations to keep your lists performant:

- Set an index for the columns you wish to filter. Always keep this in mind beforehand since you cannot change it if you have already exceeded the threshold.

- Prepare views for lists that might carry a large number of items by segments. Examples can be categories, years, and departments.

- Build your views with no more than 12 people, lookup, and managed metadata columns to avoid performance issues.

For reference on this subject, check out the following links:

- https://support.microsoft.com/en-us/office/manage-large-lists-and-libraries-in-sharepoint-b8588dae-9387-48c2-9248-c24122f07c59

- https://support.microsoft.com/en-us/office/use-filtering-to-modify-a-sharepoint-view-3d8efc52-0808-4731-8f9b-3dfaeacea3d4

Getting ready

Before diving into developing solutions with Power Apps, you are going to need a Microsoft 365 subscription. Please refer to the Preface section of this book about suggestions on getting a playground to build your apps.

How to do it...

1. Go to the SharePoint site that is going to hold the two lists. Throughout the book, we will use a fake organization called AMPI Currents, which has this site: `https://ampicurrents.sharepoint.com/sites/Trackers`

2. Select **+ New** and then **List**, which will ask for a list name and description. Please input `Clients` and leave the **Description** field blank. This action will create a list with a default structure:

Figure 1.1 – List creation procedure

3. Click on the gear icon on the top-right corner and select **List settings** to add and update the columns. This option will open all the configuration options available for a list, but we will be focusing on the **Columns** section.

4. First, click on the **Title** column to edit it. We are doing this for user interface reasons. This field lets you open the selected record quickly from the list view, so we will set it as the client's name. Once it opens, just rename the column name to `Name` and then click **OK**.

5. To add the rest of the fields, click **Create column** and then set the column name and type as seen in the following table:

Column name	Column data type	Required
Name	Single line of text	Yes
Address	Multiple lines of text	No
Phone	Single line of text	No
Email	Single line of text	No

Figure 1.2 – Clients list columns

6. Repeat *steps 2* and *3* for the **Incidents** list. Rename the **Title** column to Incident and set the columns seen in the following table:

Column name	Column data type	Required
Customer Name	Lookup	Yes
Date	Date and Time	Yes
Priority	Choice	Yes
Comments	Multiple lines of text	No

Figure 1.3 – Incident list columns

Choice means that it will use a provided list of items to choose from, and **Lookup** means that this column will link to another list that holds another set of data. In this case, we will use this column to relate the incidents to the clients.

7. Add the **Customer Name** column. Select the **Lookup** type and then, in the **Get information from** dropdown, select the **Clients** list we created before. Leave the rest of the options as default.

8. For the **Priority** column, select the **Choice** type and replace the list of choices with **High**, **Medium**, and **Low**. Set the **Default** value as **Low**.

9. Lastly, when adding the **Comments** column, specify the type of text to be **Plain text** to prevent formatting issues later when designing your app. We need to make this change because, otherwise, SharePoint will store this data in HTML to maintain the formatting and will make the text look different from the rest of the app.

Now that we have our lists in place, let's see how this list and its relationships come together.

How it works...

After setting up our data source, we can now start building some test data to use in our Power App.

Click on the gear icon in the top-right corner, select **Site contents**, and select the **Clients** list:

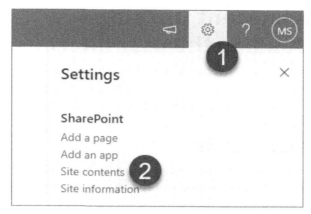

Figure 1.4 – Site contents option

Now, let's click on **+ New** to add some random test data:

- **Name**: Yennu Enterprises
- **Address**: One Yennu road
- **Phone**: +1 555 800 5555
- **Email**: sales@yennu.com

Add as much data as you like. Now, repeat the same steps with the **Incidents** list by clicking on the gear icon and selecting the list from **Site contents**.

For **Customer Name**, you will see data loaded from the **Clients** list, and the **Priority** column will let you choose from the previously defined elements:

- **Incident**: Failure in the programming of the executive elevator
- **Customer Name**: Yennu Enterprises (link)
- **Date**: 11/17/2020
- **Priority**: High
- **Comments**: The elevator returns itself to the last floor when idle.

Again, add as much data as you want, and now we are moving forward to the next section, where we will build a Power App from this data structure.

Creating an incident tracking solution – Building the user interface

Before designing interfaces, we need to ask ourselves what needs our application will solve. This analysis will help us decide which technology we will use, what infrastructure is holding every piece of our solution, and even how our end users will consume it.

Explanation and overview

We know the technology, and, with the help of the previous recipe, we have the data source section of our infrastructure solved. It's time to leverage Power Apps to automate the creation of the building blocks of our application.

Power Apps integrates deeply inside SharePoint as a tool to build solutions rapidly with its low-code principles. This integration allows the creation of a completely functional application in a few steps.

How to do it...

1. Go to the SharePoint site that has your lists. Click the gear icon on the top-right corner, select **Site contents**, and select the **Incidents** list.

2. On the list's toolbar, select **Power Apps** and then **Create an app**. This action will open up a dialog asking you the name of your application:

Figure 1.5 – Power Apps integration inside SharePoint

3. After a little while, a brand-new application gets created with the base functionalities: records manipulation, search, listing, and sorting. It's now time to polish our application to have the desired results.

4. First, let's edit our application title to match our application name and not the list. Go to **Tree view**, expand **BrowseScreen1**, and select the **LblAppName1** label. On the right pane, change the value of the label by changing the **Text** value. Do the same for the rest of the screens.

5. If you followed our example list data, you might see that some of the incident's text is not complete. To fix this, select the **Title1** label from **BrowseScreen1** and, in its properties, deselect **Wrap**. This change will add an ellipsis, making the user aware that there is more information:

Figure 1.6 – Disabling Wrap for long text

6. Next, let's fix **EditScreen1** to allow more space for the comments data card. At this moment, we won't be using the attachments data card, so by expanding **EditForm1** and selecting **Attachments_DataCard1**, we can uncheck its visible property.

7. Increase **Comments_DataCard2**'s **Height** value and then increase the **DataCardValue10** control to match the new size, and finally, set the **Mode** property to Multiline to fix the text's vertical alignment. Do the same for the **Incident** data card if you want it to have more space as well.

8. Finish up by changing the colors, fonts, and control alignment to match your style. In *Chapter 6, Improving User Experience*, we will cover some techniques to apply a style makeover to your application.

How it works...

Now that we have created our app from SharePoint data, we can take it for a test drive. The Power Apps Studio gives you a preview functionality for testing while you are developing it. You can do it in two ways:

- Go back to **BrowseScreen1** and then press the play button on the top right of the Studio interface. This action will execute the application to interact with it, just as if you were running it from your device of choice.

Figure 1.7 – Power Apps studio preview feature

- Press the *Alt* key (*Option* on a Mac) to test a particular control. For example, if I press *Alt* and then click on a button, it will perform its `OnSelect` action. This way, you can test a specific control without leaving the design mode of the studio.

Important note

Never rely on these testing methods to deploy an application to production. Power Apps Studio gives you a responsive simulator to test your app based on a low resolution. While it serves you well for functionality testing, it's no match for real device testing. You need to check your app on the user medium of consumption. Examples include SharePoint, Teams, and mobile devices.

This application will allow you to have an incident tracking system for your organization. You can now test it by creating new incidents or editing existing ones. The Power Apps template should have taken care of the core functionality already, so verify your specific requirements, such as maximum text length, user interface design changes, and the like. Making subtle user interface changes such as font names and sizes can improve the overall look of the application:

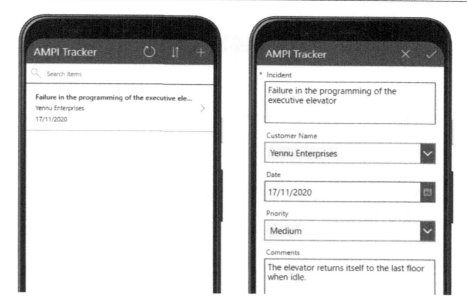

Figure 1.8 – User interface changes for the incident tracking solution

Embedding an expense tracking list with SharePoint list Power Apps

Earlier, in the *Creating an incident tracking solution – setting up the data source* recipe, we discussed how to design our SharePoint data source. We will use the same steps to create our data source for this recipe.

Explanation and overview

Planning for this data source requires the creation of related columns to track expenses. As a template, we could use the following options.

Projects

This list will hold project information, which will help us link the fees and the customer who owns the project. For this connection, we will use the customer list created in the previous recipe.

Expenses

This list will save the information related to the expense.

How to do it...

1. Go to the desired SharePoint site and create the projects lists by selecting **+ New** and then **List**:

Figure 1.9 – List creation process

2. Once the list gets created, click on the gear icon at the top right and select **List settings**. Add the following columns by clicking on the **Create column** link inside the **Columns** section:

Column name	Column data type	Required
Name	Single line of text	Yes
Client	Lookup	Yes

Figure 1.10 – Projects list columns

3. To create the expenses list, click on the gear icon at the top right, and then **Site contents**. From there, select **+ New | List** from the toolbar. Repeat *step 1* with the following columns:

Column name	Column data type	Required
Expense	Single line of text	Yes
Date	Date	Yes
Category	Choice	Yes
Project Name	Lookup	No
Amount	Currency	Yes
Comments	Multiple lines of text	No

Figure 1.11 – Expenses list columns

For the **Category** column, use these choices as an example: **Travel**, **Transport**, **Supplies**, and **Meals**. Add as much data as you like.

4. Click on the gear icon on the top-right corner, select **Site contents**, and then select the **Expenses** list.

5. On the list's toolbar, select **Power Apps** and then **Customize forms**. This action will automatically create an app based on the list structure. This time, it will build an app with only one form and one particular control called **SharePointIntegration**:

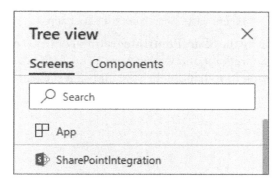

Figure 1.12 – SharePointIntegration control inside Power Apps

6. Make relevant changes to your app, such as increasing the comments' height, resizing the attachments' control, and making style changes.

7. Save and publish your app.

How it works...

As you can see, the new application differs from the one that we created earlier because this one gets embedded inside the SharePoint list. It replaces the regular list's data entry mechanism by displaying the Power App whenever you want to view, edit, or add new records:

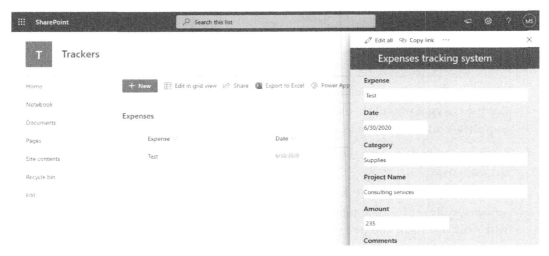

Figure 1.13 – SharePoint list power app

This integration gets done by the **SharePointIntegration** control we mentioned earlier. It acts as a bridge between SharePoint and Power Apps to catch the data events (view, create, and edit) while also allowing us to handle the save and cancel events:

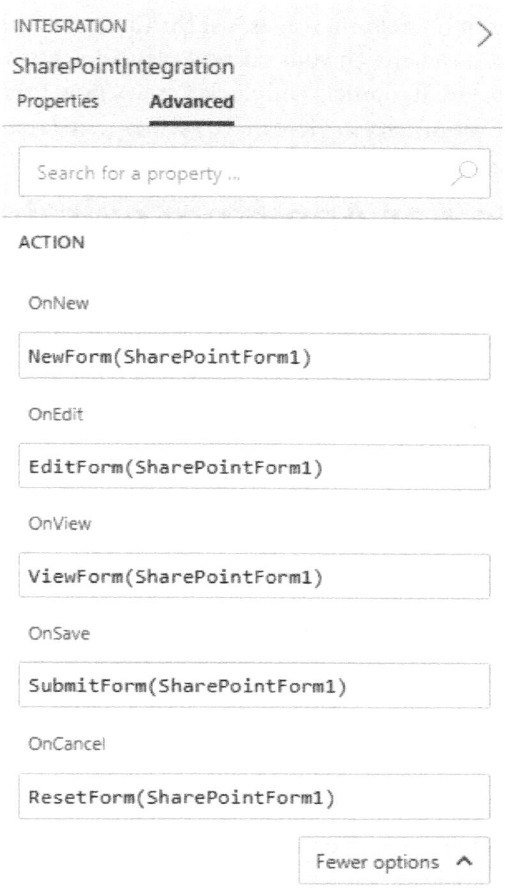

Figure 1.14 – SharePointIntegration actions

These actions are regular code blocks that get triggered depending on each event.

Embedding Power Apps inside a SharePoint list gives us the flexibility to control how the data gets entered, improve the data validation, and even allow connections to other services besides SharePoint, just to name a few examples.

See also

Think outside the box when building embedded Power Apps. They are not only there to improve data entry forms. You can create full-fledged solutions inside your lists. Please refer to the following example showcased on the Power Apps blog: `https://powerapps.microsoft.com/en-us/blog/island-council-of-tenerife-organizes-community-events-using-the-power-platform`

Embedding Power Apps in SharePoint lists is just the tip of the iceberg. There are many more scenarios where you can enrich your current platforms by integrating Power Apps: Teams and SharePoint pages, to name a couple. Want to know more? Please refer to *Chapter 7, Power Apps Everywhere*, to view more recipes that extend the use of Power Apps.

Creating a Power App from existing data

Power Apps is the ideal choice when it comes to building solutions for the enterprise. These solutions are often needed to improve a particular process when it comes to data handling. Sometimes, you will start from scratch, but most of the time, the data structure will already exist but in need of a robust and flexible application to handle it.

For these situations, there are some ready-made processes in the Microsoft ecosystem that allow the creation of applications from a particular set of data. We will discover these processes from Azure, SharePoint, and the Power Apps platform itself.

Getting ready

Azure is a platform that provides a wide range of cloud services for all kinds of scenarios, for example, application development, data analysis, and cognitive services. To work with Azure, you will need to have an active subscription. To test the capabilities of this platform, you can apply for a free account by signing up here: `https://azure.microsoft.com/en-us/free/`

As this recipe requires that we start from data, we will need to have an Azure SQL database provisioned. If you don't have one already, please follow the steps of this quickstart to create one: `https://docs.microsoft.com/en-us/azure/azure-sql/database/single-database-create-quickstart?tabs=azure-portal`

How to do it...

To gather data from an existing Azure SQL database, take the following steps:

1. Go to the Azure portal, `https://portal.azure.com`, and from the main search, enter `SQL databases` and select the service from the list, as seen in the following screenshot:

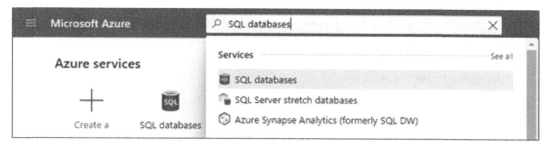

Figure 1.15 – Azure SQL databases

2. A list of databases will appear for you to pick. Select the one that has the data needed for your application. This action will open the configuration page, sometimes called the blade, with all the settings to configure the database.

3. On the left pane of the configuration page, you will find a section called **Power Platform**, in which you can start working with any of the services available:

    Power BI, to connect and visualize the data from this database

    Power Automate, to automate processes using SQL server templates

    Power Apps, to use this database as one of the data sources of your application

4. Select **Power Apps** and then **Get started**, as seen in the following screenshot:

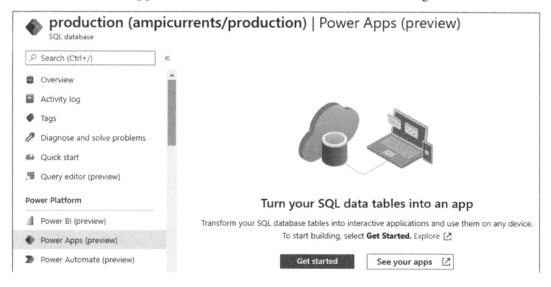

Figure 1.16 – Power Apps option in Azure

5. The Azure portal will open a **Create an app** form that will gather the required settings for your app. If this form is disabled, it means that you don't have an active Power Apps plan. You can apply for a trial one by clicking on the **Start trial** link on the form's header.

6. Enter the app name and the credentials to authenticate to the database in the **SQL Authentication** section. Finally, select a table from the list of tables in the database. The following is a sample form to create an app:

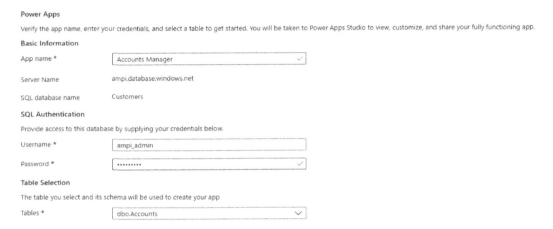

Figure 1.17 – Create an app form

7. Click **Create** to start the app building process. If the Power Apps portal doesn't open, check whether your browser of choice has blocked the popup. In the following screenshot, you can see what happens in Microsoft Edge; you can click the link or select to always allow popups from the Azure portal:

Figure 1.18 – Pop-up blocking in Microsoft Edge

8. When the process finishes, you will see an application created from the table data with a browse screen and a detail screen:

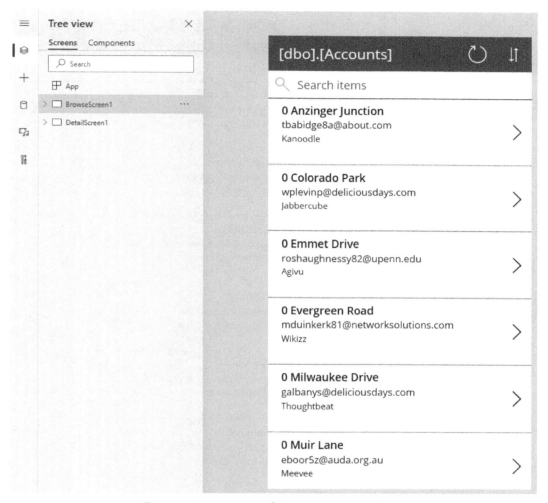

Figure 1.19 – Power app from Azure SQL Database

Getting data from a SharePoint list is done as follows:

1. Go to your SharePoint site and open the list you want to use in your app. From the toolbar, select **Power Apps | Create an app**. On the right, a new pane will open, asking you the name of the app. Enter it and click **Create**.

2. The Power Apps portal will start building the application from the selected list. This time, the template used to generate the app will also include an edit screen:

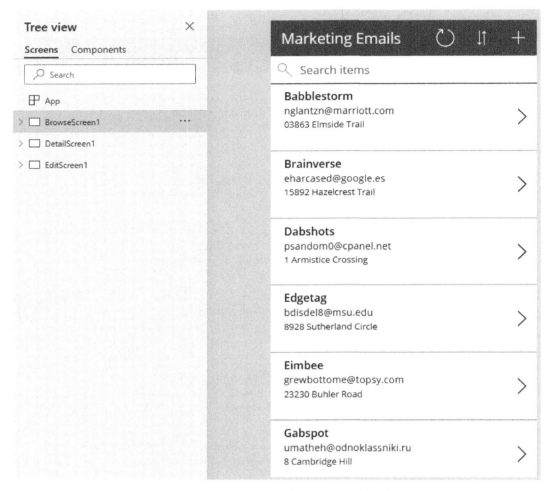

Figure 1.20 – Power app from SharePoint list

Creating apps from data using the Power Apps portal is done as follows:

1. Go to the Power Apps portal, `https://make.powerapps.com`, and from the left pane, select **Create**. Under the **Start from data** section, you will see some of the most popular data sources in the Microsoft ecosystem and an option of **Other data sources**. Selecting any of the choices will open a **Connections** page where you will be able to configure the service, as follows:

    SharePoint: You will be able to choose from the available sites and lists.

OneDrive for Business: A list of Excel files will appear to select as your data source.

Using any other option will prompt you to create a connection to that service and, depending on the service, will let you configure more options regarding the application data source connectivity.

In the following screenshot, you can see OneDrive and SharePoint on the **Connections** page:

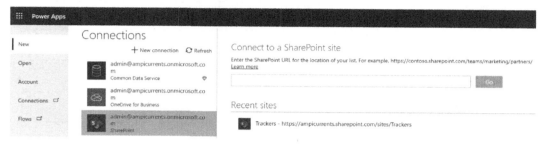

Figure 1.21 – Connections page

2. After selecting a data source, the Power Apps Studio will create an app based on the existing fields or columns.

How it works...

Depending on your selection, the application will have the required screens to handle the data source's information. When you create an application from an existing data source, Power Apps generates a minimum of two screens:

- **BrowseScreen**, to list records and interact with actions such as sort and filter

- **DetailScreen**, to present a complete set of fields related to the selected record in **BrowseScreen**

A third screen only appears if you have the requirements necessary to update the records, **EditScreen**.

For instance, if you connect to a SharePoint list in which you only have read-only permission, you will only get **BrowseScreen** and **DetailScreen**. On a list with update permissions levels such as **Contribute** or **Edit**, the **EditScreen** will handle the creation and update of records, as seen in the following screenshot:

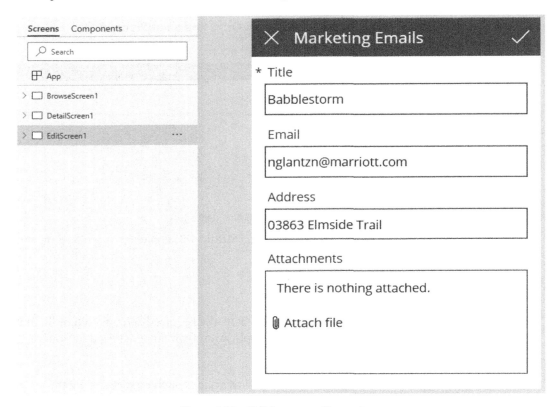

Figure 1.22 – EditScreen on Power Apps

When working with Azure SQL databases, there is an additional requirement for **EditScreen**. From Power Apps, you can only update tables with primary keys, including the deletion of records. If the table you select when creating the app from data doesn't have a primary key defined, you will only get **BrowseScreen** and **DetailScreen**, as seen in the previous *How to do it...* section when using Azure SQL as our data source.

Keep in mind that there are other known issues and limitations when working with Azure SQL databases. Visit https://docs.microsoft.com/en-us/connectors/sql/#known-issues-and-limitations for more information.

Please refer to the connector documentation of your data source of choice to learn more about possible issues or limitations that could compromise your solution: `https://docs.microsoft.com/en-us/connectors/connector-reference/`

There's more...

The applications created in this chapter are fully functional for handling data but lack appeal in the user interface department. To enhance their design, please refer to *Chapter 6, Improving User Experience*, to see how to apply an application makeover.

2
Building from data with model-driven apps

Model-driven apps are the data-centric siblings of canvas apps. They get their foundation from the business data model, taking an approach of placing building blocks on top of data. These blocks build up in a standard responsive layout, which allows the creation of a solution that adapts to any device.

Even though analyzing and setting up the data source is one of the main objectives of any application solution, this is the primary objective in these types of apps. Having a complete understanding of the business process gives you the ability to design your data model with a strong structure in mind to support the proposed solution. The last step would be to build the app on top of this model.

This chapter will explore the model-driven world of Power Apps while building a help desk solution. Through these recipes, you will get a clear view of all the components available in this platform:

- Exploring Dataverse
- Building a help desk solution
- Defining data structures
- Building the model-driven app
- Setting up business process logic
- Designing dashboards to visualize data
- Integrating canvas apps inside model-driven apps

Technical requirements

Working with apps that are born from data requires a particular structure detailed in this chapter; this means that the following recipes need to be addressed in sequence to build a complete model-driven solution.

The complete version of this application is available from our GitHub repository at `https://github.com/PacktPublishing/Microsoft-Power-Apps-Cookbook/tree/master/Chapter02`

Licensing requirements

When building model-driven solutions, there are some specific licensing requirements from Power Apps. Please refer to the Preface section of this book to get more information about the licensing model of this platform.

Exploring Dataverse

For model-driven apps, when we talk about the data model, we mean Dataverse. The data gets stored in tables just like regular databases. The difference lies in the rich set of business-oriented features:

- Leverage a set of standard business tables out of the box with the ability to add your own custom tables.

- Create a table, and it will automatically add all columns to address the underlying process requirements, such as owner info, tracking, status, versioning, and the like.

- Structure your data with various column data types, which helps in complex data modeling scenarios.

- Design **relationships** and define **keys** to standard and custom tables to ensure data integrity across the service.

- Enforce security on roles, records, and column levels, giving you complete flexibility when setting up data access.

- Add business features right from the table configuration: data consumption through **views**, data manipulation through **forms**, data visualization through **dashboards** and **charts**, and last but not least, **business rules** to apply a set of validations and logic without writing code.

Here's an example of what tables look like:

Entities > **BookTest**

| Fields | Relationships | Business rules | Views | Forms | Dashboards | Charts | Keys | Data |

Display name ↑ ∨		Name ∨	Data type ∨
BookTest	⋯	cr95e_booktestid	🔲 Unique Identifier
Created By	⋯	createdby	🔢 Lookup
Created By (Delegate)	⋯	createdonbehalfby	🔢 Lookup
Created On	⋯	createdon	🗓 Date and Time
Import Sequence Number	⋯	importsequencenumber	🔢 Whole Number
Modified By	⋯	modifiedby	🔢 Lookup
Modified By (Delegate)	⋯	modifiedonbehalfby	🔢 Lookup
Modified On	⋯	modifiedon	🗓 Date and Time
Name Primary Field	⋯	cr95e_name	🔤 Text

Figure 2.1 – Table example in Dataverse

To store these tables, Dataverse uses **environments** that act as a container not only for data but also for all the components that interact with it, such as applications, flows, and business processes.

Besides these features, Dataverse also manages **solutions** to package apps and components from one environment to another. This feature allows the implementation of **application life cycle management** (**ALM**) for the whole Power Platform. For more information, please refer to `https://docs.microsoft.com/en-us/power-platform/alm/basics-alm`

Dataverse is also the service Dynamics 365 applications use to store data; this means that you can interact with the data that your business is already using.

Building a help desk solution

When you configure Dataverse for the first time, it will help create business-centric applications with a set of base tables, such as **Account**, **Contact**, and **Organization**. Starting from those, you would only need to add custom tables that your processes might need to achieve their goal. With this recipe, we will create an application that will help handle a help desk service.

Getting ready

To build our solution, we will start by setting up a new environment and use it as our development area. Then, we can pack our solution and deploy it wherever it is needed.

How to do it...

1. Go to the Power Apps admin center by opening this URL: `https://admin.powerplatform.microsoft.com`, or `https://aka.ms/ppac` for short. You can also navigate from Power Apps by clicking on the upper-right gear icon and selecting **Admin center**.

2. Once in the admin center, select **Environments** on the left menu and then click on **New**. This action will open a panel where you will need to describe your new environment. Choose a name and a region close to you, and describe the purpose. For the **Type**, you can select **Production**, **Sandbox**, or **Trial**. **Production** is where your solutions operate for end users, **Sandbox** is for testing solutions, and **Trial** is a 30-day environment meant to test new features. It will also ask you whether you want to have a database created for this environment; as we will need one for our solution, please select **Yes** and then click on **Next**:

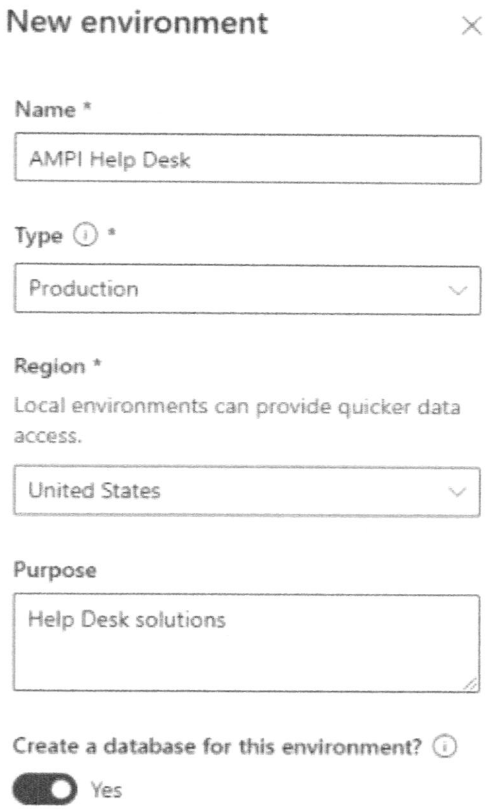

New environment   ×

Name *

AMPI Help Desk

Type ⓘ *

Production   ∨

Region *

Local environments can provide quicker data access.

United States   ∨

Purpose

Help Desk solutions

Create a database for this environment? ⓘ

🔘 Yes

Figure 2.2 – Environment settings

3. In the next panel, you will need to set the default language for the interface, the URL prefix to access your new environment, for example, `ampihelpdesk`, and the required currency for reporting purposes. Select whether you want to enable Dynamics 365 apps (given that you have the required licenses and only for the default region) and whether you're going to add sample apps and data. Finally, pre-define the security to access your environment by selecting a security group, and then click on **Save**:

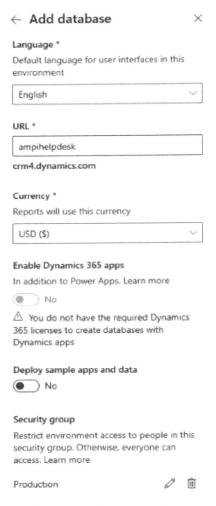

Figure 2.3 – Database settings

4. The admin center will start the provisioning of your environment. After a couple of minutes, it will appear as **Ready**, and then you can go to Power Apps to begin working with it.

How it works...

From Power Apps, select your newly created environment from the list by clicking on the current one on the top right of the interface:

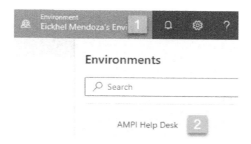

Figure 2.4 – Environment list

After making this selection, we will only see information related to this environment, such as apps, flows, and connections.

We will define the custom tables needed for our help desk solution in the *Defining data structures* recipe.

Defining data structures

To support our help desk solution, we are going to use related tables as our data source. We will design a base column template to keep track of all the information needed. You can customize it to your own needs.

Explanation and overview

The following tables will make up our solution's data structure with the main focus on the Ticket table; this will be the one from which all other tables will have their relationship. Let's start with this one and then move on to the rest.

Ticket

This table will hold the base information of the help desk ticket, and it's going to be the primary object of our data model. The column structure is as follows:

- **Title** [Text]
- **Description** [Text Area]
- **Ticket Status** [Choice]
- **Priority** [Choice]

- **Customer validation** [Choice]
- **Resolution** [Text Area]

Ticket operation

Related to the Ticket table, this will hold the specific operations executed to solve the ticket. The structure is as follows:

- **Title** [Text]
- **Description** [Text Area]
- **Operation Status** [Choice]
- **Duration** [Duration]

Project

All tickets are going to be associated with a customer's project. The structure is as follows:

- **Title** [Text]
- **Description** [Text Area]
- **Start** [Date Only]
- **End** [Date Only]

Account

We will take advantage of one of the default business tables that comes with Dataverse when a new database gets created. This table holds our customers' information.

How to do it...

1. In the **Tables** section, select **New Table** from the top toolbar. On the panel that opens, fill in the required information to create the structure.

   For the table section, set **Display name** and the plural form, such as `Ticket` and `Tickets`. For the **Name** field, you can put the same as the display name; the system will automatically generate a prefix to help make your name unique.

2. **Primary Name Column** is the main identifier in this table. For the Ticket table, input `Title`. Choose something that your users can also use to select the rows when the system is listing them.

3. Depending on the needs of your table, you might want to **Enable attachments**. For example, it might be useful in the Ticket table to include extra information about the incident that started the ticket, such as screenshots or PDF files.

4. Once we have entered all the required information, you can click on **Done**. The system will then start creating the table with the specified primary name column and the rest of the business-oriented columns.

The following is an example of the Ticket table:

Entities > **Ticket**

Fields   Relationships   Business rules   Views   Forms   Dashboards   Charts   Keys   Data

Display name ↑ ⌄		Name ⌄	Data type ⌄
Created By	⋯	createdby	Lookup
Created By (Delegate)	⋯	createdonbehalfby	Lookup
Created On	⋯	createdon	Date and Time
Import Sequence Number	⋯	importsequencenumber	Whole Number
Modified By	⋯	modifiedby	Lookup
Modified By (Delegate)	⋯	modifiedonbehalfby	Lookup
Modified On	⋯	modifiedon	Date and Time
Owner	⋯	ownerid	Owner
Owning Business Unit	⋯	owningbusinessunit	Lookup
Owning Team	⋯	owningteam	Lookup
Owning User	⋯	owninguser	Lookup
Record Created On	⋯	overriddencreatedon	Date Only
Status	⋯	statecode	Option Set
Status Reason	⋯	statuscode	Option Set
Ticket	⋯	cr1c1_ticketid	Unique Identifier
Time Zone Rule Version Number	⋯	timezoneruleversionnumber	Whole Number
Title Primary Field	⋯	cr1c1_title	Text
UTC Conversion Time Zone Code	⋯	utcconversiontimezonecode	Whole Number
Version Number	⋯	versionnumber	Big Integer

Figure 2.5 – Ticket table base structure

5. Now we can start shaping the table by adding the rest of the required columns. Click on **Add column**, and in the **Display name** field, input Description, and for the **Name** field, change it back to lowercase as description. Set **Data type** to **Text Area** and click on **Done**.

6. Repeat *step 5* to add the Resolution column.

7. Click on **Add column** again to include the Ticket Status column. For **Data type**, select **Choice**. Selecting this will display a new dropdown to choose from the existing choice columns. Choose + **New choice** from this dropdown, and in the **Items** section, remove the existing one and add these: New, Pending, Resolved, and Closed. Finally, click on **Save** and then **Done**.

8. Repeat *step 7* for the Ticket Priority column, adding the following items: Low, Medium, and High.

9. Again, repeat *step 7* for the Ticket Validation column, adding Phone and Email for the items.

    Here's an example of the Ticket Status column settings:

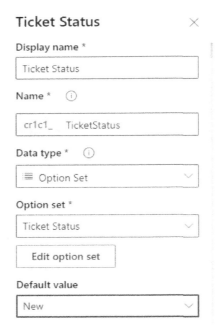

Figure 2.6 – Status column sample

10. When you complete the creation of the columns, click on **Save Table**.

11. Click on **Tables** on the left pane and then on **New Table** to add the **Ticket operation** table. For **Primary Name Column**, use `Title`. Remember to change the **Name** fields to lowercase, and then click **Done**.

12. When the table completes the provisioning, click on **Add column** to add the `Description` column using **Text Area** as its **Data type** value, and then click **Done**.

13. Click on **Add column** again to add the `Operation Status` column. For **Data type**, select **Choice**, and from the dropdown, choose the one we created in *step 7*, `Ticket Status`, and then click **Done**.

14. Again, click on **Add column** to create the last column on this table, `Duration`. For **Data type**, select **Duration** and click **Done**, and then click on **Save Table**.

15. Go back to the tables list by click on **Tables** on the left pane, and then click on **New Table** to add the `Project` table. Use `Title` for **Primary Name Column** and set the **Name** fields to lowercase. Click **Done**.

16. Once the provisioning completes, click on **Add column** to add the `Description` column using **Text Area** as its **Data type** value, and then click **Done**.

17. Click on **Add column** to create the `Start` column. Set **Data type** to **Date Only** and then click **Done**. Repeat this step to make the `End` column.

18. Click **Save Table** to complete the configuration of the `Project` table.

19. Let's configure the relationship between tables to maintain data integrity in our solution. From the **Tables** list, select to open the `Ticket` table, and then click on the **Relationships** tab. In the toolbar, click on **Add relationship** and then choose **One-to-many**. This kind of relationship roughly means that one element from one side (**Ticket**) can have many child items on the other (**Ticket Operations**).

20. When the panel opens, select **Ticket Operation** from the **Related (Many)** list. This action will create a lookup column to connect both tables. You can configure more settings in the advanced section regarding which action gets taken when a record gets deleted. To keep data integrity, you might want to avoid a ticket deletion without removing the ticket operations first. In this case, we are going to restrict deletions. When finished, click on **Done** and then **Save Table**. For more information on relationships, please refer to `https://docs.microsoft.com/en-us/powerapps/maker/common-data-service/data-platform-entity-lookup#add-advanced-relationship-behavior`

21. Repeat *steps 8* and *9* to configure the **One-to-many** relationship between
    Project (one) and Ticket (many), and finally between Account (one) and
    Project (many):

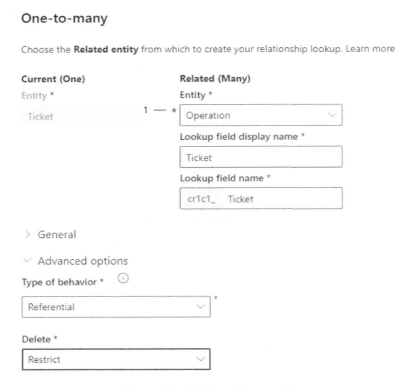

Figure 2.7 – Relationship example

How it works...

We now have the data structure and relationships in place. To start entering data in our
tables, we need to complete the required modifications in the next recipe's data forms,
Building the model-driven app. However, the Account table comes by default in the
system, so everything is already configured to enter data.

From the **Tables** list, select to open the Account table, and then select the **Data** tab. In
the toolbar, click on **Add record**. This action will open up a new browser tab with a form
to load data. Fill in all the desired columns and then click **Save & Close** from the toolbar if
you want to add only one account, or click **Save** and then **New** to add more records.

Building the model-driven app

Creating an application using a low-code approach brings a different methodology when setting up the application building process. On other technologies, you might need to choose the language, infrastructure, database system, and more. For model-driven applications, one of the essential principles is to build everything inside solutions.

Explanation and overview

A solution creates a container where you can store all the pieces that compose your application, which in turn aids in deployment, distribution, and management—more information on this subject at `https://docs.microsoft.com/en-us/powerapps/maker/model-driven-apps/distribute-model-driven-app`

The application we will create through all the recipes will get packed into a solution, so all elements can be exported in just one package and then imported into your environment.

How to do it...

1. First, let's create a solution. From Power Apps, select **Solutions** from the left menu, and then click on **New Solution**. Give it a display name and a name, and create a publisher by selecting **+ Publisher** from the dropdown. The publisher identifies the developer and also specifies the prefix for all your custom tables and columns. Finally, set the solution version or keep the default one.

2. Select to open your recently created solution from the list, and let's start adding items. First, we will include the existing tables. Click on **Add existing** from the toolbar, and then click on **Table**. Select **Ticket**, **Ticket Operation**, and **Project** from the list, and then click on **Next**. Mark **Include all components** on both tables and finally, click on **Add**.

3. Now, let's create the model-driven app. Click on **New** from the toolbar and then **App | Model-driven app**. Input the **Name**, **Unique Name**, and **Description** values for the app, and then click on **Done**. Leave the rest of the options as default:

Figure 2.8 – New model-driven dialog

4. The first thing that we need to set for our application is the sitemap. This component allows us to configure the navigation inside our app. Following the Power Apps platform's design, it will give you a left menu to add items for the user to select. Click on the pencil next to this component to set it up.

    The navigation is composed of **areas**, **groups**, and **subareas**. Let's define ours by clicking on **Add** to include these elements.

5. Use the following options as a template, and for the `Ticket` subarea, select the **Entity** type, so it opens our previously created table. Once you've made the changes, press **Save** and then **Publish**. Finally, click at the top left on the **App Designer** breadcrumb to go back to the model-driven app:

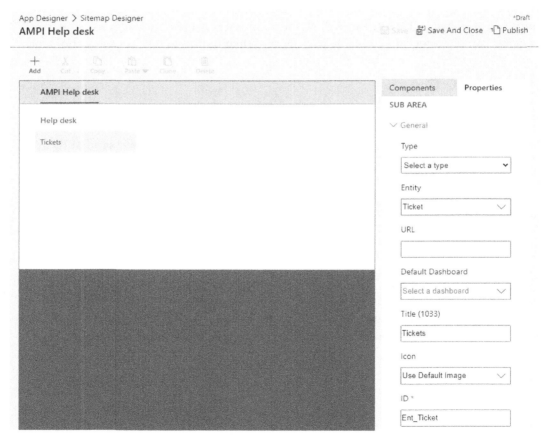

Figure 2.9 – Sitemap example

6. You might have noticed that the `Ticket` table now appears on the entity view. This change is due to the designer adding every related component to the app. Let's complete the table design, starting with the forms.

7. A form is a screen designed to manage the records of the tables. To configure it, click on the **Forms** element of the `Ticket` table. You will see a panel that opens on the right with the list of all forms selected by default. When setting up an application, it's best to select only the ones that will be available, so in this case, deselect the **All** checkbox. Click on the pencil that appears on the right of the `Information` form to modify it.

8. Once the form designer opens, you will see that only the **Primary** column appears. Any change after the creation of the table needs to get included in the respective forms.

    Select all the columns we created for this table from the left to add them to the form. You can also drag and drop the columns and components to place them as you see fit. Make these changes and then click on **Save**, and finally on **Publish**. Close the designer afterward:

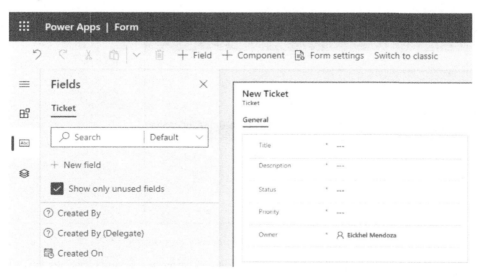

Figure 2.10 – Form designer for the Ticket table

9. Let's continue with views. A view is a list of records organized, filtered, and sorted as needed. Active tickets, tickets by creation date, and pending tickets are examples of views. As with the forms, uncheck **All**, and let's create a view by clicking on **Create New**.

10. When **View Designer** opens, set the name on the right panel under the **Properties** tab as Pending tickets. On the **Components** tab, click on **Column Attributes Primary Entity** and drag and drop the desired columns from the right panel to the view in the order you see fit. Be sure to include the **Created On** column. Click on the header of each column to set the width as desired.

11. Select the **Created On** column's dropdown and click on **Primary Sort**, so we have the newest items on top.

12. Expand the **Filter Criteria** section, located on top of the **Columns** section, and click on **Add Filter** to add a filter row. Choose **Ticket Status** from the list of columns, select **Does Not Equals**, and click the next field to select from the **OptionSetType** values. Click the right arrow to add Closed or Resolved, and then click **OK**. Finally, click on **Save** and then **Publish**. Close **View Designer**.

The pending tickets view should look like the following screenshot:

Figure 2.11 – Pending tickets view example

13. Now that we have configured both the forms and views of our table, we can save, validate, and publish our app—the validation step checks for any inconsistencies in our application that need to get fixed.

How it works...

After completing the previous steps, we can test our application to verify whether it is working as intended.

From the **Solutions** section, select to open your solution and look for the model-driven app. Select it, and from the toolbar, press **Play**. This action will open the application with a menu on the left with a `Tickets` option inside a `Help desk` group and in the main display, the new **Pending tickets** view.

Add some records by clicking on the **New** button from the toolbar. If you create one with a Ticket Status of `Closed` or `Resolved`, it should not appear on the main view. To solve this, change the selected view in your application. In your solution, add as many views as needed to make it easier for your users to track information:

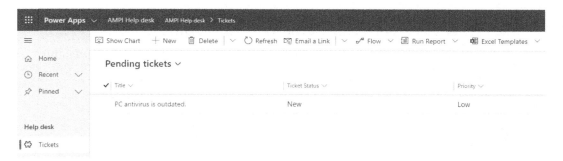

Figure 2.12 – Model-driven application running

In the next recipes, we will add application logic to have data validation. We will also include a dashboard to offer a more informative view of the business process data.

Setting up business process logic

For every business process, there is always a step-by-step procedure that defines every requirement, objective, and resolution from start to end. Companies build on and improve these procedures depending on the business needs, and they even create departments to work exclusively on this.

Explanation and overview

Model-driven apps help set up these rules by providing several tools to define business logic on various platform levels. You can incorporate data validation rules and structured data flows to guide the end user, and even trigger workflows for defined events on your processes. These are just some examples of what you can achieve with this platform.

Let's improve our help desk app by adding business logic to the solution we created in the previous recipe:

- Hide or make a column visible depending on the status of a ticket using a business rule. In our case, there is no reason to have the `Customer Validation` column visible unless the case is in the `Resolved` state.

- Guide the ticket processing by making sure the user inputs the required information on each defined step with the help of a **business process flow** (**BPF**). This component also allows you to execute processes, Power Automate cloud flows, or workflows when a defined trigger gets fired.

How to do it...

1. First, open the help desk solution, and let's start by adding data validation rules to the `Tickets` table. Select the table and then click on **Edit**.

2. Go to the **Business rules** tab, and on the toolbar, click on **Add business rule**; this will open a designer where you can define actions based on a condition.

3. Select the default condition, **New condition**, and on the right panel, set these properties:

   Display Name: Customer validation visibility

   Under **Rules**, set to check when `Ticket Status` equals `Resolved` or `Closed`, and then click on **Apply**.

4. Click on **Add** on the main toolbar to include an **Add Set Visibility** action. Once you choose this option, two plus signs will appear next to the condition, when it is valid (**checkmark**) and another when it isn't (**X**). Place one on the **checkmark** and then add another for the **X**.

5. Select each new action and set the following properties on the right pane, and then click on **Apply**:

- Condition is met:

   Display Name: `Show Customer Validation`

   Field: `Customer Validation`

   Visible: `Yes`

- Condition isn't met:

    Display Name: Hide Customer Validation

    Field: Customer Validation

    Visible: No

6. Finally, click on **Ticket: New business rule**, located at the upper left of the screen, to set the business rule's name. Enter Customer validation visibility and then hit **Save** on the toolbar, and then on **Activate** to make it available for this table:

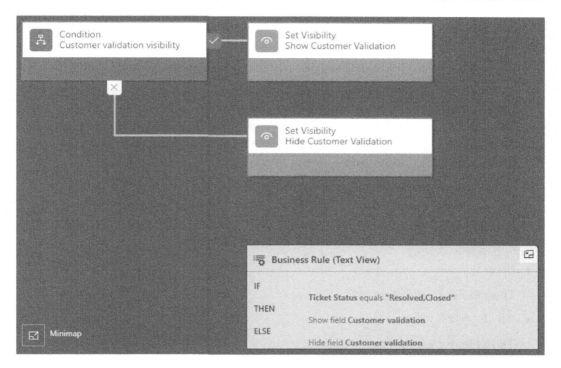

Figure 2.13 – Customer validation business rule

7. Now, let's create a BPF to guide our users during the ticket processing:

- From your solution, click on the ellipsis on the toolbar and select **Switch to classic**. This process still requires the classic interface to use the proper solution prefix for the BPF.

- Once the classic solution designer opens, click on **Processes** on the left pane and then click **New** in the toolbar; this will open a new dialog to gather properties for your BPF. Set the following values for the `Ticket` table and click **OK**:

Figure 2.14 – New BPF dialog

8. Once the designer opens, you will find a default stage. These are the steps of your guided flow. Let's create three more stages by dragging them next to each other from the components panel. Click on each one and set **Display Name** to the following: `New`, `In Progress`, `Resolved`, and `Closed`. For each one, click on **Apply** afterward.

9. Each stage comes with a data step by default, which lets us specify the column that gets displayed in each step of our BPF, as well as, most importantly, which ones are required when moving from one stage to the other. Let's configure the data steps for each stage by clicking on **Details** and setting these values:

- `New`:

  Data Field: Description

- `In Progress`:

  Data Field: Description – Required

- `Resolved`:

  Data Field: Resolution – Required

- `Closed`:

  Data Field: Customer validation – Required

10. After completing these changes, on the top toolbar, click on **Validate** to check everything is correct, and then click **Save**. Finally, click on **Activate** to enable this BPF.

How it works...

Once we have configured the business process logic for `Tickets`, every time this table gets invoked, it will carry on these defined components. To see them working, go to your solution, select the model-driven app, and click on **Play**; this will open the app on the `Pending Tickets` view. Click on **New** to add a ticket.

You will see that the form now includes your BPF, which lets you have a clear visualization of which step of the process your ticket is. After saving it, if you try to move beyond the `Resolved` stage, it will ask you to set the value for the required columns:

Figure 2.15 – BPF in action

As for the business rule, the `Customer Validation` column will remain hidden until the ticket status gets changed to `Resolved`. Once we enter this column's data, it is then that we can finish the BPF:

Figure 2.16 – Ticket processing completed

Designing dashboards to visualize data

When working with business processes that deal with data, one of the main goals for organizations is to gain insights. Knowing where your operations are failing or where there is a market opportunity is vital, so having an easy way to interact with data is very important.

Dashboards are a Dataverse feature that gives you the ability to display a mix of graphs, grids of data, and web resources in one place. Let's give more value to the help desk solution by including a ticket dashboard.

How to do it...

1. Let's create the charts that we are going to use in our dashboard. Starting from our solution, click on the `Tickets` table, and from the toolbar, click on **Edit**.

2. Go to the **Charts** tab and click on **Add chart** at the top; this will open a new configuration window to define the data that the graph will use, the type, and the data visualization rules.

3. First, choose the view that will filter the data, then select the legend entries, which are the series of your graph, and finally, the horizontal axis, which will categorize your data. Let's create three charts using the following configurations; after completing each one, click on **Save & Close**:

   - Standard settings for all charts:

     View: Active tickets

     Legend Entries: Ticket

   - **Chart name**: `Ticket by Priority` – Pie chart:

     Horizontal Axis: Priority

   - **Chart name**: `Ticket by Project` – Pie chart:

     Horizontal Axis: Project

   - **Chart name**: `Ticket by Ticket Status` – Column chart:

     Horizontal Axis: Ticket Status

4. Now that we have defined the charts, we can place them on our dashboard. From the solution, edit the model-driven app, and on the **Dashboards** component, click on **Create New** and select **Classic Dashboards**. On the dialog that opens, click on **3-Column Overview Dashboard**. We will use this layout as a template:

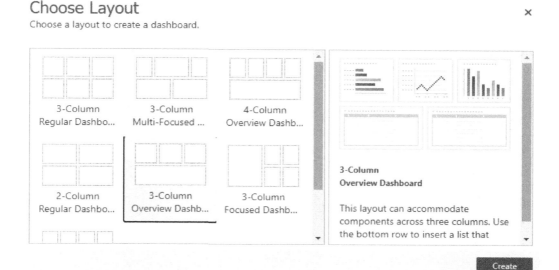

Figure 2.17 – Dashboard layouts

5. In the dashboard designer, set the name of your dashboard and then start placing the sections' elements. Click on each placeholder, and from the top toolbar, select the desired resource.

6. For the top section, select the first placeholder and click on **CHART**. Then, in the dialog, choose `Ticket` as **Record Type** and `Active tickets` from the **View** list, and pick one of the charts we created in *step 3*. Repeat this for the other two placeholders.

7. As for the lower section, click on the placeholder and select **LIST**. Choose `Ticket` as **Record Type** and `Active tickets` from the **View** list; this will display a grid of records for easy access.

8. Hit **SAVE** on the toolbar and close the window to return to the model-driven editor.

9. To make our dashboard accessible in our application, we need to modify the sitemap by clicking on the pencil icon next to it.

10. Let's update the `Tickets` subarea by changing the type to **Dashboard** and selecting our newest one from the **Default Dashboard** list. Click on **Save** and then on **Publish**.

How it works...

After completing the dashboard setup, we can see it working in our model-driven application by selecting it from our solution and then clicking on **Play**.

When the app opens, you will see the dashboard instead of the list of records we used to have. At a glance, this display gives insight into the current state of the help desk system.

If you don't see the changes immediately, you might need to do a hard refresh of your browser window. This behavior is due to the cache mechanism:

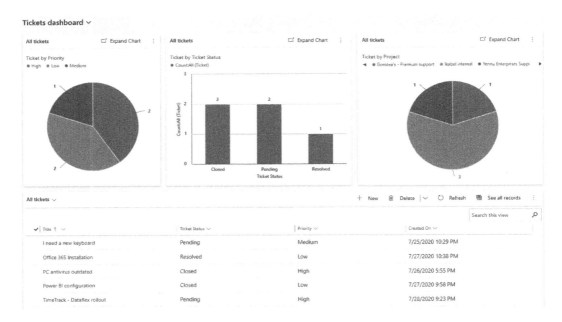

Figure 2.18 – Tickets dashboard

Integrating canvas apps inside model-driven apps

One of the best features present in canvas apps is the ability to access multiple external connectors from the same app. We can leverage this strength by embedding a canvas as a component.

These are sample scenarios in which this can be very helpful:

- A canvas application that is already in production that we want to integrate into our model-driven system.

- A canvas app that connects to a legacy system using the on-premises data gateway.

- An employee tracking system that gives us information about in which of our customer locations our support staff is working at any given moment. This data could be useful to see whether we already have someone from support at the client location from which a new ticket has arrived.

Now let's see how we can integrate a canvas into our model-driven solution.

How to do it...

1. From our solution, select to open the `Project` table. Then, go to the **Forms** tab to edit the main form.

2. Once the designer opens, select the **Switch to classic** option from the toolbar. The Power Apps platform is still evolving the form designer experience, so we still need to use the standard version to add some components.

3. Select where you want your canvas app to appear, and then, from **Field Explorer** on the right, drag a column to that position. Keep in mind that this column needs to have data to make the app visible, so make sure you select a required column. In this example, I've selected `Title`.

4. Double-click on the column and, under the label section, uncheck **Display label on the form** so that it doesn't appear next to our app.

5. Go to the **Controls** tab and click on **Add Control…**, select Canvas app from the list, and click on **Add**. This action will add the Canvas app property section. On the list of controls, select the canvas app and choose **Web**, **Phone**, and **Tablet**.

6. In the Canvas property section, you will see the settings needed to link an app. To add a new one, click on **Customize**; this will create a new canvas app with a form using the `Project` table as its data source. You will notice a new control called **ModelDrivenFormIntegration**, as shown, which acts as a gateway between the model-driven form and the canvas app:

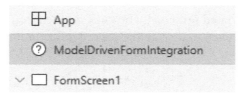

Figure 2.19 – ModelDrivenFormIntegration

It works just like the **SharePointIntegration** control we saw in the previous chapter's *Embedding an expense tracking list with SharePoint list Power Apps* recipe but with only one action available. Its primary purpose is to act on data refresh.

7. Design your app to match your needs. Keep in mind that one of the primary purposes of this integration is to have the ability to link the data from the Dataverse table with our canvas app. This connection gets done by the integration control using the **Item** property, which carries the column data from the selected item in the model-driven app:

Figure 2.20 – Project columns in the canvas app

8. Once you finish building your app, click on **Save**, and publish it to make it available in our model-driven app. Close the canvas app studio.

9. Back in the classic form designer, you will see that the canvas properties were updated to reflect the new app's link. Click **OK** to save the field properties, and then save the form, and finally, publish it. Close the classic form designer.

10. Go back to your solution. You will see that the canvas app appears automatically in the list of components.

How it works...

Let's pretend our company is in the middle of its cloud migration, and we still use a legacy ERP system to control customers' support rights. We can build a canvas app with a custom connector, a data gateway, or a Power Automate cloud flow to get data from the on-premises system. This solution can give support representatives more insight into the customer's rights related to the ticket.

Open a ticket with an associated project. If you click on the Project column value, it will navigate to the project form to display the related information about the project:

Figure 2.21 – Project table navigation

As soon as the project table form appears, the model-driven integration control will notify the canvas app of the currently selected record. That will execute the `OnDataRefresh` action logic you specified in your app:

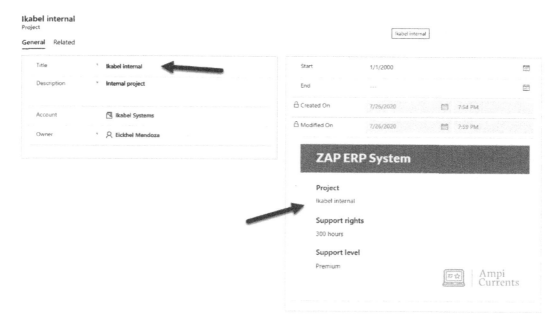

Figure 2.22 – Canvas app integrated into the model-driven form

This integration shows just one of the situations where a canvas app can aid a model-driven solution to accomplish something that would require adding a code solution or a third-party component. Make sure you know all the possibilities of each type of app to leverage each one's skills.

3
Choosing the right data source for your applications

Selecting the right data source is one of the most critical decisions when designing your application infrastructure. Many factors come into play, such as features, security, speed, pricing, and integrations.

Thankfully, the needs of your solution will help you to select the right one. For example, it would be better to use a database with a certified connector if you're going to use Power BI; or if your application needs to store a specific data type, it's best to choose a database that has it natively. Another example is when working with canvas apps, where setting up data sources using different connectors opens a whole range of possibilities when interacting with data.

Before we dive into this chapter, we will also cover a key topic regarding the Power Platform's licensing model. Having understood this concept, we can discuss data concerning the Power Platform with the help of these recipes:

- Reducing your application complexity by using Azure SQL database views
- Choosing the right data source – real-world tests
- Integrating on-premises data with the data source flexibility of canvas Power Apps

- Improving application speed and responsiveness by using static data
- Consuming external data by using dataflows

Technical requirements

To thoroughly test all the recipes tackling various forms of data sources, we will need either of the following licensing plans. In each recipe, there is going to be a clarification on which ones we could use. Please refer to the Preface section of this book to get more information about the licensing requirements. The complete version of this application is available from our GitHub repository at `https://github.com/PacktPublishing/Microsoft-Power-Apps-Cookbook/tree/master/Chapter03`

Data sources and the licensing model

We need to understand the unique differentiator that makes us need a license: whether a connector is labeled premium or not. This tag activates the users' license requirement using our app, even if you have one when building it.

The current licensing model reminds of the SQL Server **client access licenses** (**CALs**), in which every user accessing the server requires a pass. It is the same for the Power Platform. You add capacity to your environments to allow unlicensed users to access your app.

The platform recognizes which apps are built with premium connectors to access data or services. When you access the details of your apps or flows, you will see a **License designation** or **Plan** section that will inform you about this:

Figure 3.1 – License designation in apps and flows

These changes came on October 1, 2019, when many apps were already using premium connectors, mostly Azure services, which were initially standard. Microsoft then decided to offer a **grandfathering period** that allowed using these apps without the license requirement for apps published before October 1. More information regarding this exception can be found at `https://docs.microsoft.com/en-gb/ power-platform/admin/powerapps-flow-licensing-faq#how-does- the-change-to-power-apps-and-power-automate-use-rights-for- microsoft-365-applications-affect-me-if-i-purchased-the- subscriptions-prior-to-oct-1st-2019-will-my-existing-power- apps-applications-and-power-automate-workflows-continue-to-work`

When designing your infrastructure, always consider the licensing model beforehand to avoid surprises at the end of your project when the user base starts growing.

However, you need to be conscious about the value of this consumption model where previously you would need to buy licenses for every user that might use your app at any given moment instead of purchasing passes only for the actual users. Let me explain this with an example.

Let's pretend we have an organization with 10 employees that would use your app at some specific points in time:

- Five administrative employees will use the app daily
- Four managers will use the app quarterly
- One employee from marketing will only use the app occasionally

If the license price were 10 USD, previously, you would have had to pay 100 USD per month. With the consumption model, you can make calculations based on usage to allow a certain amount of simultaneous users, say six, which would reduce the price to 60 USD per month.

Power Apps/Power Automate for Microsoft 365

You don't always need an add-on license to work with Power Apps or Power Automate. Starting from the regular Microsoft 365 Business Basic license, you can build apps in the context of Microsoft 365 using standard connectors. Real-world applications use SharePoint as their data source without incurring extra costs, even for mobile apps with offline capabilities. Besides this, there is also a new addition called Dataverse for Teams, which allows using a light version of Dataverse in the Microsoft Teams platform. More information on this can be found at `https://go.microsoft.com/ fwlink/?linkid=2085130`

Let's deep dive into the data source recipes with a clear concept of the licensing model in mind.

Reducing your application complexity by using Azure SQL database views

Performance is one of the main objectives of almost all data source engines. Database developers tweak the innards of their core systems to make them as efficient as possible while also adding new features for app makers. Knowing this, why not leverage the efficiency of these platforms?

That's the primary purpose of this recipe, to learn how to improve our apps' responsiveness and complexity by making the data sources work for us.

Getting ready

We will improve the application's complexity and performance when connected to an Azure SQL database to build our use case. The database needs five tables that will make up our data catalog. The scripts to create them and the base apps are available in our GitHub repository: `https://github.com/PacktPublishing/Microsoft-Power-Apps-Cookbook/tree/master/Chapter03`

If you don't have an Azure subscription, you can request a free version with credit for 30 days to test all the services available on this cloud platform.

Apply for it at `https://azure.microsoft.com/en-us/free/`

How to do it...

First, download all the files from the repository and have them ready. The following steps will help you build the Azure SQL database needed for the sample power app.

Provisioning the data source

1. Go to the Azure portal, `https://portal.azure.com`, and click on **Create a resource**. This action will open the Azure Marketplace. Using the search field, enter `SQL Database`, and hit *Enter*.

2. From the list of services, select **SQL Database** and then click **Create**. This action will open the **Create SQL Database** page, as seen in the next screenshot:

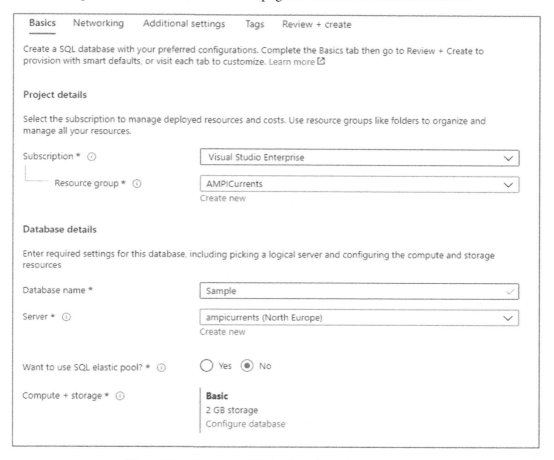

Figure 3.2 – Creating a SQL database from the Azure portal

3. Select your subscription and resource group. Enter the name of the database in the **Database name** field and select a server. If you don't have an existing server, click on the **Create new** link just below the servers list and enter the required information: **Server name**, **Server admin login**, and **Password**. For the **Location** input, select one closest to your location for better response times.

4. Select **No** for the elastic pool setting and then click on **Configure database** in the **Compute + storage** setting. When the **Configure** page opens, select the pricing tier you want for your database. For testing purposes, click on **Looking for basic, standard, premium?** link and then choose **Basic** for the lowest pricing tier, and then click on **Apply**.

5. Back on the **Create SQL Database** page, click on the **Additional settings** tab and select **Sample** from the **Use existing data** setting.

6. Select the **Review + create** tab and then click on **Create**. This action will start the provisioning of the database. Once it finishes, you can continue to the next step.

7. Connect to your Azure SQL database and execute the provided scripts from the `Azure SQL scripts` folder; this will prepare the tables needed for our app. To complete this task, you can use either SQL Server Management Studio, `https://docs.microsoft.com/en-us/sql/ssms/download-sql-server-management-studio-ssms?view=sql-server-ver15`, or the Azure portal itself. Accessing the portal is straightforward, as you don't need to install any software. Load the scripts using the **Open query** option in the toolbar and execute them one by one. In the following figure, you can see how to access Query editor:

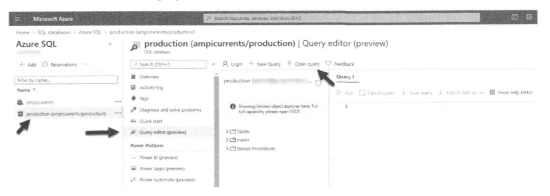

Figure 3.3 – Query editor in the Azure portal

8. Go to the Power Apps maker portal, `https://make.powerapps.com`, and then add the connection to your database by clicking on **Data | Connections** on the left pane. From the toolbar, click on **New connection** and look for **SQL Server**. Select the authentication type you want to use, set the required credentials, and then click on **Create**.

9. Now, click on **Apps** from the left pane and select **Import canvas app** from the toolbar. Click on **Upload** and pick the `PowerTrack SQL.zip` package file you downloaded from the `Apps` folder. After the upload is complete, the review screen will open the list of resources to import. If you want to rename the app, click on the wrench icon under actions; if not, just click on **Import** to finish the process.

When the import completes, you will get a dialog letting you know that the process has finished successfully with a link to open the app. You can also open it from the list of your apps:

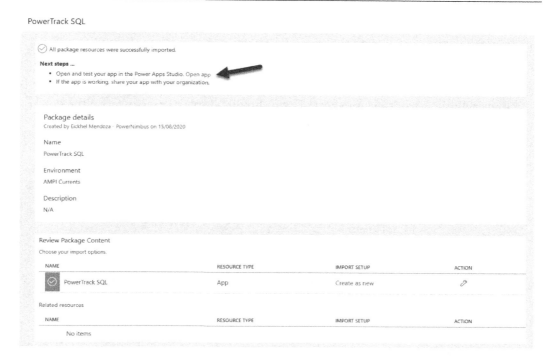

Figure 3.4 – Successful Power App import

10. The app used Azure Active Directory authentication for the database, so the first time it loads, it will ask you for permission to allow the use of the SQL server connection. Still, you won't be able to connect to the specified database; you will need to remove the current tables and connect them again to your Azure SQL database. Remove the connections as shown in the following screenshot:

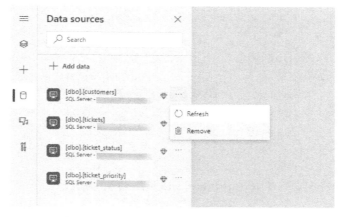

Figure 3.5 – Application's data connections

11. After removing all tables, on the same **Data sources** panel, click on **Add data**, search for SQL, and pick **SQL Server**. Select your previously configured connection, and choose the customers, tickets, ticket_status, ticket_priority, and technicians tables from your database.

    If everything is working as expected, you should be able to press play on the Power Apps Studio to test your app. When selecting customers from the combo box, the related tickets should appear in the gallery.

12. Let's inspect the gallery's Items property:

```
Filter(
    AddColumns(
        AddColumns(
            AddColumns(
                '[dbo].[tickets]',
                "Technician",
                LookUp(
                    '[dbo].[technicians]',
                    id = technician_id,
                    full_name
                )
            ),
            "Status",
            LookUp(
                '[dbo].[ticket_status]',
                id = status_id,
                description
            )
        ),
        "Priority",
        LookUp(
            '[dbo].[ticket_priority]',
            id = priority_id,
            description
        )
    ),
    customer_id = CustomersCbx.Selected.id
)
```

As you can see, there are several complex formulas to accomplish the relations between the five tables. First, we filter the tickets for the selected customer, and then we add columns to get the technician's name and the descriptions for the statuses and priorities. Having many formulas to query data reduces performance and adds a maintenance overhead for your app. Let's improve this by using an Azure SQL view.

13. On your Azure SQL database, execute the provided script, `VIEW - TicketData.sql`.

14. Include the view you just created in the app as you did in *step 6*; the database views appear next to your database's tables. Using this database view, we can accomplish several tasks:

- Reduce the complexity of the gallery's `Items` property by removing all the `AddColumns` formulas leaving just the filter for the selected customer:

```
Filter(
    '[dbo].[vw_TicketData]',
    customer_id = CustomersCbx.Selected.id
)
```

- Remove the need for the "lookup" tables as they don't need to be connected to our app to discover the descriptions of the statuses, priorities, or technician data. You can even remove the `tickets` table because the view is providing all the information needed.

How it works...

The application performance gets improved because the relationship process is executed at the database level and not from the Power App. We also decreased the data transfers between the data source and our app when we reduced the tables connected to the app. The code also looks cleaner, and it's easier to maintain.

The following view script links the tables in our database by using the SQL built-in language. To put it into words, it gets only the fields we need and joins the four tables by their identity fields:

```
CREATE VIEW vw_TicketData
AS
SELECT tickets.customer_id,
       tickets.date,
       tickets.location,
```

```
        technicians.full_name AS Technician,
        ticket_status.description AS Status,
        ticket_priority.description AS Priority
FROM dbo.tickets
    INNER JOIN dbo.ticket_status
        ON ticket_status.id = tickets.status_id
    INNER JOIN dbo.ticket_priority
        ON ticket_priority.id = tickets.priority_id
    INNER JOIN dbo.technicians
        ON technicians.id = tickets.technician_id;
```

This approach also adds another enhancement in terms of development workload. The team in charge of database maintenance and performance can provide us with better insights on obtaining data most optimally.

There's more...

This recipe was just an example of how our chosen data source's capabilities can improve our app. You need to get to know the features available in your data service to take advantage of them when building your apps.

Another similar example is to use Dataverse table views. It works on the same principles of the SQL database views, giving us just the columns we need with the data we require. We can then use these views in our apps by invoking them in our `Filter` clause:

```
Filter(Tickets, 'Tickets (Views)'.'Active Tickets')
```

The list doesn't stop here; you can use store procedures to build code into your SQL database, apply business rules to your Dataverse tables, improve user authentication, and more. These are just examples of the capabilities available for these two data sources. Make your application building process more straightforward by leveraging them.

Choosing the right data source – real-world tests

Every data source has unique features that make it ideal for specific scenarios, whether you need a robust relational database, a document-centric infrastructure, or a lightweight approach for mobile applications.

This recipe will test some of the most well-known players of Microsoft's data source world: Dataverse, SharePoint, and Azure SQL Database. With the help of Power Automate, we will test both the reading and writing speeds of these three contestants.

Getting ready

The first requirement is to have the same data structure in each service:

- A list with the default **Title** column in SharePoint
- A table with a **Title** field in Azure SQL using the Basic tier
- A table with a **Title** column in Dataverse

After creating these sources, we head to Power Automate to build our tests at `https://powerautomate.microsoft.com/`

How it works...

1. To run our test, we will need some data, so let's build a cloud flow to write data into SharePoint. First, go to **My flows**, and then click on **New flow**, select **Instant cloud flow**, and then choose **Manually trigger a flow**.

2. We will load 500 records into each data source; to do this, we need to create a loop that will load the data. Click on the plus button to add an **Initialize variable** action, name it `autoNumber` of the **Integer** type, and set **Value** to 0:

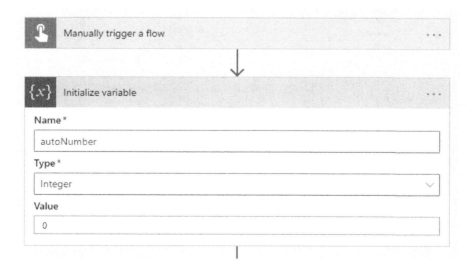

Figure 3.6 – Loop variable initialization

3. Add a new **Do until** action, which will run our data input loop. Set this action to execute until `autoNumber` is equal to `500`. Insert an action inside this loop. Search for **SharePoint** and then look for **Create item**. Configure it to use your SharePoint site address and your list name, and set the title to `Element` and the `autoNumber` variable.

4. Add one last action of **Increment variable** to increase the value of `autoNumber` by 1; this will make sure our loop keeps running until 500:

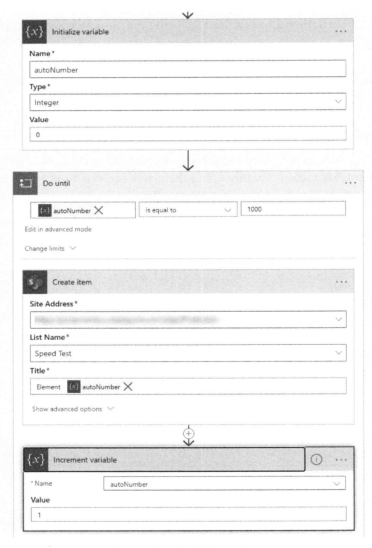

Figure 3.7 – Load data actions

5. Save this cloud flow and run it. It will create the items in SharePoint.

6. Create a new cloud flow repeating *steps 1* to *5* for Azure SQL, using **Insert row (V2)** in *step 3* with your server name, database name, and table name.

7. To build our last test, create another cloud flow and repeat *steps 1* to *5* for Dataverse (also known as Common Data Service) using the **Create a new record** action in *step 3*, setting the Power Platform environment and table name.

8. Now is the turn for the reading tests. Create a cloud flow for SharePoint, repeat *step 1*, and then add an action called Get items. Configure it to your site address and list name, and then save and run your cloud flow.

9. For Azure SQL, create a cloud flow and repeat *step 8* with the **Get rows (V2)** action. Map it to the previously used server name, database name, and table name.

10. Lastly, for Dataverse, create one last cloud flow and repeat *step 8* using the **List records** action with the same environment and table name as before:

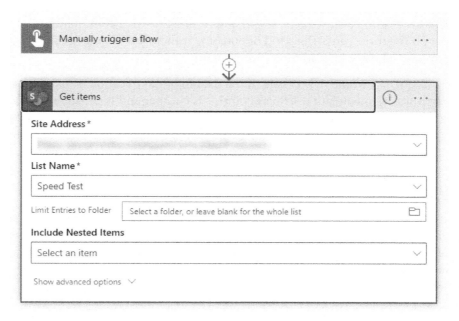

Figure 3.8 – Read data actions

How it works...

The six cloud flows we have just created will help to get an overview of these data sources' data-handling speeds. The load cloud flows need to get executed first so that we can have data for our reading tests. In my test scenarios, these were the execution times I've obtained on an average of three runs:

- **SharePoint**: 5.3 minutes
- **Azure SQL**: 3.3 minutes
- **Dataverse**: 3 minutes

Even though these are low times, only Dataverse got a constant runtime of 3 minutes. Azure SQL was a minute later on the second test, and SharePoint was more inconsistent with runs of 4, 9, and 3 minutes. We need to keep in mind that not only is it a matter of speed, but it is also a case of consistency, and this could be critical for the success of your application.

If we look at the reading test, we get a surprising result. The three contestants got 0 seconds flat on the three runs. This kind of outcome is mainly due to the caching mechanisms that all three have in their infrastructure.

However, this opens a whole new debate. If the data in our application is mainly for reading purposes, then why not use SharePoint? It is cheaper and is constant in the reading test; this, of course, will depend on the complexity of your entities. It is not the same using just one field than also including complex data types in the mix. Still, this specific SharePoint result is something to bear in mind.

There's more...

The platform used for SharePoint and Dataverse has predefined performance limits to comply with SLAs and response times. When using Azure SQL, we executed our tests on a database configured at the Basic tier level. Increasing this level improves performance on memory or throughput levels. You can even upgrade the database to a more robust and performant level. These skills should also be taken into account when deciding on your data sources.

I hope this workshop sparks your curiosity regarding the complexity behind the data sources you will be using in your developments.

Integrating on-premises data with the data source flexibility of canvas apps

Not all data lives in the cloud; sometimes, there are some organizational restrictions, legacy platforms that are too expensive to migrate, or complex network infrastructures, making our job a little more complicated.

There are different ways to overcome these challenges: synchronization processes, exposing application interfaces outside the local infrastructure, to name a couple. Thankfully, one of the most significant features of the Power Platform is the ability to connect to on-premises services using a data gateway.

The on-premises data gateway acts as a bridge between the local services and Azure. There is no need to set authentication for the services you need to access; this only allows the platforms to be visible between each other—authentication takes place afterward.

Gateways not only connect to databases; they also include access to the filesystem, local SharePoint servers, and other on-premises services.

Getting ready

Once you have identified the on-premises system that you want to access, you need to choose the type of gateway you want to use: regular or personal mode. As the name implies, the difference lies in the number of users. The personal mode only allows one user, and the other shares the gateway between multiple users.

There are specific use cases for each. For example, why configure a gateway for the entire organization if only the data analyst is the one that needs to gather information from the local SQL server to use it in Power BI? They can install the personal gateway on their computer to collect data whenever required.

Regarding technical requirements, to access on-premises data, you will need a Power Apps license. As discussed at the Preface of this book, you can use a **per-app plan** or a **per-user plan**. For personal use, you can also take advantage of the Power Apps Community plan license, which lets you access premium connectors and on-premises gateways.

The sample application and the mock-up Excel file are available from the GitHub repository located at `https://github.com/PacktPublishing/Microsoft-Power-Apps-Cookbook/tree/master/Chapter03`

How to do it...

1. For this recipe, we are going to use a personal gateway. To add one, go to the Power Apps maker portal, and from the left pane, go to **Data | Gateways** and select **New gateway** from the toolbar; this will open a new web page prompting you to download the installer. Execute it and follow the installation wizard:

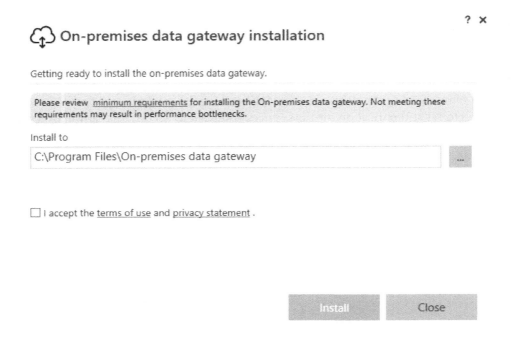

Figure 3.9 – Data gateway installation

2. Configure it by using an organizational email account to sign in. Register the new gateway and then give it a name, for example, `Personal connection`. Set a recovery key if you need to recover the gateway and hit **Configure**. After it completes the configuration, you should see a green check beside Power Apps, Power Automate, and Power BI, as shown:

Figure 3.10 – Successful gateway installation

3. To verify the visibility from the cloud, go back to the Power Apps maker portal, and you should see your newly created gateway:

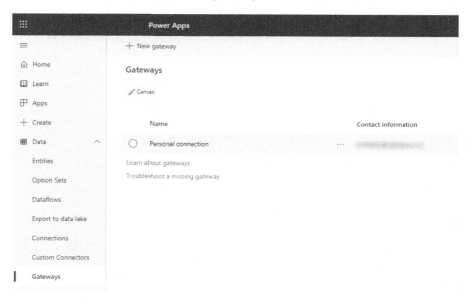

Figure 3.11 – Local gateway in the Power Apps maker portal

4. From the portal, create a new canvas app, with either the phone or tablet layout. From the left pane, select **Data sources**, click on **Add data**, and search for `file system`, and then click on **Add connection**.

5. A right pane will open where you need to set the root folder from where the connection will display the list of files and folders, for example, `C:`. As for authentication, you will need to enter a local username and password to ensure the platform can connect.

> **Tip**
> If you are using Windows 10 configured to log in using an organizational account, you can find your actual username by going to **System Settings | Accounts | Other users**. Your username will be on the list of **Workplace** or **school users** starting with `AzureAD\<YourFullName>`.

6. We are going to connect through the gateway to get data from a local Excel file. We have provided one for you to test, `Mock data.xls`, in the GitHub repository.

7. Once we have the connection, you will start browsing your filesystem from the root folder you specified, as shown in the following screenshot:

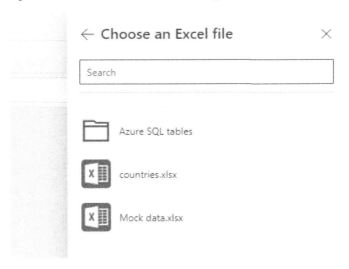

Figure 3.12 – Local file browser from Power Apps

Look for the provided file and select it; this will open the list of tables inside the Excel file. Select **Table1**, and then click on **Connect**. This action will add the table to the list of available data sources.

How it works...

Having an Excel table as a data source works the same way as any other source in Power Apps. You can add it to a gallery or perform formulas on the data to shape it as you see fit.

In the following screenshot, we designed an example application in which we are grouping by `Departments` on a combo box by using this formula:

```
Sort(GroupBy(Table1, "department", "Departments"), department)
```

The result is a grouped table of the Excel data by departments sorted in ascending order:

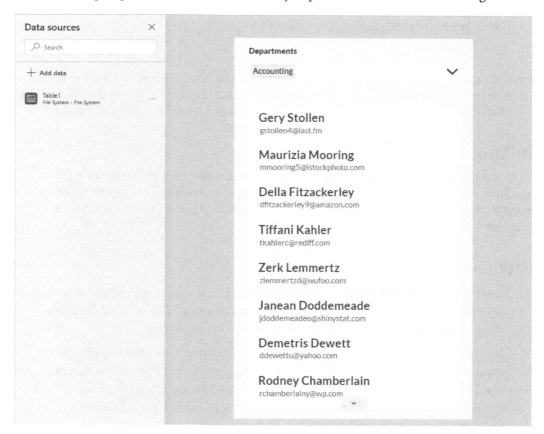

Figure 3.13 – Canvas power app using local data

As for the gallery, the `Items` property gets filtered by this formula:

```
Filter(Table1, department = DepartmentCbx.Selected.department)
```

As you can see, we can use the gateways for other services besides relational data. With the capability of canvas apps to use several connectors at once, the possibilities are endless.

Improving application speed and responsiveness by using static data

When working with data in the cloud, there are situations where the data collection process can be slow. Many factors can add delays when obtaining data: network speed, signal strength, and data source infrastructure, to name a few.

That's why you need to think about the data you are working with in your solutions:

- Where is it located?

- What is its availability?

- How changeable is it?

In this recipe, we are going to try to add a solution to the last question. If data doesn't change, why not make it static? We are not talking about adding the data in the actual code; we will add the data as a resource for the application, just like when adding an image.

Getting ready

As an example of data that rarely changes, we have provided a list of countries in an Excel file, `countries.xlsx`, in this chapter's repository: `https://github.com/PacktPublishing/Microsoft-Power-Apps-Cookbook/tree/master/Chapter03`

How to do it...

1. Go to the Power Apps maker portal and create a new canvas app; select either phone or tablet layout. From the left pane, select **Data sources**, click on **Add data**, and search for `import from Excel` and choose this connection.

2. This action will prompt you to select an Excel file from your system; pick the provided one, or any other from your computer, given that the data on this file has a table defined. More information on this can be found here: `https://support.microsoft.com/en-us/office/overview-of-excel-tables-7ab0bb7d-3a9e-4b56-a3c9-6c94334e492c`

3. Once the file has been uploaded, the right pane will display a list of tables inside the file for you to select. Choose one and then click on **Connect**. The selected one will appear on the list of data sources as if it were a connected one.

How it works...

If your data rarely changes, you can opt to add it as a resource in your application. Keep in mind, though, that the amount of data will increase the size of your app. A 3 MB Excel file is no candidate for this. Think of these resources as you would think about images. The smaller the file size they occupy, the better.

With the provided file, you can build an app that can help you search for a list of countries:

Figure 3.14 – List of static countries data

The gallery's Item property can then use a formula to filter the data by the text input:
Filter(Data, Find(SearchTxt.Text, name) > 0).

Now, you can check your apps for static data candidates and improve their performance by reducing data sources' connections.

Consuming external data by using Dataflows

The data for your solutions can come from very different sources: relational databases, on-premises data, analytics data, APIs, and even from regular files. This variety of data sources can be in any location or without an infrastructure to provide data.

Dataflows aim to be an instrument to gather all kinds of data sources into Dataverse. With this tool, you will be able to consolidate all the required data, related or not, into Dataverse, where you can then improve the collected information by adding views, relationships, and the like. Dataflows not only gather information but also allow you to transform it while doing it.

Using Power Query, the same technology used in Power BI, gives you a full set of features to shape your data. For more information about Power Query, please refer to `https://docs.microsoft.com/en-us/power-query/power-query-what-is-power-query`

Dataflows can run manually or on a schedule. They live in your environments, so you can have them running in your test environment, gathering data from test sources and have different ones in production.

For this recipe, we are going to use a different approach other than connecting to a database. We will get weather data and save the forecast into a table in our Dataverse database, thanks to the AccuWeather developer API.

Getting ready

You need a license to use Dataflows and you can't use a Power Apps Community plan because it is not part of the included features. You either need to use a per-app plan or a per-user plan. To get more information about licensing, please refer to `https://powerapps.microsoft.com/en-us/pricing/`

The next thing we are going to need is to register for a free developer account with AccuWeather at `https://developer.accuweather.com/`. Once registered, from **MY APPS**, you will need to create an app that will grant you access to their system through an API key. The limited trial is a free service that allows 50 calls a day and just one key per developer, but it suits our objective well.

How to do it...

1. Go to the Power Apps maker portal, and from the left pane, select **Data | Dataflows**, and click **New Dataflow** from the toolbar. Name the Dataflow in the dialog that opens, for example, `Weather data`, and then click on **Create**.

2. Next, the Power Query dialog displays the built-in data sources available for you to use. Every option has different kinds of settings. The authentication type and credentials get configured by their connection parameters and privacy levels, depending on the isolation you want for the data source. For this example, select **Web API**:

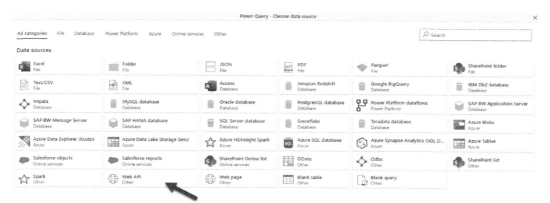

Figure 3.15 – List of data sources available for Power Query

3. On the Web API configuration dialog, enter the following URL, `http://dataservice.accuweather.com/forecasts/v1/daily/5day/349727?apikey=` plus your API key. This URL gets the 5-day daily forecast of New York City (location code `349727`). Set the desired name for **Connection name** and leave all the other values as default. The information we are going to receive gets structured as one record, as shown here:

```
{
    "Headline": {
        "EffectiveDate": "2020-08-16T08:00:00-04:00",
        "EffectiveEpochDate": 1597579200,
        "Severity": 5,
        "Text": "Rain today",
        "Category": "rain",
        "EndDate": "2020-08-16T20:00:00-04:00",
        "EndEpochDate": 1597622400,
        "MobileLink": "http://m.accuweather.com/en/us/new-
        york-ny/10007/extended-weather-
        forecast/349727?lang=en-us",
        "Link": "http://www.accuweather.com/en/us/new-
        york-ny/10007/daily-weather-
        forecast/349727?lang=en-us"
```

```
  },
  "DailyForecasts": [
    {
      "Date": "2020-08-16T07:00:00-04:00",
      "EpochDate": 1597575600,
      "Temperature": {
        "Minimum": {
          "Value": 65,
          "Unit": "F",
          "UnitType": 18
        },
        "Maximum": {
          "Value": 71,
          "Unit": "F",
          "UnitType": 18
        }
      },  ...
```

4. The next dialog is the actual Query editor, where you can transform the incoming data. Depending on the displayed data, the toolbar gives you hints on actions to execute. Let's start by selecting **To table** from the toolbar:

Figure 3.16 – Query editor for Power Query

5. This action converts the unstructured data into a table with columns and rows. Still, the data needs more transformation to get it right. On the **Transform** tab, select **Transpose**. This function interchanges rows per column and vice versa.

6. Now that we've rotated the data, we need to select **Use first row as headers** to promote the first data row as column names:

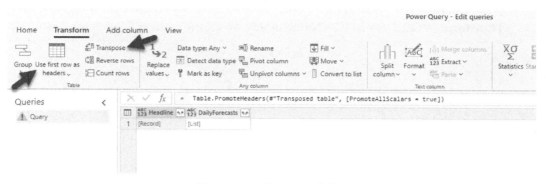

Figure 3.17 – Transposed data

7. The next step is to expand the data from the columns. We have a headline record and a list of forecasts. Let's remove the **Headline** column because we don't need it for our table—right-click on this column and select **Remove columns**. Then, click on the upper right of the DailyForecasts column to expand the data, as shown in the following figure:

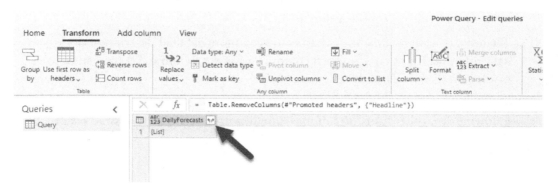

Figure 3.18 – Expand button

8. This action will expand the record to a list of rows with data. Click on the expand button again, and this time it will show the list of fields to choose. Select **Date** and **Temperature** and click on **OK**.

9. We already have the date and the temperature records. Let's get the day of the week by changing the data type. Right-click on the `DailyForecasts.Date` column and select **Change type | Date/Time/Zone**. Now, we can click on **Date** at the right of the **Transform** tab and format it as **Name of day**, as shown in the following screenshot:

Figure 3.19 – Name of day transformation

10. Now, let's expand the actual weather data by selecting the expand button on the `DailyForecasts.Temperature` column. Select the **Minimum** and **Maximum** fields. This action will create two columns with record data. Expand each of these columns and only select the **Value** field.

11. The last step is to rename the columns to get a more detailed description of the data columns. Right-click on each column and select **Rename**. Set the names to `Weekday`, `Minimum`, and `Maximum`.

12. Once all these changes are in place, we should see the data transformed like the following. Try other transformations if you like until you get the desired result. Click on **Next** when done:

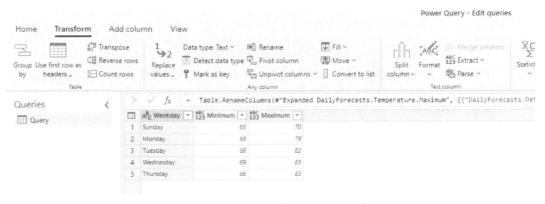

Figure 3.20 – Data transformation complete

13. Now is the time to place the transformed data into Dataverse. You will get the option to load the data into a new table or use an existing one. Let's use a new one by giving it a name and display name of New York Forecast. Set an auto-generated unique primary column and name it ID. Set the destination data types of each column to **Text**. Once ready, click on **Next**. You should get the following result:

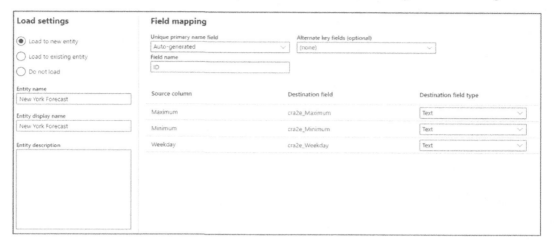

Figure 3.21 – Data load settings

14. Now on to the refresh settings; you can set it to manual or automatic. If we are gathering forecast data, the best thing might be to execute it automatically once a day. Set it to run every 1 day, starting from the desired date and time. Now, click **Create** to complete the process.

15. Once the configuration is complete, you should see your dataflow in the list, and, in a minute or two, you should see the **In progress** status, meaning that a first refresh is executing. When it completes, you will see the updated timestamp in the **Last Refresh** column and the scheduled **Next Refresh**.

How it works...

Now that we have completed the steps to build the dataflow, we can verify that the data is, in fact, in our Dataverse. Go to **Data | Tables** and look for the table you defined in the dataflow's load data step, in our case, New York Forecast.

Go to the **Data** tab and, by changing the view to **All columns**, verify that we got the 5-day forecast data:

Figure 3.22 – Current forecast view

Now go to the **Views** tab and create a new view. We defined a `Current Forecast` view to gain a better visualization. Please refer to *Chapter 2*, *Building Model-Driven Apps* for detailed information on table and view handling.

There's more...

We have learned that Dataflows are a great tool to ingest data from different sources on the same principles of low-code technologies, without the need to build a web app to connect to an API, transform the data using code, and then insert the results back into Dataverse.

Another feature of Dataflows is that they also serve as a synchronization tool. When defining the load data settings, there is a check option called **Delete rows that no longer exist in the query output**. This change requires the alternate key field to be mandatory as it uses it for comparison purposes when loading new data:

Figure 3.23 – Dataflow load settings for sync

This setting, tied to a scheduled refresh, turns Dataflows effectively into a sync mechanism. In our tests, we loaded data from an Azure SQL database into a `Technicians` table with these columns: `ID`, `Full name`, `Email`, and `Location`. After the first load, we deleted a record from the SQL database, and on the next refresh, the deleted one was removed.

Another concept that we need to consider is that you can configure a Dataflow to load several tables simultaneously. As you can see from the previous figure, we are loading both `SalesLT Products` and `technicians` on the same Dataflow.

As you can see, this is a great tool for integrating external data into Dataverse. Once there, you can have complete control over security, automatization, and data consumption.

4
Automating processes with Power Automate

The Power Platform provides different solutions to solve business organizations' needs; Power BI to analyze data, Power Apps to build applications, Power Virtual Agents to interact with users, and Power Automate to effectively automate processes.

In this chapter, we will talk about Power Automate, which aims to improve business processes with a series of actions to help streamline existing operations. Examples of these actions include executing procedures based on specific events, building data integration systems, automating repetitive tasks, and more.

Before we dive into this chapter, we will also cover a key topic regarding the different types of flows. Having understood this concept, we can then build recipes using examples for diverse scenarios:

- Creating a sales survey solution with Power Automate and Microsoft Forms
- Building a file processing automation for SharePoint document libraries
- Overcoming Power Apps delegation with Power Automate
- Creating a modular solution with Power Automate

Technical requirements

Depending on the services we are connecting when working with Power Automate, there might be a license requirement. Please refer to *Chapter 3, Choosing the right data source for your applications*, to get more information regarding this. For these situations, we could use either of the following plans. The complete version of this application is available from our GitHub repository at `https://github.com/PacktPublishing/Microsoft-Power-Apps-Cookbook/tree/master/Chapter04`

Paid plans

In Power Automate, three licensing plans allow access to data using premium and custom connectors and also on-premises data with data gateways. The difference lies in the capacity of these plans and who will be the end user of them:

- There are two plans for users: the **Per user plan** and **the Per user plan with attended RPA (Robotic Process Automation)**. Both let you create unlimited flows, but the latter adds robotic process automation of legacy systems and includes AI builder service credits.

- On the other hand, the **Per flow plan** allows the entire organization to use five flows without needing to license each user.

Using either of these options depends entirely on the analysis of the business process that requires automation. For detailed information about the pricing of these plans, please refer to `https://flow.microsoft.com/en-us/pricing/`

The different types of flows

Power Automate offers five types of flows to provide organizations with as many options as possible. There is a type for all kinds of scenarios.

Automated

These cloud flows get executed when a specific action triggers them, for example:

- When a new email arrives in Gmail

- When a new tweet gets posted on Twitter

These are examples of triggered actions. You can build your solutions around them by doing the following:

- When I receive a new email having the word *invoice* in the title, extract the attachments and copy them to the Finance SharePoint document library.

- When a new tweet gets posted, send the content to the AI builder for sentiment analysis, and then send a Teams notification to Marketing if the result is negative.

Instant

If you want to trigger a cloud flow manually, this is your option. You can execute this by doing the following:

- Clicking a button from your mobile phone
- Running them from a canvas app
- Selecting a file in a SharePoint document library

Those were some examples of actions that can trigger a cloud flow manually. We can create solutions such as the following:

- Creating an on-demand report from the current sales records
- Notifying a user via Teams from a canvas Power app
- Requesting a signature for a selected file in SharePoint

Scheduled

As the name implies, these cloud flows get executed at a specific date and time and with a defined recurrence. These are some use cases:

- Performing a monthly backup of a particular folder into my personal OneDrive
- Creating and sending the timesheets report every 2 weeks
- Performing a daily cleanup of an Azure SQL table

Business process

As mentioned in *Chapter 2, Building Model-Driven Apps*, these flows act as a guiding system for our Dataverse tables to help users through the data gathering process. Examples include the following:

- Turning leads into opportunities for the sales department
- Guiding a support case in a help desk system

UI

These desktop flows bring **Robotic Process Automation** (**RPA**) to Power Automate by recording your interaction with web and desktop applications to avoid repetitive tasks by automating the playback of these interactions. Using these can help in the following cases:

- Data entry on a legacy ERP system that has no API to interact with
- Recording the customization of a particular application and then replicating it in different virtual machines

As you can see, there is a diversity of flows aimed at solving almost every business requirement, and the platform keeps evolving to offer even more features to help you achieve your goals.

Creating a sales survey solution with Power Automate and Microsoft Forms

Web forms are a great tool for gathering information. Whether you require feedback for a new organizational process, an event registration, or even a simple contact form, you need to define the fields to collect the data correctly in these forms.

Microsoft Forms gives you an easy way to create them with an easy-to-use interface that allows you to create forms, quizzes, and polls in no time. We will take advantage of this and complete our solution by integrating an automated cloud flow using Power Automate.

The first step is to design a sales survey, and then, depending on the answers received, we will notify a team to further engage with the customer.

The way we notify people in our organizations has evolved since the use of email messages. Using email for external users and collaboration tools for the internal business is the norm. We are also accustomed to receiving rich notifications in which we can interact directly using our platform of choice.

Adaptive cards help improve notifications by using user interface code pieces, which act and look native in the platform where they are delivered.

The following is an example of an adaptive card:

Figure 4.1 – Adaptive card examples in Microsoft Teams and Web Chat

Targets of adaptive cards can be mobile devices, desktop applications, bot platforms, and collaboration tools, such as Microsoft Teams. To get more information, please refer to `https://adaptivecards.io/`

Getting ready

To recreate this recipe, you will need a regular Microsoft 365 business plan (Microsoft 365 Business Basic and up) or a Microsoft personal account (Outlook, Hotmail, or Live). Both account types let you use Microsoft Forms for free.

On the Power Automate side, we will use a standard connector so we can go with the same licensing requirements; either account type works for our scenario. We will also make use of a marketing team in Microsoft Teams as an example.

How to do it...

1. Browse to Microsoft Forms by typing this address, `https://forms.office.com`, and once there, click on the **New Form** button. This action will open the designer where we can start setting up our form.

2. Click on **Untitled form** to define the name, description, and image. You can also click **Theme** on the toolbar to take advantage of built-in themes.

The following is an example of the *Office* theme:

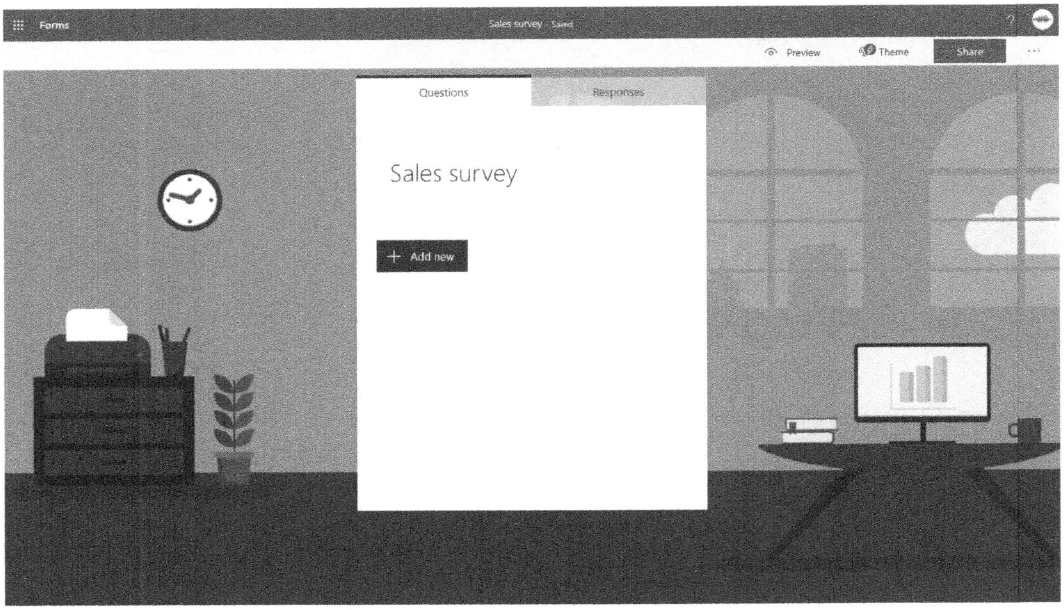

Figure 4.2 – Microsoft Forms theme

3. Now, let's click on **Add new** to start including fields. A list of options appears to select the type. You can choose from the following field types:

Figure 4.3 – Field types available in Microsoft Forms

4. To build our sales survey, let's create the following fields:

- **Text**

  Customer name

- **Choice** – Required

  How did you first learn about our services?

  Advertisement, Trade show, Search engine, Other

- **Text** – Long answer

  Please describe the main reasons you selected our services

- **Rating** – 5 stars – Required

  Overall rating of our services

- **Choice** – Required

  Would you like a follow-up call?

  Yes, No

5. Click on **Preview** on the toolbar. You should have a form just like the following:

Figure 4.4 – Sales survey preview

6. On the toolbar, click on **...** | **Settings** to configure who can fill out the form. For our recipe, we are going to select **Anyone with the link can respond**. You can change it as desired.

    Now that we have our form ready, we can start building actions that will be triggered when we start receiving the responses.

7. Go to the Power Automate portal, `https://flow.microsoft.com/`, to create a new cloud flow by clicking on **My flows** and then **New flow** | **Automated cloud flow**. This will open a dialog to choose the trigger.

8. Give it a name such as `Sales survey flow`, search for the trigger `When a new response is submitted` on Microsoft Forms, and then click on **Create**:

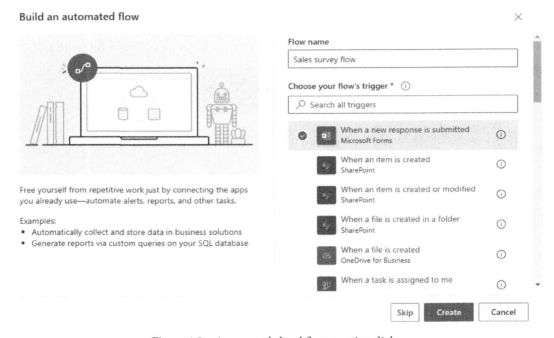

Figure 4.5 – Automated cloud flow creation dialog

9. When the designer opens, you will have to select the form from which we will expect answers by providing its `Form Id`.

10. The next step will be to get the actual response data by choosing the **Get response details** action using the previous step's result as the input data.

11. Now we need to redirect the flow depending on the *Would you like a follow-up call* question. To do this, we need to add a condition action to check whether the answer was `Yes`. Select this question in the left value field, select `is equal to` in the condition dropdown, and then, in the right value field, enter `Yes`:

Figure 4.6 – Response details action and condition

> **Experimental features**
>
> If the Power Automate interface differs from what these screenshots display, it's because of the experimental features' activation. To view this new interface, go to the Power Automate portal, click on the screen's top-right gear, and then on the **View all Power Automate settings** link. Enable this feature from the dialog that opens.

12. On the `If yes` route, let's add a Teams notification to our Marketing team using an adaptive card. Add a new action and search for `Post an Adaptive Card to a Teams channel and wait for a response`. By using this, we can send a notification to a specific channel and wait for feedback. Select the **Team** and **Channel** fields where you would like to send it, and in the **Message** section, add the keys and their respective values to bind them in the message. We can use these keys in the adaptive card designer to define where to display the data. For example, the `rating` key links to the `Overall rating of our service` response.

13. Click on **Create Adaptive Card** to open the designer. We have designed a message that displays the form's response and asks for a confirmation on the follow-up. You can get the code of our adaptive card in our GitHub repo: `https://github.com/PacktPublishing/Microsoft-Power-Apps-Cookbook/tree/master/Chapter04`

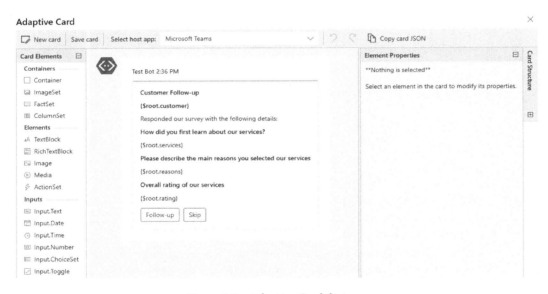

Figure 4.7 – Adaptive Card designer

14. Lastly, in the cloud flow action, select **Yes** under `Should update card` to change the notification with the `Update message` field's contents. We can use this to notify everyone on the team when someone accepts or discards the follow-up.

15. On the `If no` route, we could, for example, add a record to a `Ratings` table in Dataverse to keep track of the ratings we are receiving from our customers. Then, we could build **Key Performance Indicators** (**KPIs**) using table charts or Power BI. The following screenshot represents the condition routes configured:

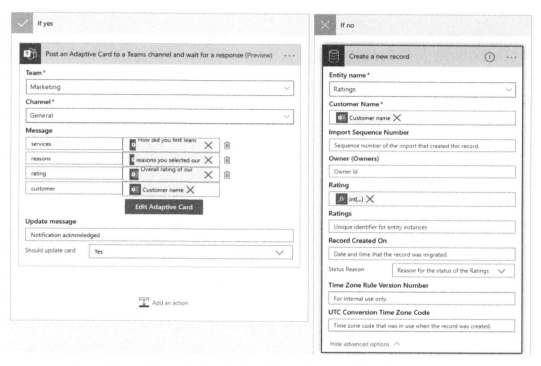

Figure 4.8 – Adaptive Card and Create Dataverse record actions

You can change either of these actions to your specific needs when automating responses from Microsoft Forms.

How it works...

To test our recipe, we need to send some responses using our form. Whenever you select Yes in the follow-up question, a message will be sent to the Marketing team, letting them know that a customer wants to continue engaging with our company. In the following screenshot, you can see the notification:

Figure 4.9 – Adaptive Card in action

We can continue to iterate with the responses from our notification by executing more activities, including the following:

- Creating a follow-up Teams meeting
- Sending an automated email to the customer
- Updating the customer record in the CRM system

These are just examples of what you can achieve by automating customer satisfaction feedback using Power Automate, but it doesn't end here. Imagine being an educator who builds quizzes using Microsoft Forms and then auto-grades his students using Power Automate while feeding a database with the scores for further analysis. The possibilities are endless.

Building a file processing automation for SharePoint document libraries

Improving business activities, especially the recurring ones, is a top priority in every organization. The tedious work of repeating a set of actions for a business process can be prone to errors because the personnel tends to act by replication and without validation.

Power Automate builds upon this need to help organizations automate their tasks so people can focus on the business.

In this recipe, we will automate a business process using a SharePoint document library that handles the quotes of a given company. These quotes get created using Microsoft Word with defined metadata to help classify its contents.

When a quote is complete, users can manually execute a cloud flow, which converts the document into a PDF file with the same metadata as the original file. It also notifies the Finance team if the quote is over $100,000.

Getting ready

When using SharePoint, as far as licensing goes, a regular Microsoft 365 Business Basic is required to include this service for your organization. On the Power Automate side, we will use standard connectors, so there is no need for an additional license.

How to do it...

1. First, let's start by building a document library. Go to your desired SharePoint site, click on the gear icon located in the top-right corner, and then select **Site contents**.

2. Below the site title, you will find a toolbar. Click on **New | Document library**. A panel will open on the right side where you can input the name of your library. For our example, name it Quotes. Add a description if you like and deselect **Show in site navigation**, so it doesn't appear in the site's navigation (unless you want it to).

3. On the new library, click on the **Add column** indicator at the end of the column titles. Let's add the following columns:

- **Single line of text** – Quote number
- **Choice** – Department

  Choices: Finance, HR, Marketing, IT

- **Currency** – Amount
- **Single line of text** – Fiscal year

  Default value (calculated value): =YEAR(TODAY)

4. Reorder the columns to get the desired result. The following image displays a Quotes library with the previous columns and a few loaded files:

Quotes

		Name	Quote number	Department	Fiscal year	Amount
○						
		202054454.docx	202054454	Finance	2020	$350,000.00
		2020546589.docx	2020546589	HR	2020	$65,000.00
		2020564541403.docx	2020564541403	Marketing	2020	$25,000.00

Figure 4.10 – Quotes document library

5. From the library toolbar, select **Automate | Power Automate | Create a flow**. This action will display a panel with ready-made templates to create a flow. Click on **See your flows** to build your own. Please note that this cloud flow needs to be created in the default environment in order for it to work.

6. Once in the Power Automate portal, go to **My flows** on the left pane and then click on **New flow | Instant cloud flow** to build an on-demand flow. On the dialog that opens, set a name, choose For a selected file in SharePoint, and then click **Create**.

7. The first action that appears acts as a link from our cloud flow to the selected document library. Choose your SharePoint site address and the Quotes library. Add a new step to get the actual properties for the file requesting the automation. Click on **New step** and look for Get file properties in SharePoint. Set the same site address and library as the previous action, and for the **Id**, select it from the result of the last step:

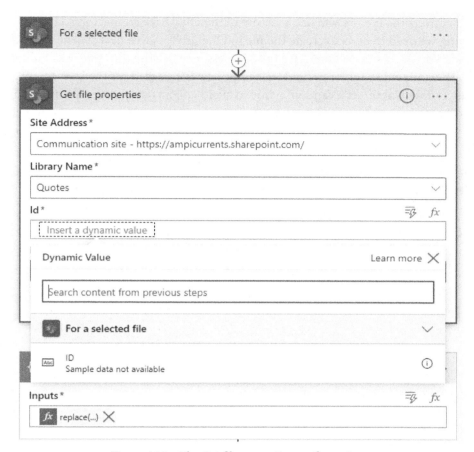

Figure 4.11 – The Get file properties configuration

8. To create our resulting PDF file, we need to define its name. For this, we are going to use the `Compose` action to build a formula to generate it. Add this new action and, for **Inputs**, use the following command:

```
replace(triggerBody()?['entity']?['fileName'], '.docx',
'.pdf').
```

With this formula, we are using the same filename but changing the file extension from Word (`.docx`) to PDF (`.pdf`). To tidy up our cloud flow, let's rename this action from `Compose` to `PDF filename` by clicking on the ellipsis and then **Rename**.

9. Now that we have all the metadata, we can start the actual automation. Let's get the file content so we can use it in the conversion. Click on **New step** and look for `Get file content` in SharePoint. Set the same site address as before, and for the file identifier, use the `Identifier` collected from the previous step.

10. To convert the file, we will use a feature of the OneDrive connector, so the first thing we need to do is to create the file in OneDrive. Add a new step and search for `Create file` in OneDrive for Business. Choose the root folder as **Folder Path** or any other folder to hold the temporary file needed for the conversion. As for **File Name**, set a random name to avoid concurrency issues if this cloud flow gets executed more than once. We can use a formula for this, for example, `concat(ticks(utcNow()), '.docx')`. As regards **File Content**, select the result of the previous step.

11. To do the conversion, we need to add a new step. Look for `Convert file` in OneDrive for Business. For **File**, select the Id of the previous step and PDF as **Target type**.

12. Let's add a new step to delete our temp file and avoid clutter in our OneDrive. Look for `Delete file` on OneDrive. For **File**, select the ID of the *Create file* step:

Figure 4.12 – OneDrive actions

13. We need to get this result back to SharePoint, but before we do, we need to consider that this might be a second execution of the cloud flow, so we will need to do some cleanup first. Add a new step and look for `Get file metadata using path` on SharePoint to check whether the PDF file already exists. Set the same **Site Address** as before and, in **File Path**, input `/Quotes/` and then, from the Dynamic content selector, pick the **Outputs** from the **PDF filename** action.

14. If the file exists, let's delete it. Add a new step called `Delete file` in SharePoint. Set the same **Site Address** as before and use the ID from the previous step as the input of **File Identifier**. Rename this action to `Delete PDF file`:

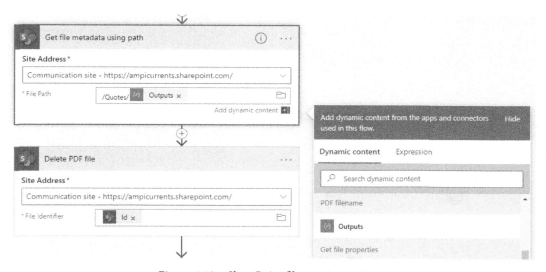

Figure 4.13 – SharePoint file creation actions

15. We need to keep in mind that the first time this cloud flow gets executed, the PDF file won't exist, so we need to inform Power Automate that if any of the previous two steps fail, it should continue to run the rest of the actions. To do this, we are going to add a new action called `Scope`. This action allows us to encapsulate several steps together. If one fails, the entire scope fails.

16. Drag the `Get file metadata using path` and `Delete PDF file` actions inside the scope.

17. Add a new step and look for `Create file` in SharePoint. Set the same site address and path as in the previous actions. For **File Name**, use the **Outputs** from the **PDF filename** action, and for **File Content**, get the conversion result of the *Convert file* step. Rename this action to `Create PDF file`. Going back to the scope structure, this is where we inform Power Automate that, if the scope fails, execution should be continued. Click on the ellipsis of this action and then on **Configure run after**. Select **has failed** and then click on **Done**. If any of the steps inside the scope fail, this step will continue:

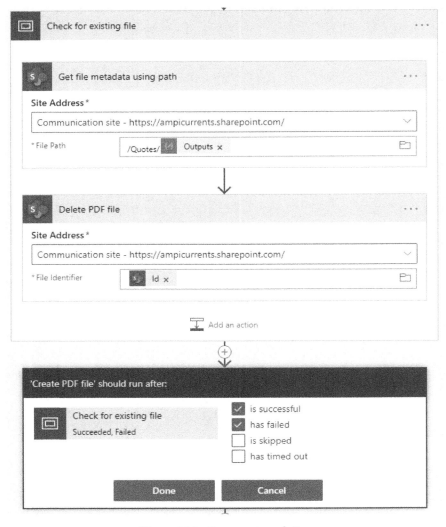

Figure 4.14 – Scope encapsulation

18. We now need to replicate the same metadata as the original file. Add a new step and look for `Update file properties`. Set the same site address and library as before, and the **ItemId** from the last file creation step as the ID. The rest of the fields come from the **Get file properties** result. Keep in mind that the Department field, being of the Choice type, needs to get the actual value, so look for `Department Value`:

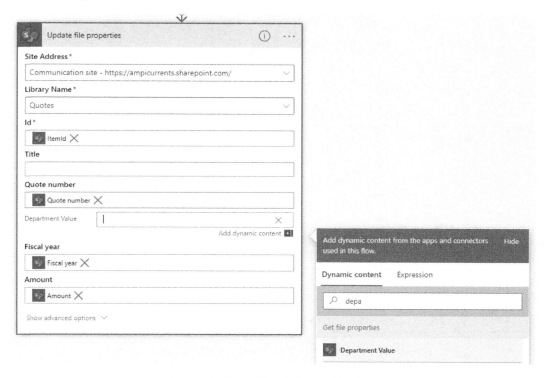

Figure 4.15 – Field metadata replication

19. Our last step is to notify the Finance team if a quote is over $100,000. Add a new action called `Condition`. Let's check whether the amount of the **Get file properties** result is greater than 100,000. Rename this condition to `Check the amount`.

20. On the `If yes` route, add a new step called `Post a message` on Teams. Set the desired **Teams** and **Channel** fields and build a message using the fields from the `Get file properties` result. Rename this action to `Post a message to Finance`. This is what the amount condition and the notification message look like:

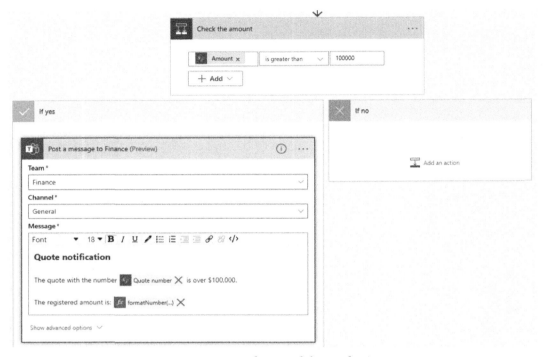

Figure 4.16 – Amount condition and the notification message

How it works...

Back in the document library, you will notice that if you select a file and then click **Automate** on the toolbar, you will get your cloud flow listed and ready to process the chosen file. On the first execution, it will ask for permission to use the connectors defined in your cloud flow, in our case, SharePoint, OneDrive, and Microsoft Teams. Click on **Continue** and then on **Run flow** to start processing the file:

Figure 4.17 – Flow activation on a selected file

When the process finishes, the converted file will appear in the document library with the .pdf extension. If the amount is over $100,000, a notification will appear in the Finance team channel, alerting them about this quote, looking like this:

Figure 4.18 – Teams channel notification

This solution is an all-round example of a quote processing system. You can add more steps, validations, and notifications depending on the needs of your Finance department.

This cloud flow is available in our GitHub repository here: https://github.com/PacktPublishing/Microsoft-Power-Apps-Cookbook/tree/master/Chapter04

You can improve it by doing the following:

- Adding actions to the **If no** route of the **Check the amount** condition
- Including a document signing solution to sign the final quote
- Sending the final quote via email to the customer

Overcoming Power Apps delegation with Power Automate

Canvas apps offer a wide range of features. Among them, we can highlight the ability to connect to multiple data sources simultaneously for a given application.

Delegation is a term used in canvas apps, which means that the platform is delegating the data processing to the data source rather than doing it in the application itself. We need to acknowledge this if we want to have applications with quick response times.

Querying data uses memory and processing power; the less of these our application uses, the better. That's why we need to use data sources that support delegation. To get more insight on this matter, please refer to `https://docs.microsoft.com/en-us/powerapps/maker/canvas-apps/delegation-overview`

Another critical aspect is the network bandwidth used when getting data. By default, Power Apps limits the number of records retrieved to 500. Even if your data source supports delegation, getting more items than that will throw a warning because the platform won't be able to get all the requested data. In the following screenshot, you can see the sign on top of the label that calculates the number of records of our Speed Test list. The list has 3,000 items, and the app can only count the first 500 received by the SharePoint connector:

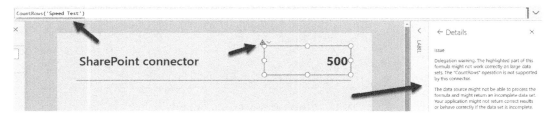

Figure 4.19 – Delegation warning for a SharePoint list with 3,000 items

> **User experience advice**
>
> When designing your application, the best approach is to work with filtered data. It makes no sense to throw 3,000 items into a gallery for the user to browse. The best method should be to filter data by categories, indexed fields, or any other column that lets you work with limited sets of data.

There are times when delegation does not play in our favor. As indicated in Figure 4.19, if we need to count the total number of records of our data source, we will hit delegation issues sooner or later. Showing all the items of a given table using a gallery will end up in the same situation.

In the development phase of our app, we might have missed this, or perhaps the client requests to show all data, irrespective of the number of records. For these situations, we will leverage Power Automate and the strength of the formulas available in Power Apps to solve these issues.

Getting ready

To use this recipe, we need to have a SharePoint list with at least 3,000 items. Please refer to *Chapter 3, Choosing the right data source for your applications*, for a cloud flow example that loads 500 items to a list as a template.

The files needed for this recipe are available through the GitHub repository located at `https://github.com/PacktPublishing/Microsoft-Power-Apps-Cookbook/tree/master/Chapter04`

How to do it...

1. Go to the Power Automate portal, `https://powerautomate.microsoft.com`, to create a new flow by clicking on **New flow | Instant cloud flow**. Give it a name and select Power Apps as the trigger, and then click **Create**.

2. The first step is to get data from our SharePoint list filled with 3,000 elements. There are ready-made actions to get this data from this data source, but we will introduce you to the SharePoint REST API to acquire these items. Why? A picture is worth a thousand words:

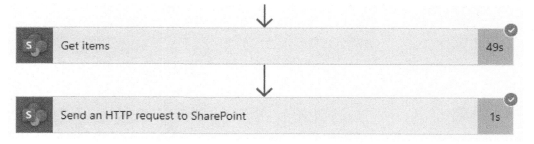

Figure 4.20 – Speed comparison between two actions

Imagine a user waiting almost a minute to get the data; this won't help with your solution's user adoption. Add a new step and look for `Send an HTTP request to SharePoint`. Set **Site Address** to the SharePoint site, leave **Method** as GET, as we are querying data, and for the **Uri**, you will need to enter the following command:

```
_api/web/lists/GetByTitle('Speed test')/
items?$select=Title,Department&$top=3000
```

Let's break this code down:

- `_api` – SharePoint endpoint where we are going to establish the communication.
- `web` – Methods to access information from a given site.
- `lists` – Endpoint for lists handling methods.
- `GetByTitle('Speed test')` – We indicate that it should look for the list with the name speed test.
- `items` – Get all the items of the list.
- `select` – Modifier to specify that we only want the Title and Department columns.
- `top` – Modifier to indicate that we want to limit the result to the first 3,000 elements. Keep in mind that going over 5,000 items requires further tweaking and pagination.

  In the **Headers** section, add these items:

  a. **Key**: `accept` – `Value: application/json`

  b. **Key**: `odata` – `Value: nometadata`

`nometadata` indicates that we don't want extra metadata information. We do this to clean as much data from the response as possible, thereby reducing bandwidth.

3. Querying SharePoint data using this action returns data in a JSON format. To understand this data and use it, we need to parse it. Add a new step and look for `Parse JSON`. For **Content**, select the body of our previous step, and for **Schema**, copy the contents of the `schema.json` file provided from our GitHub repository. Another way to get this schema is to run the cloud flow with just the query action and get the body from the outputs, as seen in the following screenshot:

Figure 4.21 – Response output from SharePoint

4. Now let's clean up the response even further by using the **Select** action. This option allows us to select only the necessary columns from the previously received data. Add a new step and look for `Select`. Use `value` from the **Parse JSON** action in the **From** field. In the **Map** section, set these values:

- **Key**: `Name – Value: Title field`

- **Key**: `Department – Value: Department field`:

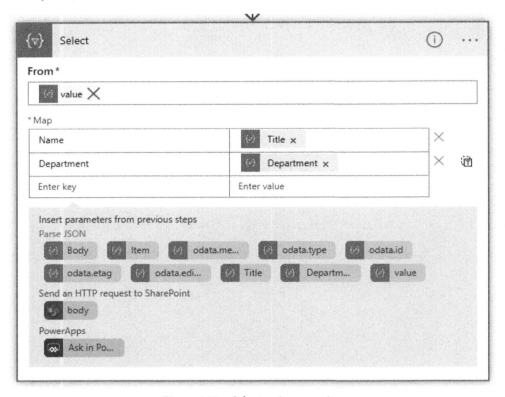

Figure 4.22 – Select action mapping

5. To send the response to Power Apps, we only have a handful of data types: Text, Yes/No, File, Email, Number, and Date. None of these is a complex data type as an object or an array. To solve this, we are going to use the `Join` action. As the name implies, this action joins an array to a string using a delimiter. Add a new step and look for `Join`. Use `Output` from the **Select action** in the **From** field. For the **Join with** field, use the semicolon.

6. Our last step is to send the data back to Power Apps. Add a new action and look for `Respond to a PowerApp or flow`. Click on **Add an output**, select **Text,** and use `data` as the **Title**. For the value, select **Output** from the **Join** action.

7. Go to the Power Apps portal, `https://make.powerapps.com/`, to make use of our newly generated cloud flow. First, make sure you are in the same environment as the cloud flow, click **Apps** in the left panel, and then click on **New app | Canvas**. Choose either Phone layout or Tablet layout.

8. Insert **Button**, **Label**, and **Gallery** controls. Change their visual properties to match your desired style.

9. Click on the button and, on the **Action** tab of the main toolbar, click on **Power Automate**. This action will open a list pane of all the instant cloud flows in this environment. Select yours from the list. This action will associate it with the app and will place the calling code to the `OnSelect` method.

10. From the **Action** tab of the main toolbar, click on **On select** to open the formula bar of this action. Change it to the following code:

```
ClearCollect(
    Elements,
    ForAll(
        Split(
            Delegationhelper.Run().data,
            ";"
        ),
        With(
            Match(
                Result,                      "\
{\""Name\""\:\""(?:(?<name>.+))\""\,\""Department\""\:\""
(?:(?<department>.+))\""\}"
            ),
            {
                Name: name,
                Department: department
            }
        )
    )
)
```

Let's break down the previous code:

- `ClearCollect` creates a new collection to hold the data coming from Power Automate.

- `ForAll` iterates through the array in parallel threads.

- `Split` creates an array from the string received from Power Automate by breaking it using the semicolon used to join it. Please note that `Delegationhelper` is the name of the connected cloud flow. Change it accordingly.

- `With` executes a regular expression formula by using the `Match` function, exposing the result to the name and department variables.

11. *Alt*-Click the button to execute the code and create the collection.

12. Select the gallery control and set its data source to the `Elements` collection. Adapt the elements inside this control to display the collected data, using `ThisItem. Name` and `ThisItem.Department` as their values.

13. Select the label and set its text property to `CountRows(Elements)`. Counting the elements of the collection won't throw the delegation warning.

How it works...

After completing the steps, you can have an application just like the following screenshot:

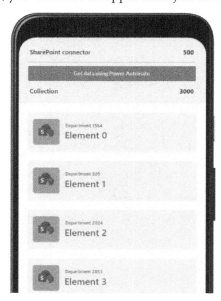

Figure 4.23 – Delegation example Power App

As you can see, the SharePoint connector can only count the first 500 elements, while the data received from Power Automate handles the whole 3,000.

We are taking advantage of various actions to get data from our data sources to overcome the delegation issues. Until Power Apps can learn to resolve JSON data, we can use the regular expression method to make use of the data in our apps.

The code we used to transform back the data in Power Apps consists of an iteration through the data received from Power Automate, extracting the fields from each record, and collecting the result in the `Elements` collection.

The extraction expression looks for patterns that match this data, `{ "Name" : "Element 2088" , "Department" : "Department 1578" }`, and then uses capture groups to extract the fields into one record:

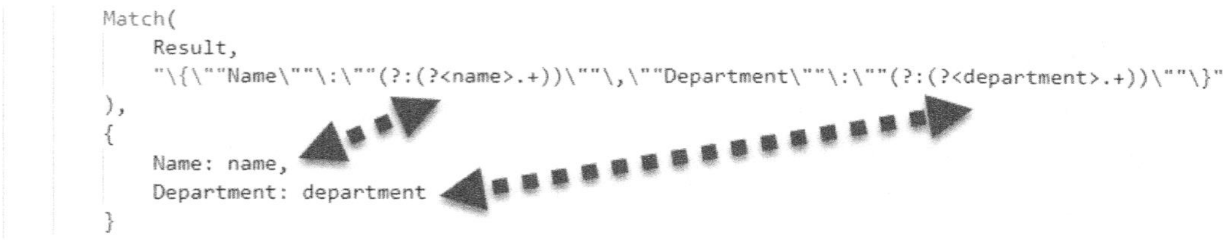

```
Match(
    Result,
    "\{\""Name\""\:\""(?:(?<name>.+))\""\,\""Department\""\:\""(?:(?<department>.+))\""\}"
),
{
    Name: name,
    Department: department
}
```

Figure 4.24 – Capture groups in regular expressions

For more information regarding this technique, please refer to `https://www.regular-expressions.info/refcapture.html`

Power Automate is an integration tool from its inception, so it's prepared to handle a large amount of data without having to deal with application responsiveness, user interaction, or adoption. This plays well in our favor to solve this kind of issue. We still recommend taking advantage of delegation when interacting with data sources, but this approach can solve the dilemma for those particular situations.

The demo application, as well as the cloud flow, are available in our GitHub repository at `https://github.com/PacktPublishing/Microsoft-Power-Apps-Cookbook/tree/master/Chapter04`

There's more...

There is a setting in Power Apps that can bend the limit of 500 records when delegation issues appear, but it only raises the limit to 2,000.

To access this, from the Power Apps Studio go to **File** in the main toolbar, then **Settings | Advanced settings,** and then change the value of **Data row limit for non-delegable queries**. If you can't solve your delegation issue at the data source level and your data is under the 2,000 items limit, this might be another escape route. Again, these are only workarounds for specific situations; remember: data always grows.

Regarding the use of SharePoint REST APIs, there is much more that you can do than just query data: create, update, or delete elements, lists, or even SharePoint sites. To get more information about the features available in this API, please check the following link: `https://docs.microsoft.com/en-us/sharepoint/dev/sp-add-ins/get-to-know-the-sharepoint-rest-service`

Creating a modular solution with Power Automate

Power Automate is an excellent tool for automating repetitive tasks to solve business needs with a great set of features. There are some occasions where you might have built a great solution to a process using a flow that takes care of several tasks with just one click.

To set an example, let's imagine you have an instant cloud flow used by the marketing department that takes care of these activities using an email address as input:

- Sends a pre-built email to that address
- Saves a logging record to a table in Dataverse
- Sends a notification to the marketing team in Microsoft Teams, letting them know that an email activity has completed

What would happen if another process in your company that takes care of other activities also needs the activities already created in your flow? One solution would be to recreate the same actions in the new flow, but what about maintenance? If, later on, you need to change something in the marketing process, you would need to make the change twice.

In this recipe, we will learn how to create modular solutions in Power Automate that let us break one big solution into pieces or reuse existing ones to improve your flows' maintenance and readability.

Getting ready

To create a modular solution, we need to work with Power Platform Solutions, a feature that lets you pack several components into a single distribution package. Examples of these components may include canvas apps, model-driven apps, Power Automate cloud flows, and Dataverse tables. To get more information about Solutions, please refer to *Chapter 2, Building Model-Driven Apps*.

We'll start with our previous example, *Building a file processing automation for SharePoint document libraries*, and then we will create a *parent* flow that will call our marketing flow.

A SharePoint list, called `Marketing Emails`, is also required with the following structure:

Column name	Column data type	Required
Customer	Single line of text	Yes
Address	Multiple lines of text	No
Email	Single line of text	Yes

Figure 4.25 – Marketing Emails SharePoint list structure

Add sample data to this list using, for example, mock data from this service: `https://mockaroo.com/`

The complete solution package is available in our GitHub repository at `https://github.com/PacktPublishing/Microsoft-Power-Apps-Cookbook/tree/master/Chapter04`

How to do it...

1. Go to the Power Automate portal, `https://powerautomate.microsoft.com`, and click on **Solutions** on the left pane. From the toolbar, click on **New solution**. This action will open a pane on the right to configure your new solution. Set its **Display name** and **Name** fields and then select **Publisher**. Leave the rest of the options as their default settings and then click on **Create**:

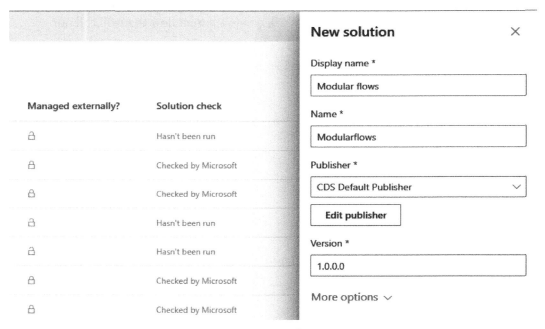

Figure 4.26 – New solution pane

2. When the solution gets created, open it from the list of available solutions. Let's add components by clicking **New | Flow** from the toolbar. This action will open the flow designer to start building our automation. Let's select **Flow button for mobile | Manually trigger a flow** as the trigger. On this new action, click on **Add an input** and choose Email as the type. Name it as you wish; we are naming it `Marketing Email`.

3. Add a new step and look for `Send an email` on Office 365 Outlook. Set the email parameter in the **To** field and set a test **Subject** and **Body** email:

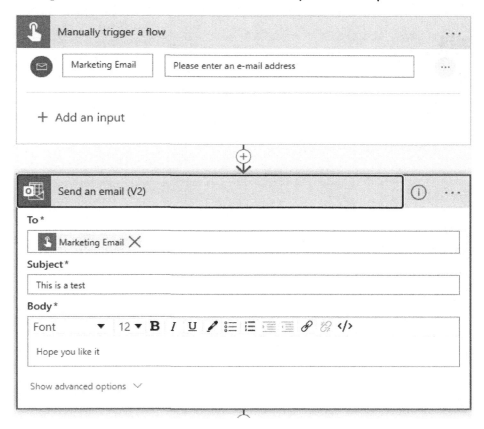

Figure 4.27 – Cloud flow parameters and Email action

4. Add another step and look for `Create a new record` under Common Data Service (or Dataverse when updated). Select a table from the list and save the email parameter for logging purposes. If you don't have a table created, Go to **Data | Tables** to create one. Refer to *Chapter 2, Building Model-Driven Apps*, to learn more about data table handling.

5. Add one more step and look for `Post a message as the Flow bot to a user` on Microsoft Teams. As an example, set **Headline** to `Email notification`. Input `Marketing Email` as the **Recipient** and write a message such as `The marketing email was delivered and logged`.

6. For both flows to work, the last step must be a response, so add a new action and look for `Respond to a PowerApp or flow`. Click on **Add an output** and select a data type to respond, for example, a text output with the value `Logged`:

Figure 4.28 – Logging actions and response of the marketing process flow

7. Now that we have this cloud flow complete, we can name it by clicking on **Untitled** in the top left of the screen, for example, `Marketing Process`, and hit **Save**.

8. Click the back arrow beside the cloud flow name to go back to its settings. Click on **Edit** on the **Run only users** section and, under **Connections Used**, set all connectors to use a specific connection and not **Provided by run-only user**, as shown in the following screenshot:

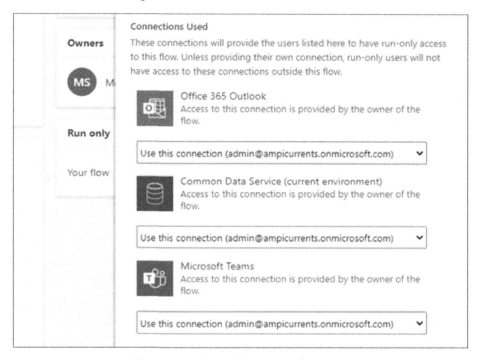

Figure 4.29 – Run only users configuration

9. Once all the connections have the right setting, click on **Save** and close this browser tab.

10. Back on the solution editor, let's create another flow by clicking **New | Flow** from the toolbar. For demo purposes, use the same trigger as before, **Flow button for mobile | Manually trigger a flow**, without adding parameters.

11. As an example, we will create just one action that gets emails from a SharePoint list and use them as input parameters for our **Marketing Process** flow. Add a new step and look for Get items on SharePoint.

12. Add one more step and look for Run a Child Flow on Flows. This action only appears when designing flows inside solutions. Select the previously created flow from the list. This list only shows flows that are within solutions. Once selected, it will ask for the email parameter. Use the column coming from the SharePoint list.

13. Being a list of items received from SharePoint, an **Apply to each** section will be autogenerated to handle all elements in the list:

Figure 4.30 – Main flow calling the child flow

14. Give the flow a name by clicking **Untitled** in the top left of the screen and hit **Save**.

How it works...

To test the connected flows, edit the **Parent** flow and click on **Test** in the screen's top-right corner. Choose **I'll perform the trigger action** and then click on **Test**, **Run Flow** on the next pane, and **Done** on the last one.

The flow should start getting the emails from the SharePoint list and send them as a parameter to the *Child* flow, Marketing Process.

> **Run only users**
>
> This configuration is necessary because when a cloud flow gets executed, it uses the credentials for the user that is running it. When a *Parent* flow calls a *Child* flow, the latter loses the security context of the *Parent*. For this reason, we need to configure the *Child* flow to use the connection credentials configured in each action.

Each action has its associated connection, as you can see in the following screenshot:

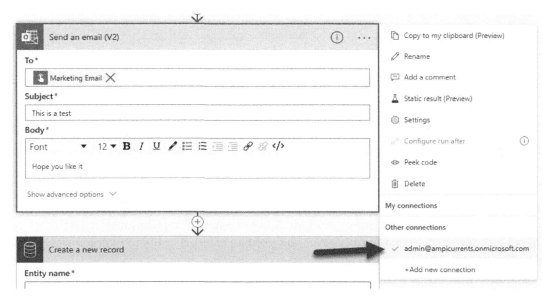

Figure 4.31 – Connections used by actions

Here you will see a list of all the connections configured in your environment for the action's specific service. You can review all of them by going to either the Power Apps portal or the Power Automate portal and, in the left pane, click on **Data | Connections**.

There's more...

Using this technique requires that your flows are part of a solution. However, there's a workaround to make this available for flows outside solutions.

If you change the *Parent* flow trigger to be an HTTP request, anyone with the POST URL can call it. When you make this change, the platform creates a random URL that can only trigger this cloud flow. In the following screenshot, you can see the URL created after the cloud flow gets saved:

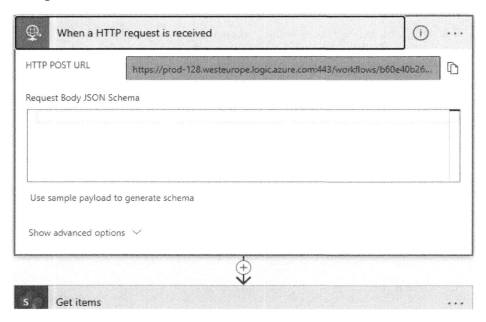

Figure 4.32 – HTTP request trigger

With this alternative, you can organize all your cloud flows inside a solution and call them using the address provided from other cloud flows or external applications. Using this trigger also serves as a solution whenever you need an external entity to interact with your organization's resources.

5
Extending the Platform

The Power Platform is composed of several tools and services dedicated to building solutions that help improve organizational procedures. The tools we use to create applications and integrations offer a range of standard features in their field while also leaving room for extensibility.

When building applications, you need to create interfaces that interact with your end users, and in this process, you might need to repeat a set of controls such as headers, menus, loaders, and the like. This task can be tedious as it slows down development when a new change is needed.

In this chapter, we will learn how to speed up the application building process by using **components**. These elements allow the creation of small building blocks that focus on a specific task by encapsulating a set of controls to be reused across your application.

Before we dive into this chapter, we will also cover a key topic regarding *user interface guidelines*. In this chapter, you will also learn how to create custom connectors in your environments to connect to data sources using tools your developers are already using, such as Postman.

The following recipes are going to define these concepts:

- Setting up your first canvas Power Apps component
- Building a floating action button component
- Creating a vertical navigation component
- Developing template fields using components
- Using the Power Apps component library
- Expanding communications with custom connectors

Technical requirements

Building and using components for Power Apps application development doesn't require an additional paid license. However, the use of custom connectors requires the use of any of the plans described in the Preface section of this book. Regarding the Power Automate licensing, you can use either of these plans:

Power Automate paid plans

Depending on the target, there are two plans for Power Automate:

- Specific users can take advantage of these two plans: the **per-user plan** and **the per-user plan with attended RPA (Robotic Process Automation)**.
- The entire organization can use the **per-flow plan,** allowing five flows without needing to license each user.

These plans include the use of custom connectors needed for the related recipe.

For a more in-depth insight into licensing, please review *Chapter 3, Choosing the right data source for your applications*, to get a better understanding with some real-world examples. The complete version of this application is available from our GitHub repository at `https://github.com/PacktPublishing/Microsoft-Power-Apps-Cookbook/tree/master/Chapter05`

User interface guidelines

Designing intuitive applications has become a work of art over the years. In the beginning, developers did not consider applications' usability; they only focused on providing the required functionality.

Since the mobile revolution, back in 2007, an app's design has become as important as its purpose. Applications that are easier to use have had more success than others with more features but less user interface appeal.

All major players in the mobile industry started to define their approaches to user interface design by creating guidelines for their devices. Toolbars were initially at the bottom, then at the top, now they're back at the bottom again. There have been many iterations depending on device sizes, screen aspect ratios, and more.

The main guidelines in use today come from Google, Apple, and Microsoft. It doesn't matter the device, there is a guideline for it. The idea is to give app designers and developers cues on how to design their apps. The approach is to have one unique backend but different interfaces depending on the mobile ecosystem.

The applications we develop should use cues from these guidelines because users already know what these designed controls do. Let's take the floating action button, for example. The function of this button is quite well known; it is the main activity in the application. The following screenshot represents the use of this element in an app:

Figure 5.1 – Floating action button in action

This control is just an example of all the definitions you can find from these guidelines. To gather more ideas from them, refer to these links:

- Google Material Design: `https://material.io/design`

- Human Interface Guidelines: `https://developer.apple.com/design/human-interface-guidelines`

- Fluent Design System: `https://www.microsoft.com/design/fluent`

Setting up your first canvas Power Apps component

After discussing the advantages of using cues from design guidelines, let's mix this concept using canvas Power Apps components. With the help of this recipe and the others that fall into the components category, we will recreate the most common controls seen in the design guidelines as components, so you can reuse them in your apps.

Imagine building a Power Apps canvas application with 30 screens using the same main menu copied over and over. Eventually, the organization would require a new option to be added to the menu. You would have to apply the change to each of the screens of your application.

As we mentioned before, a component is an encapsulation of controls that will serve one purpose. Working with them is like creating a new screen; the designer and the available controls are the same. The difference lies in that you can set the dimensions to match a specific size.

Going back to our previous example, creating a menu component will allow replicating instances of this element on every screen while giving you one single place to update your menu. Once updated, all screens will reflect the change automatically.

Components also have custom properties that will allow communication between them and the application itself. We will create one from scratch to see these concepts in action.

Getting ready

The components feature comes enabled by default on new apps, but you need to activate it from the app settings if you are maintaining an older application. To enable it, go to **File | Settings | Advanced settings** and set **Components** to **On** as seen in the following screenshot:

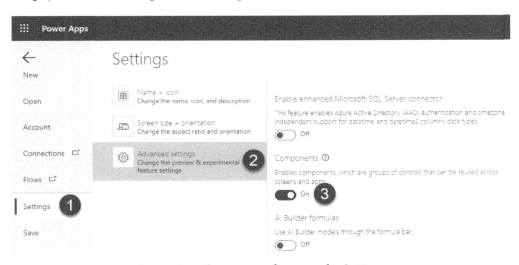

Figure 5.2 – Components feature under Settings

When this option gets enabled, you will see a new tab in the **Tree view** called **Components**, where you will find the list of components available in the application. You can also import existing ones or export them to other apps. Here, you can see these options under the **Components** tab:

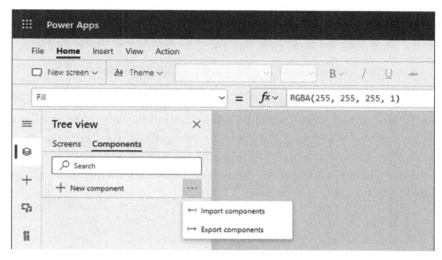

Figure 5.3 – Components tab

Now that we have prepared our app to use components, let's create our first one.

How to do it

1. Go to the **Components** tab and select **New component**. This action will create a new one in the list and will adapt the canvas designer for editing.

2. From the right pane, change the height of the component to `100` and set **Width** to `App.Width`. Changing these values to formulas or variables requires the change to be done in the formula bar, as seen in the following screenshot:

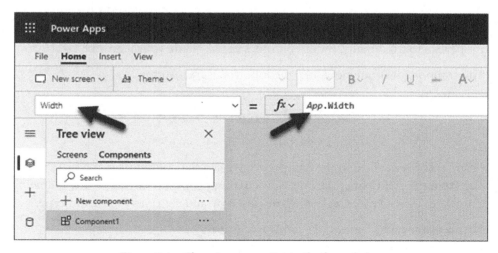

Figure 5.4 – Changing properties in the formula bar

> **Speed trick**
>
> If you click on the label of the control's properties, it will make the formula bar jump to that property.

3. Change the **Fill** property to your color of choice. We will set it to a dark blue.

4. Go to the **Insert** toolbar and select **Label** to add it to the canvas. Set its **X** and **Y** positions to 0 and **Width** and **Height** to Parent.Width - 100 and Parent.Height, respectively. Change the **Left** padding to 20. Set the font color to white and the size to 28. Click the edit icon next to the control's name to set the name of the label to TitleLbl as seen here:

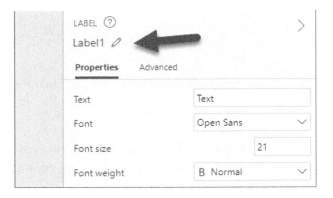

Figure 5.5 – Control naming in Power Apps

5. From the **Insert** toolbar, select **Icons** and then choose Home. For the positioning, set **Y** to 0 and **X** to TitleLbl.X + TitleLbl.Width. Set **Width** and **Height** to 100. It might look weird, but we'll fix it with the padding. Set all **Padding** properties to 20. Finally, set its color to white. Name your icon TitleIcn.

The component should look like the following screenshot:

Figure 5.6 – Title component in progress

6. From **Tree view**, click on the component we created and set its name to TitleCmp, and from the right pane, click on **New custom property** for each of the following properties using Input as their **Property type** and Text as their **Data type**:

Display name and **Name**: Title; **Description**: Title

Display name and **Name**: IconName; **Description**: Name of the icon

The custom properties will look like the following screenshot:

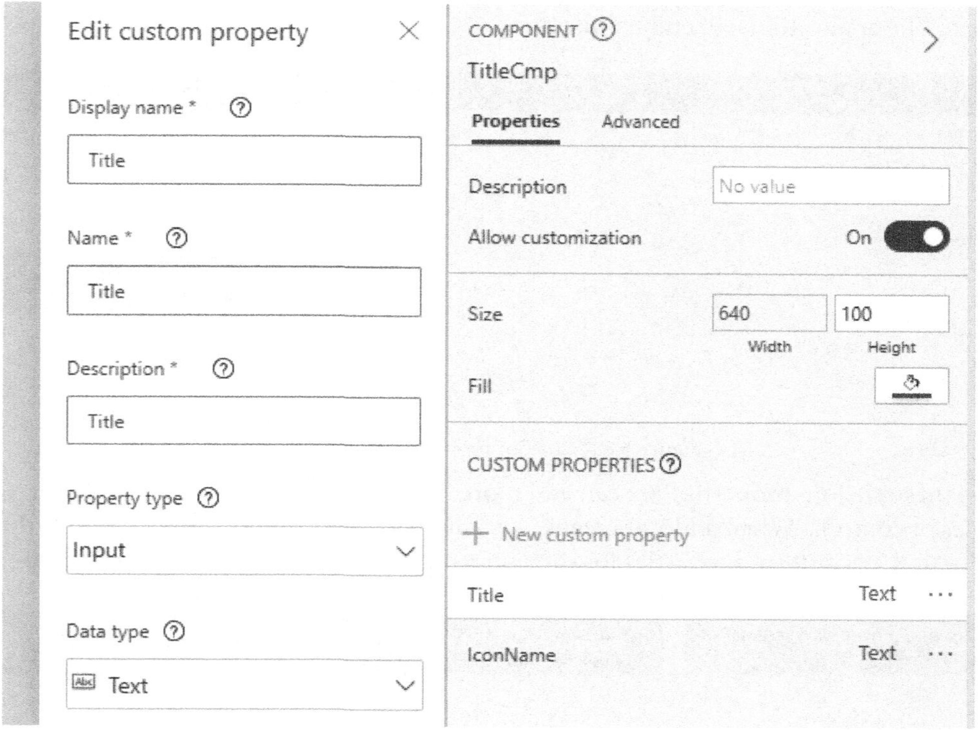

Figure 5.7 – Component's custom properties

7. Select the label from **Tree view** and set its **Text** property to `TitleCmp.Title`
    by using the formula bar. Now select the icon and change its **Icon** property to
    `TitleCmp.IconName`, again, from the formula bar.

This component is now ready. Let's take it for a test drive.

How it works

We have built a header-like component using custom properties, which allows the change
of its internal properties from the app using it. To use it, select the **Screens** tab from **Tree
view** and, from the **Insert** toolbar, click on **Custom** and then choose the component
we just created, `TitleCmp`, from the list.

This action will add it to our canvas and because we've set the width to `App.Width`,
it will expand automatically, no matter the layout of your app. The same goes for the
controls inside the component. When using `Parent.Width`, they will adapt to the width
of their parent; in this case, the component.

While selected, let's head to the right pane to complete its configuration. Using the formula bar, change the **Title** property to My component, and **IconName** to Icon. Items. The application will end up like this:

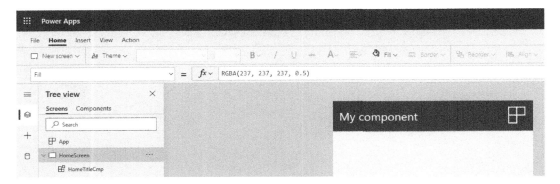

Figure 5.8 – Custom properties in action

Using these custom properties, we can add more functionality than just encapsulating a series of controls. When adding screens, you can reuse this component and change the Title and IconName properties for each screen as seen in the following screenshot:

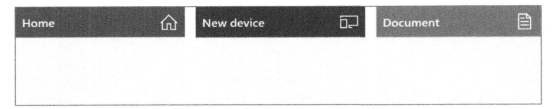

Figure 5.9 – Header component examples

Another added value to this technique is that it lets you maintain design consistency across your app by giving the user the same look for all the screens. Let's learn more about components' functionality in the following recipes.

The application holding this component is available from our GitHub repo at https://github.com/PacktPublishing/Microsoft-Power-Apps-Cookbook/tree/master/Chapter05

There's more

Knowing the concept of components will make you think in a different way when designing your applications. From the very beginning, you will start thinking about which elements can be made into a component to help you build applications faster.

Keep an eye on existing ones created by Microsoft or the community, such as the ones seen here: `https://powerusers.microsoft.com/t5/Canvas-Apps-Components-Samples/bd-p/ComponentsGallery`

Building a floating action button component

One of the most recognizable features in mobile design is the use of **floating action buttons (FABs)** in user interfaces. It represents the primary action of the active screen. Almost every user will know its purpose because they have seen it in all major applications, such as Microsoft Outlook:

Figure 5.10 – Write and email FAB action in Microsoft Outlook

We will learn how to replicate this element using components in this recipe.

Getting ready

To use components, refer to the *Getting ready* section of the *Setting up your first canvas Power Apps component* recipe to follow the steps to enable it for your Power App if it is not enabled by default.

How to do it

1. Create a new app using the phone layout, and from **Tree view**, go to the **Components** tab and click on **New component**. From the right pane, name it FABCmp. Set its **Width** and **Height** to 95, and its fill color to transparent: RGBA (0, 0, 0, 0).

2. Go to the **Insert** toolbar, click on **Icons**, and select the Add icon. Set its **X** and **Y** positions to 5 and its **Width** and **Height** to 80. All padding properties should be 20. Lastly, set its color to white and name this control IconIcn.

3. Using the **Insert** toolbar on the left, select **Circle** from the **Shapes** group. Set the same position and size as the icon we just inserted. Set the name of this control to `BackgroundCrl`. Change the order to place it at the bottom of the canvas, so the icon is on top. Go to the **Home** toolbar, click on **Reorder** and then **Send to back**.

4. To make this component more fashionable, we will add a shadow to the circle. From the **Insert** toolbar, click on **Text** and then **HTML text**. Set its **X** and **Y** positions to 0 and **Width** and **Height** to 95. All padding properties should be 5. Set the **HTML Text** property to this value:

```
"<div style='height: 80px; width: 80px; border-radius:
50px; -webkit-box-shadow: 2px 2px 5px 0px rgba(0, 0,
0, 0.75); -moz-box-shadow: 2px 2px 5px 0px rgba(0, 0,
0, 0.75); box-shadow: 2px 2px 5px 0px rgba(0, 0, 0,
0.75);'></div>"
```

5. Reorder the HTML text control to the back as we did in *step 3* and name it `ShadowHTML`. Your FAB should have this look:

Figure 5.11 – FAB component

6. Go to the component properties and click on **New custom property** for each of the following properties as their `Input` property:

    Name: `IconName`; **Description**: `Name of the icon`; **Data type**: `Text`

    Name: `CircleColor`; **Description**: `Color of the circle`; **Data type**: `Color`

    Name: `Screen`; **Description**: `Screen name`; **Data type**: `Screen`

    Move to the **Advanced** tab of the component and change the **IconName** default value from `Text` to `Icon.Add`.

    Select the `IconIcn` control and, on the right pane, change the `Icon` property in the formula bar to `FABCmp.IconName`. Continue by selecting the **Advanced** tab and click on the **OnSelect** property inside the **ACTION** section. On the formula bar, add this code:

    ```
    Navigate(FABCmp.Screen, ScreenTransition.Fade)
    ```

7. Select the `BackgroundCrl` control and change its **Color** property (being the **Fill** property) using the formula bar to `FABCmp.CircleColor`.

You will see that your component changes its appearance to black. This variation is due to the change of its visual properties to formulas or variables:

Figure 5.12 – Visual properties using variables

This component is now ready to transform depending on the values set by the custom properties.

How it works

Go back to the **Screens** list in **Tree view** and from the **Insert** toolbar, click on **Custom** and select `FABCmp`. Set it at the bottom right of your screen. You can refer to this guideline for information about placement: `https://material.io/components/buttons-floating-action-button#placement`

From the properties, change its `CircleColor` to match your application style. As for the rest, change the icon name that best reflects the primary action and also set the screen name where you want to navigate when the user selects it. The following are examples of using this control:

Figure 5.13 – FAB component examples

If you run the application, selecting the FAB control will change the active screen to the one set in the custom properties, giving you the ability to redirect your user to a new screen where the main action will take place.

The application that includes this component is available here: `https://github.com/PacktPublishing/Microsoft-Power-Apps-Cookbook/tree/master/Chapter05`

Creating a vertical navigation component

Guiding users through navigational controls is a known technique in almost all interfaces. There are many ways to design them; examples are tutorials, tabs, and next steps indicators.

The Power Apps Studio includes a ready-to-use template screen that uses a tutorial-like approach from the **New screen** selector:

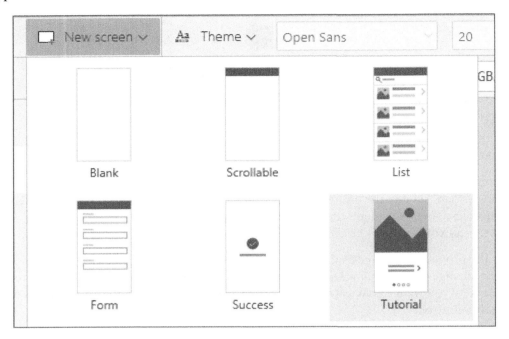

Figure 5.14 – Tutorial screen template

You can take advantage of this feature if you want to add a short tutorial for your new users.

This recipe will create a vertical navigational component suitable for desktop applications that will serve as a tool to guide your users.

Getting ready

As mentioned in all the other component-related recipes, to use the components feature, we need to activate it in our Power App if it hasn't been enabled by default. Refer to the *Getting ready* section of the *Setting up your first canvas Power Apps component* recipe to learn how to do it.

How to do it

1. Navigate to the Power Apps portal, https://make.powerapps.com, and from the left pane, select **Apps** and then, on the toolbar, click on **New app | Canvas**. Select the Tablet layout as this component is more suitable for this form factor.

2. Go to the **Components** tab in the **Tree view** screen of the Studio and click on **New component**. Name this component NavCmp. Set its **Width** to 180 and **Height** to App.Height using the formula bar.

3. From the **Insert** toolbar, select **Media | Image** and set the **X** and **Y** properties to 20. For the size, set **Width** to 140 and **Height** to 60. Name this control LogoImg.

4. Select **Rectangle** from the **Shapes** group of the **Insert** toolbar on the left and set these properties: **X** to 15, **Y** to 100, **Width** to 150, and **Height** to 1. For the **Fill** property, enter the following value in the formula bar: RGBA(237, 237, 237, 0.5). Set the name of this control to TopDividerRct.

5. Add a gallery by selecting **Gallery | Blank vertical** from the **Insert** toolbar. Position it to 10 on **X** and 120 on **Y**; set **Width** to 160 and **Height** to App.Height - 200. Change its **Template size** property to 50. Name this control OptionsGly.

6. Edit the gallery by clicking on the pencil icon as seen in the following screenshot:

Figure 5.15 – Gallery pencil icon

Add these controls from the **Insert** toolbar:

- From the **Media** dropdown, select **Image** and place it like this: 5 for **X**, 10 for **Y**. For the size, set **Width** to 140 and **Height** to 35. Set **Border radius** to 12 and reset its **Image** property to None. Name this control OptionBGImg.

- Add a label and set its **X** value to 5 and the **Y** value to 10. Change **Width** to 140 and **Height** to 35. For the padding, put the top and right to 5, the left to 15, and for the bottom, 7. Set its **Color** to white and name this control OptionLbl.

- Click on **Icons** and select the **Add** icon. Place it on 0 for **X**, 10 for **Y,** and set **Width** to 160 and **Height** to 40. Set all padding to 160. Name this control OptionIcn.

7. Copy the rectangle created in *step 4* and change its properties to `15` for **X** and `App.Height - 60` for **Y** using the formula bar. Name this control `BottomDividerRct`.

8. From the **Insert** toolbar, add a label and place it on `0` for **X** and `App.Height - 53` for **Y** using the formula bar. Set **Width** to `Parent.Width` and **Height** to `40`. Set the **font size** to something low like `11`, **Text alignment** to `Center`, and **Color** to `white`. Set the **Text** property to `Back` and name this control `BackLbl`.

9. Now click on **Icons** and select the **Add** icon. Place it using `BackLbl` as the reference; **X** would be `BackLbl.X` and **Y** `BackLbl.Y`. Do the same for its size: **Width** would be `BackLbl.Width` and **Height** `BackLbl.Height`. Set all padding to `160`. Go to the **Advanced** tab of this control's properties and input `Back(ScreenTransition.Fade)` on the **OnSelect** property. Set the name of this control to `BackIcn`.

10. Go to the component's property pane and click **New custom property** for each of these as an `Input` property type:

   - **Name**: `ApplicationLogo`; **Description**: `Application Logo`; **Data type**: `Image`

   - **Name**: `NavColor`; **Description**: `Navigation primary color`; **Data type**: `Color`

   - **Name**: `Screens`; **Description**: `List of screens`; **Data type**: `Table`

   - **Name**: `ActiveScreen`; **Description**: `Active Screen`; **Data type**: `Screen`

11. To use these custom properties, we can set their values using sample data from the component itself. Go to the **Advanced** tab of the `NavCmp` properties and set the following data:

   - **NavColor**: `ColorValue("#2A4365")`

   - **Screens**: `Table({Name: "Home", Screen: App.ActiveScreen}, {Name: "Departments", Screen: App.ActiveScreen})`

12. Let's link these custom properties to the respective controls using the formula bar:

   - Change the **Fill** property of the component to `Self.NavColor`.

   - Set the **Image** property of `LogoImg` to `NavCmp.ApplicationLogo`.

- Change the **Data source** of `OptionsGly` to `NavCmp.Screens`.

- Set the **OnSelect** property in the **Advanced** tab of the `OptionIcn` control to `Navigate(ThisItem.Screen, ScreenTransition.Fade)`.

- Change the `OptionLbl` **Text** property to `ThisItem.Name`.

- Set the `OptionBGImg` **Fill** property to `ColorFade(NavCmp.NavColor, -25%)` and the **Visible** property to `ThisItem.Screen = NavCmp.ActiveScreen`.

With the sample data and the custom properties in place, it's easier to see how the component might look. Check the following screenshot as an example:

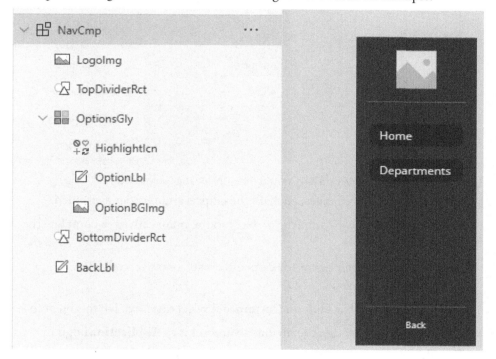

Figure 5.16 – Navigation component with sample data

Make sure the placement of all the controls follows the pattern seen in the following screenshot:

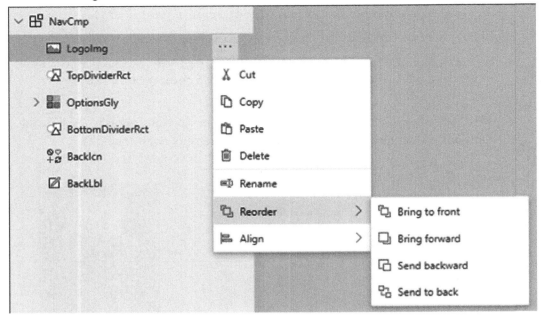

Figure 5.17 – Control order inside the component

If you need to make changes, click on the ellipsis and reorder as needed.

The component is now complete; go back to the main canvas to complete the configuration:

1. Name your first screen HomeScreen and create a new screen called DocumentsScreen.

2. From the **Insert** toolbar, click on **Custom** and select NavCmp. Do this on both screens.

3. Upload an image through the media tab and set it as **ApplicationLogo** in the component's properties.

4. Select the **App** element in **Tree view** and, in the **Advanced** tab, select the **OnStart** property and set its value as the following:

```
Set(gblMenuOptions,Table
({Name:"Home",Screen:HomeScreen},
{Name:"Documents",Screen
:DocumentsScreen})).
```

Right-click the **App** element and select **Run OnStart**.

5. Set gblMenuOptions as the component's **Screens** property.

Now that we have the component configuration finished, let's test it by running the app.

How it works

When the application starts, the component acts as a navigation system for all the defined screens, as seen in the following screenshot:

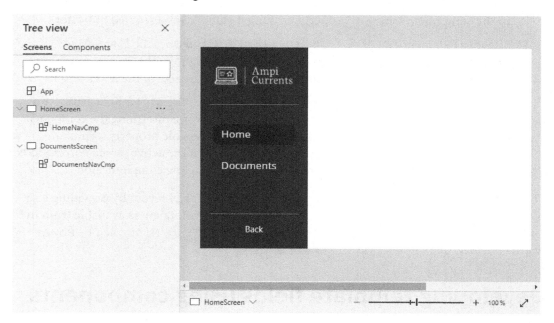

Figure 5.18 – Navigation component in action

Because the component uses the sample data, we can see examples of the data needed in each property, for instance, the required format for the **Screens** property table.

Let's explain some of the features of this component:

- If you need to add a new screen to your application, simply add a new record to the gblMenuOptions variable, and all the components will reflect the change.

- The use of the `OptionIcn` and `BackIcn` icons is to imitate a *hand cursor* instead of a *text cursor*. Users expect this kind of behavior when selecting options using the mouse. You can see the result in the following screenshot:

Figure 5.19 – Power Apps cursor workaround

- Adding a negative color fade to `OptionBGImg` creates a darker version of the color in the component's custom property, making it suitable for a *selected* indicator.

- The lower elements, such as `BottomDividerRct` and `BackLbl`, are using negative calculations based on the height of the application. This positioning technique makes them stay at the bottom, no matter the size of the application.

- Even though we created the `Active Screen` custom property without setting any value, it gets the default value from `App.ActiveScreen`, informing the component about the active screen, therefore, helping us with the **Visible** property formula, `ThisItem.Screen = NavCmp.ActiveScreen`. If the active screen corresponds to one in the gallery, `OptionBGImg` becomes visible, acting as an indicator.

This component offers a simple solution for apps using the tablet layout by providing a set of customizations to make it flexible. The package for this component is available from the GitHub repo at `https://github.com/PacktPublishing/Microsoft-Power-Apps-Cookbook/tree/master/Chapter05`

Developing template fields using components

When designing applications, any help is always welcomed. That's why application development platforms are continuously evolving to find more ways to help developers in building great solutions.

As the user interface becomes as important as the expected functionality, we need to find more ways to achieve consistent interfaces. This recipe will build a set of components to maintain the same design for controls used in data representation and gathering.

In the following screenshot, the fields and their labels come from a component, and with the use of custom properties, you can configure the behavior and even change the theme:

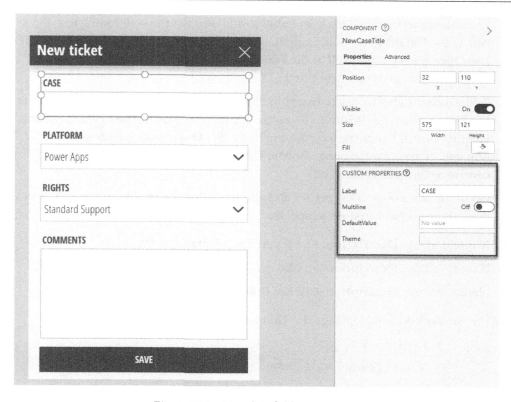

Figure 5.20 – Template field components

Getting ready

To build these components, you need to make sure your application has this feature activated. New apps come with this feature enabled by default, but if you maintain an existing one, please refer to the *Getting ready* section of the *Setting up your first canvas Power Apps component* recipe to learn how to activate it.

How to do it

1. Go to the Power Apps portal, `https://make.powerapps.com`, and from the left pane, select **Apps,** and then click on **New app | Canvas** from the toolbar. We are going to create this example based on the Phone layout, so select this option.

2. Click on the **Components** tab in **Tree view** and click on **New component**. Set **Height** to `121` from the properties pane and name it `DetailCmp`.

3. From the **Insert** toolbar, click on **Label** to add one. Set the positioning to 0 for **X** and **Y**. Set **Height** to 50 and, using the formula bar, set **Width** to Parent.Width. Use **Open Sans Condensed** as the **Font**. Set **Font size** to 20 and its weight to **Semibold**. Name this control DetailLabelLbl.

4. Add another **Label** from the **Insert** toolbar and input 1 for **X** and 50 for **Y** in the **Position** section. Set **Width** to Parent.Width - 3 using the formula bar and **Height** of 69. Change the left padding to 12. Set **Open Sans Condensed** as the font and its size to 24. Change **BorderThickness** to 1 and change the name of this control to DetailValueLbl.

5. Go to the component's properties and add the following **Input** custom properties by clicking on **New custom property**:

   - **Name**: Label; **Description**: Field label; **Data type**: Text
   - **Name**: Value; **Description**: Field value; **Data type**: Text
   - **Name**: Theme; **Description**: Theme; **Data type**: Record

Go to the **Advanced** tab and change the **Theme** default property to the following:

```
{
    PrimaryColor: ColorValue("#A61419"),
    SecondaryColor: ColorValue("#B67368"),
    BorderColor: ColorValue("#ADABAC")
}
```

With the help of a record variable, we can represent a theme by creating color properties and then assigning them as required. This technique allows you to maintain the same look and feel between the applications and the components you use.

1. Select DetailLabelLbl and set **Color** to DetailCmp.Theme.PrimaryColor and the **Text** property to DetailCmp.Label using the formula bar.

2. For DetailValueLbl, change the **BorderColor** property to DetailCmp.Theme.BorderColor and the **Text** property to DetailCmp.Value with the formula bar.

3. This component is now complete, and with the help of the associated theme, it should look like the following screenshot:

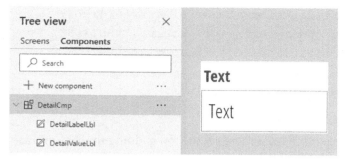

Figure 5.21 – DetailLabel component

4. Let's create the entry field component by clicking **New component** on **Tree view**. Name the component `EntryCmp` and set the properties as follows:

- Set **Height** to `121`.

- From the **Insert** toolbar, click on **Label** to add one. Set the positioning to `0` for **X** and **Y**. Set **Height** to `50` and, using the formula bar, set **Width** to `Parent.Width`. Use **Open Sans Condensed** as the **Font**. Set **Font size** to `20` and its weight to **Semibold**. Name this control `EntryLabelLbl`.

5. From the **Insert** toolbar, click on **Text | Text input**. Set `1` for **X** and `50` for **Y** in the **Position** section. Set **Width** to `Parent.Width - 3` using the formula bar and **Height** to `Parent.Height - Self.Y - 20`. Set **Open Sans Condensed** as the **Font** and its size to `24`. Change **BorderThickness** to `1` and **Border radius** to `0`. Name this control `EntryValueTxt`.

6. Go to the **Advanced** tab of the `EntryValueTxt` properties and set **OnChange** to `Set(ReturnValue, EntryValueTxt.Text)` using the formula bar.

7. Go to the `EntryCmp` properties and add the following **Input** custom properties by clicking on **New custom property**:

   Name: `Label`; **Description**: `Field label`; **Data type**: `Text`

   Name: `Multiline`; **Description**: `Multiline switch`; **Data type**: `Boolean`

   Name: `DefaultValue`; **Description**: `Default value`; **Data type**: `Text`

   Name: `Theme`; **Description**: `Theme`; **Data type**: `Record`

8. Create a new custom property, but this time select **Output** for **Property type**:

   Name: `TextData`; **Description**: `TextData`; **Data type**: `Text`

9. Go to the **Advanced** tab and change the Theme default property to the following:

```
{
    PrimaryColor: ColorValue("#A61419"),
    SecondaryColor: ColorValue("#B67368"),
    BorderColor: ColorValue("#ADABAC"),
    Multiline: false,
    TextData: ReturnValue
}
```

10. Select EntryValueTxt and set the top padding to this formula: If(EntryCmp. Multiline, 12, 5).

11. Select EntryLabelLbl and set **Color** to EntryCmp.Theme.PrimaryColor and the **Text** property to EntryCmp.Label using the formula bar.

12. Select EntryValueTxt and, using the formula bar, change the **BorderColor** property to EntryCmp.Theme.BorderColor, **Default** to EntryCmp. DefaultValue, and **Mode** to the following code:

```
If(
    EntryCmp.Multiline,
    TextMode.MultiLine,
    TextMode.SingleLine
)
```

The completed component should look like the one in this screenshot:

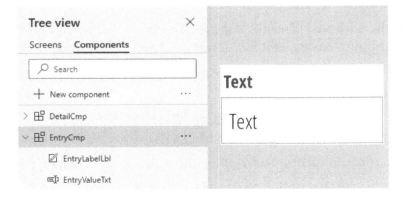

Figure 5.22 – EntryCmp component

13. Add one last component called `DropDownCmp`. Set the properties as follows:

- Set **Height** to `121`.

- From the **Insert** toolbar, click on **Label** to add one. Set the positioning to `0` for **X** and **Y**. Set **Height** to `50` and, using the formula bar, set **Width** to `Parent.Width`. Use **Open Sans Condensed** as the **Font**. Set **Font size** to `20` and its weight to **Semibold**. Name this control `DropDownLabelLbl`.

14. Click on **Input | Drop down** from the **Insert** toolbar. For **X** set `1` and for **Y** set `50`. Change **Width** to `Parent.Width - 3` using the formula bar and **Height** to `69`. Set **Open Sans Condensed** as the **Font** and its size to `24`. Change **BorderThickness** to `1` and **ChevronBackground** to `White`. Name this control `DropDownValueDrp`.

15. Go to the **Advanced** tab of the `DropDownValueDrp` properties and set **OnChange** to `Set(ReturnValue, DropDownValueDrp.SelectedText)` using the formula bar.

16. Go to the `DropDownCmp` properties and add the following **Input** custom properties by clicking on **New custom property**:

    Name: `Label`; **Description**: `Field label`; **Data type**: `Text`

    Name: `Items`; **Description**: `Items`; **Data type**: `Record`

    Name: `Theme`; **Description**: `Theme`; **Data type**: `Record`

17. Create a new **Output** custom property:

    Name: `SelectedItem`; **Description**: `Selected item`; **Data type**: `Text`

18. Go to the **Advanced** tab and change the **Theme** default property to the following:

```
{
    PrimaryColor: ColorValue("#A61419"),
    SecondaryColor: ColorValue("#B67368"),
    BorderColor: ColorValue("#ADABAC")
}
```

Also change the **Items** sample data to: `{Data: ["A", "B", "C"]}` and **SelectedItem** to `ReturnValue.Value`.

19. Select `DropDownLabelLbl` and set **Color** to `DropDownCmp.Theme.PrimaryColor` and the **Text** property to `DropDownCmp.Label` using the formula bar.

20. Select `DropDownValueDrp` and, using the formula bar, change these properties:

- **Items** to `DropDownCmp.Items.Data`

- **BorderColor** to `DropDownCmp.Theme.BorderColor`

- **ChevronFill** to `DropDownCmp.Theme.SecondaryColor`

The drop-down component is now complete; compare yours with the following screenshot:

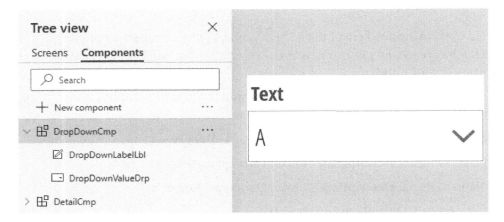

Figure 5.23 – Drop-down component complete

We are now ready to test these components in a new application.

How it works

These components will help us create application screens in no time by adding a field and its label simultaneously. You would only need to add them to the canvas screen and update the custom properties from the connected data source.

To add the components we just created, go to the **Insert** toolbar, and from the **Custom** dropdown, select the most suitable one from the list. When we add the components to the application canvas, they expose the defined custom properties to configure their behavior, as seen in the following screenshot:

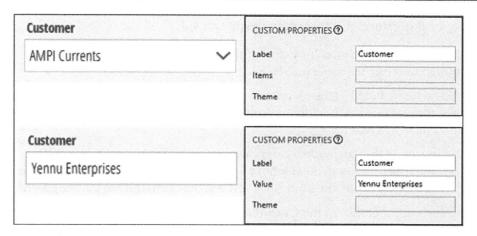

Figure 5.24 – Component custom properties

Using `DetailCmp`, `EntryCmp`, and `DropDownCmp` from this recipe, and `TitleCmp` from our first recipe, *Setting up your first canvas Power Apps component*, we can create screens like the following:

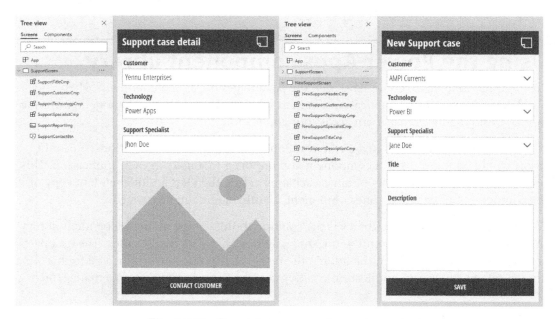

Figure 5.25 – Power App screens using components

Let's describe the features that these components provide:

- They make your tree view look cleaner than a tree view with all the controls required to create the same interface.

- Because we included a `Theme` custom property, we can reuse these components on other applications having different colors. Try extending this theme to include font names or more colors.

- We can extend the `EntryCmp` component by using the `Multiline` custom property, which allows the text input to change its **Mode** from single-line to multi-line while maintaining the same look and feel thanks to the top padding formula.

- The custom properties of the **Output** type allow the communication from the component to the application. The **OnChange** actions in `EntryCmp` and `DropDownCmp` trigger the update of these properties, giving you the text input and the selected text from the dropdown.

The application containing these components is available from our GitHub repository at `https://github.com/PacktPublishing/Microsoft-Power-Apps-Cookbook/tree/master/Chapter05`

Using the Power Apps component library

Through the chapter so far, we have seen the advantages of using components when building and maintaining applications. We encapsulate controls that work together for one purpose, and then we reuse them across our application.

However, if we wanted to use a specific component across several applications, our only resort would be to export this component and import it manually in each application. This process breaks maintainability because each application then has an independent copy of the component. If we update one component, all others remain unchanged.

The Power Apps component library is the solution to this. It acts as an independent library that can hold all the components you want to share across your applications. The best part is that if you update one from the library, the rest of the applications connected to this library will get an update notification creating seamless component lifecycle management.

Getting ready

To make use of this feature, we will use the component we created in our first recipe, *Setting up your first canvas Power Apps component*, which is available from our GitHub repository: `https://github.com/PacktPublishing/Microsoft-Power-Apps-Cookbook/tree/master/Chapter05`

How to do it

1. Go to the Power Apps portal, `https://make.powerapps.com`, and from the left pane, select **Apps**. In the list of apps, you will find a tab called **Component libraries**. If you haven't already done so, click on **Create component library**, and on the dialog that opens, give your library a name and click **Create**.

2. The Power Apps Studio will open just like when creating regular apps, but this time it will open directly in the **Components** section of the **Tree view**. From there, click on the ellipsis to import a component, as you can see in the following screenshot:

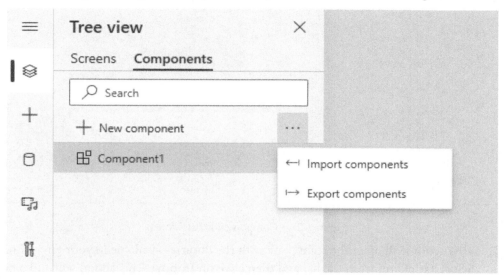

Figure 5.26 – Component import feature

3. The import action will open a right pane with a list of applications containing components. If you already have the `BaseComponents` app in your environment, select it from the list and click **Import**. Otherwise, click on the toolbar on **Upload** to include the components of a downloaded application in your environment. Notice that the Studio only imports components from `.msapp` files.

4. The `TitleCmp` component should appear in the list for you to select. You can now delete the default component called `Component1` after importing `TitleCmp`. Keep in mind that at least one should exist in the library.

5. From the toolbar, click on **File | Save** and then **Save** again to update your library. Once this process completes, click **File | Close**.

6. Go back to the Power Apps portal and create a new app with the phone layout. After the Studio is fully loaded, click on the **plus sign** on the left pane, and at the very end, click on **Get more components**, as seen in the following screenshot:

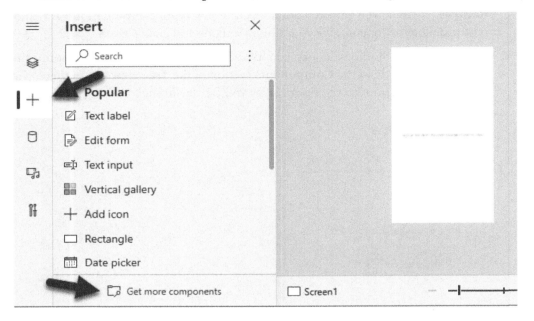

Figure 5.27 – Component library access

7. This action will open the right pane with the libraries available in your environment. Select **TitleCmp** from the list and then click on **Import**. This action will add a new section in the list of elements to insert called **Library components**. In this section, you will find the components imported from libraries.

8. Select the component to add it to the canvas, and set some custom properties for the title and the icon. Click on **File | Save** and then close your app.

9. From the Power Apps portal, go to **Apps**, click on the **Component libraries** tab to select the previously created library, and then click on **Edit** from the toolbar.

10. Once the Studio opens, set the height of the **TitleCmp** component to 110, and its **Fill** color to Transparent.

11. Change the height of TitleLbl to 85 and **Width** to 556. Set the **Fill** color to any color you like. Use the same for the **Fill** property of TitleIcn.

12. Set the **X** position of TitleIcn to 555 and **Width** and **Height** to 85.

13. From the **Insert** toolbar, click on **Text | HTML text**. Set its **X** position to 0 and its **Y** position to 85. Change **Width** to Parent.Width and **Height** to 20. Set all padding properties to 0 and, from the formula bar, set its **HtmlText** property to the following:

```
"<div style='margin-top: -15px; height: 15px; -webkit-
box-shadow: 0 8px 16px 0 rgba(0, 0, 0, 0.16); -moz-box-
shadow: 0 8px 16px 0 rgba(0, 0, 0, 0.16); box-shadow: 0
8px 16px 0 rgba(0, 0, 0, 0.16);'></div>"
```

14. Name the HTML text control TitleShadow and change its order to be at the end. The component now has a shadow, as seen in the following screenshot:

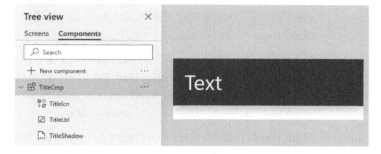

Figure 5.28 – Title component with shadow

15. Save the changes by clicking on **File | Save** and then **Publish**. Close the library afterward. Always publish the changes to make them available to all apps.

After making this change, let's see how the library plays in our favor.

How it works

Go back to the list of apps in the Power Apps portal and select to edit the application you just created. Once it opens, you will see a banner letting you know that a component inside your application has an update, like the one shown in the following screenshot:

Figure 5.29 – Component library update

Clicking the **Review** button will display a dialog that will list all the libraries with updates. From there, you can check which one you want to get updates from, and clicking **Update** will apply them.

This Power Apps feature brings a great collaboration tool for app makers, allowing them to build components in just one place and share them across an organization's solutions.

Expanding communications with custom connectors

At the time of this writing, there are more than 400 connectors available for the Power Platform. This number means that many organizations, besides Microsoft, support using this connectivity solution for Power Apps, Power Automate, and Logic Apps.

You can find connectors from Adobe, Amazon, Jira, and Twitter, just to name a few. But what happens if you need to connect to an **Application Programming Interface (API)** created in your organization, or perhaps you need to go beyond what the Twitter connector offers? For these scenarios, there are **custom connectors**.

They allow creating a set of methods that connect to a specific endpoint with the properties you define. These can then be shared across your organization and even certified by Microsoft to be available for all users of Power Apps, Power Automate, and Logic Apps.

For more information regarding this, please visit `https://docs.microsoft.com/en-us/connectors/custom-connectors/`

Getting ready

Depending on the platform using the custom connectors, they will require that the user has a Power Apps or Power Automate license. Please refer to the *Technical requirements* section of this chapter to get more details.

The service we are going to use in this recipe is AccuWeather. It's an online service that offers location and weather data. They offer an API for developers when you register at `https://developer.accuweather.com/`. Upon completing the registration and login, go to **MY APPS** to create an app that will grant you access to their system through a key. Using the trial offer, you will have a limit of 50 calls a day and just 1 key per developer for free.

To build the connector, we are going to take advantage of the **Postman** application. This tool is well-known among developers because it allows sending **Hypertext Transfer Protocol (HTTP)** requests to API endpoints. It means that developers can use it to send petitions to online services using different methods and then verify the responses.

How to do it

1. Download and install Postman from `https://www.postman.com/downloads/`. Upon running it, click on **New Collection** from the left pane. On the dialog that opens, name it `Accuweather` and click on **Create**. This action will add it to the list of collections, as seen in the following screenshot:

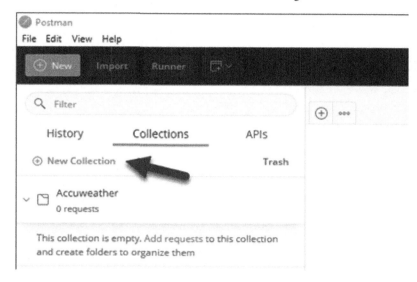

Figure 5.30 – Postman collection creation

2. Expand the new collection by clicking on it and then click on **Add requests**. On the dialog that opens, set the name to `City Search` and click on **Save to Accuweather**. From the left pane, click on the new request you just created to configure it.

3. Enter the following address in the URL: `http://dataservice.accuweather.com/locations/v1/cities/search`. This request needs parameters to work, so from the **Params** tab, enter the following:

Key: apikey; **Value**: <YOUR ACCUWEATHER API KEY>

Key: q; **Value**: Mississauga

This request will search for a city named Mississauga.

4. Click **Send** to test the request. This action will execute it, and the online service will then return the data from the requested city in the **Body** section at the bottom of the screen, as seen in the following screenshot:

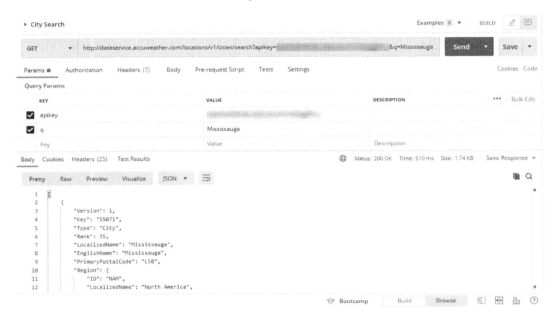

Figure 5.31 – Postman request and response

5. Now that we have a successful request, we can export the collection to build our custom connector. But first, we need to remove sensitive information such as the API key by cleaning the values from the **Params** list.

6. Click on **Save,** and from the Accuweather collection, click on the ellipsis to expand the menu. Select **Export** and pick **Collection v1** on the dialog and then click on the **Export** button, as seen in the screenshot that follows. Save the file to a location on your computer:

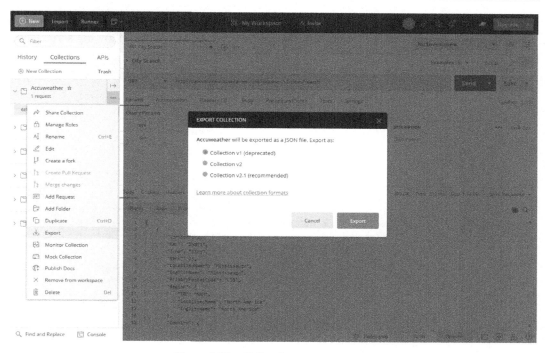

Figure 5.32 – Collection export process

7. Go to the Power Apps portal, `https://make.powerapps.com`, and from the left pane, click on **Data | Custom connectors**. On the right, click on the **New custom connector** dropdown and select **Import a Postman collection**.

8. Name your connector `Accuweather Location` and click on **Import** to upload the collection file we exported from Postman. Click on **Continue** to start building the connector.

9. The build wizard opens to the **General** tab, where you can add more properties, such as a description or a connector icon image. Set **Description** to `Accuweather location service` and then click on the **Definition** tab. We will skip the **Security** tab because our service relies on the API key configured in the **Definition** tab.

10. Review the information listed:

- In the **General** section, you can describe your service. **Operation ID** is the method that will appear in your Power Apps, for example.

- The **Request** section displays all the configuration gathered from the Postman file. Verify that the **URL** and the **Query** values are present, as in the following screenshot:

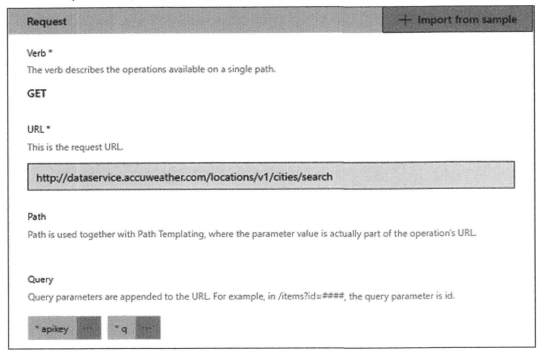

Figure 5.33 – Request section of the custom connector

- At the end of this tab, there is a **Validation** section that will let you know if there are any errors in your connector. If everything checks out, click at the top on **Create connector** to complete the connector's creation. After the process completes, click on **Close**, as we will test it directly on an app.

11. Back in the Power Apps portal, create a new canvas app using the **Phone** layout.

12. From the left pane, click on **Data** and expand the **Connectors** section to look for the `Accuweather location` connector. Select it and click on **Connect**. A dialog might pop up to remind you of the license requirements when using custom connectors. Click **Got it** to dismiss it.

13. From the **Insert** toolbar, add a **Label**, a **Text input**, a **Button**, and a **Vertical gallery**. Set the following configuration:

- Set the **Text** property of the label to `Location`. Name it `LocationLbl`.

- Set the name of the text input to `SearchTxt`.

- For the button, set the **Text** property to `Search` and, by using the formula bar, set the **OnSelect** property to the following:

```
UpdateContext({Locations: Accuweather.CitySearch("<YOUR
ACCUWEATHER API KEY>", SearchTxt.Text)})
```

Remember to set your AccuWeather service API key. Name this button `SearchBtn`.

Set the **Items** property of the gallery to `Locations`. Edit the gallery by clicking on its pencil icon, and from the **Insert** toolbar, add two labels. Name the first one `CityNameLbl` and set the **Text** property to `ThisItem.EnglishName`. For the second label, set the **Text** property to `ThisItem.Key` and name it `KeyLbl`.

Adapt the design to your liking and now let's test the connector.

How it works

Building the connector from Postman allows the previous validation that the required information gets requested correctly. It speeds up the custom connector creation process by packaging the requests in a collection, making the process straightforward.

After setting up our app, we can test it by entering any city in the world in the **SearchTxt** text input and then clicking the **SearchBtn** button to load the results into **Locations**. This variable gets a table representation of the response from AccuWeather, which is then displayed in the gallery as seen in the following screenshot:

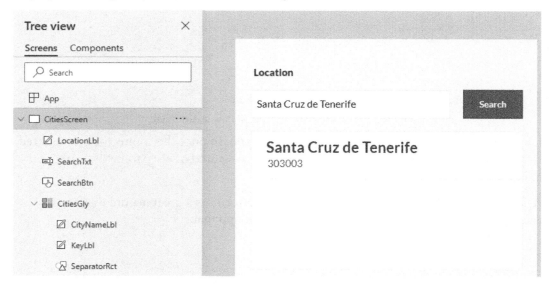

Figure 5.34 – AccuWeather custom connector in a canvas app

We can extend this connector by adding more requests such as weather data using the location key gathered in the `City search` method.

This sample application and the Postman collection file are available in the GitHub repository located at `https://github.com/PacktPublishing/Microsoft-Power-Apps-Cookbook/tree/master/Chapter05`

There's more

The custom connector can also query location information from this provider. In Power Automate, Add the actions of this connector from the **Custom** tab as seen in the following screenshot:

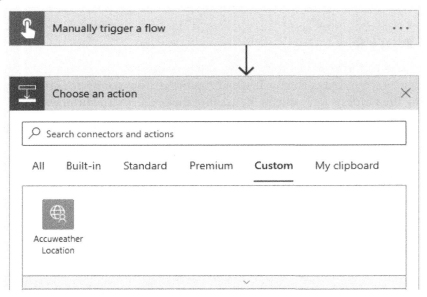

Figure 5.35 – Custom connector in Power Automate

The methods configured in the connector will be exposed once the connector gets selected to the flow, and then you will only need to fill in the required query parameters: `apikey` and `q`.

Making a custom connector that works on both platforms is a great feature that, once again, improves the application building process for app makers.

6
Improving User Experience

The process of creating applications is a complex workflow. You need to analyze the requirements, design data sources, choose existing tools and platforms, and build the **User Interface (UI)**, among others.

Power Apps, being a platform to build applications, is always evolving to help app makers create functional solutions quickly. However, this sometimes means making sacrifices in specific areas, such as including an appealing UI.

This chapter will show you how to improve the UI of full-featured applications created from data, thus promoting our solution's adoption. We will also discover how to improve our application building workflow by creating one responsive application that works the same on mobile and desktop.

The recipes in this chapter will help us to go deeper into these concepts:

- Enhancing application interfaces
- Building a responsive password manager in Power Apps – setting up the Azure Key Vault service
- Building a responsive password manager in Power Apps – designing an adaptive application

Technical requirements

Depending on the type of connector needed for your data source, you might need a license for your applications. Standard connectors, such as the one used for SharePoint, don't require licensing, apart from the existing Microsoft 365 license, but premium connectors, such as the one required for Azure SQL Database, do. Please refer to the Preface section of this book to get more information about the licensing requirements.

All the applications that we will use as examples in this chapter are available in the GitHub repository: `https://github.com/PacktPublishing/Microsoft-Power-Apps-Cookbook/tree/master/Chapter06`

Enhancing application interfaces

Having an application automatically built for us is an excellent feature in Power Apps. The main logic of a regular application gets created from the data we need to handle. Screens for activities such as listing data or manipulating records are already defined. This feature also acts as a great learning resource for makers that are new to this platform on how to get things done for these particular tasks.

However, this doesn't mean that these ready-made applications achieve high scores in the design department. Remember that end users expect appealing UIs for the apps they use on their devices. With this recipe's help, you will learn how to improve application screens by applying some design ideas to make them more good-looking. These ideas will help you enhance your applications like the one seen in the following figure:

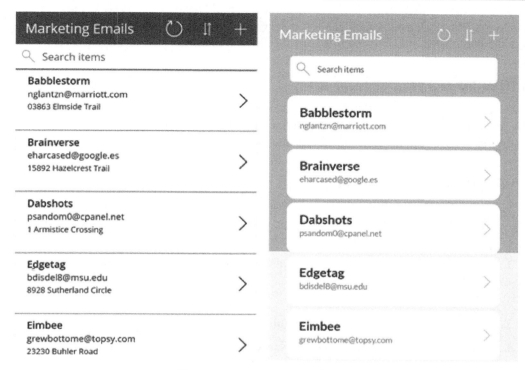

Figure 6.1 – Power Apps makeover

Let's discover how to adapt the ready-made application to be more user friendly.

Getting ready

To apply the UI changes, we will need an application created from data such as the ones we learned about in *Chapter 1, Building pixel-perfect solutions with Canvas Power Apps*. You can build your app using any data source of your choice.

For this particular example, we used a SharePoint list with the following columns of **Single line of text** column types:

- Customer (title)
- Email
- Address

As for the data, we used a data generator service called **Mockaroo** to create dummy data for the list. Check out their website for more info: `https://mockaroo.com`

How to do it...

When creating a Power App from a SharePoint list, the platform builds three screens to handle your data: BrowseScreen1, DetailScreen1, and EditScreen1. Let's follow these steps to improve each one. Keep in mind that the numbering of some controls might change.

Improving the Browse screen

1. Let's start by modifying the action bar called **RectQuickActionBar1**. Using the formula bar, change its height to `App.Height * 0.5`, so it takes half the screen's size, and then set its **Fill** color to `ColorValue("#B4D2E9")`.

2. Select the **TextSearchBox1** control and set its **X** location to `37` and **Y** to `114`. Make the **Width** value `Parent.Width - 75`. Set **Font** to `Lato` and **Font size** to `16`. Change **Border radius** to `10`.

3. Delete **Rectangle11** as we are not going to use this separator.

4. Change the **Y** property of **LblAppName1** to `11`. Set **Font** to **Lato** and **Font size** to `26`.

5. Using the *Shift* key, select all the icons, **IconNewItem1**, **IconSortUpDown1**, and **IconRefresh1**, and change all these properties at once:

    Y position to `23`

    Width and **Height** to `64`

    All padding properties to `16`

6. Change the **X** property of each icon like so:

    *   **IconNewItem1** to `Parent.Width - Self.Width - 33`
    *   **IconSortUpDown1** to `IconNewItem1.X - Self.Width`
    *   **IconRefresh1** to `IconSortUpDown1.X - Self.Width`

The header should look like this:

Figure 6.2 – Header makeover

7. Select **BrowseGallery1** and set these properties:

    X to 20 and **Y** to 208

    Width to `Parent.Width - 40`

    Template size to 117 and **Template padding** to 15

8. Expand the gallery and delete **Separator1** and the **Body1** control.

9. Click on the pencil of the gallery to edit the contents, and from the **Insert** toolbar, click on **Media | Image**. From the properties pane, set **Image** to None and change its **Fill** color to `ColorValue("#FEFFFF")`. Set the **X** and **Y** positions to 0 and change **Width** to `Parent.TemplateWidth` and **Height** to `Parent.TemplateHeight`. Set **Border radius** to 20 and send the image to the back of the gallery canvas by right-clicking on the image control then selecting **Reorder | Send to back**.

10. Change the **NextArrow1** control to have a **Width** and **Height** value of 64 and set all padding properties to 16. For the **Fill** color, set a lighter one, such as `RGBA(202, 202, 202, 1)`.

11. Select **Title1** and set the **Y** property to 25, **Font** to **Lato**, and **Font size** to 22.

12. As for the **Subtitle1** control, change its **Y** property to 68, **Font** to **Lato**, and **Font size** to 16. Lastly, change the color to `RGBA(149, 149, 149, 1)`.

13. Finally, to obtain a better contrast, change the **Fill** color of **BrowseScreen1** to `RGBA(237, 237, 237, 0.6)`.

Refining the Detail screen

1. Click on the **RectQuickActionBar2** control and change its **Color** property to `ColorValue("#B4D2E9")`.

2. Using the *Shift* key, select all the icons, **IconDelete1**, **IconEdit1**, and **IconBackArrow1**, and change all these properties at once:

   Y position to `12`

   Width and **Height** to `64`

   All padding properties to `16`

3. Change the **X** property of each icon like so:

   • **IconEdit1** to `Parent.Width - Self.Width - 20`

   IconDelete1 to `IconEdit1.X - Self.Width`

4. Select **LblAppName2** and change its **Font** property to **Lato** and **Font size** to `24`.

5. Change the **Y** property of **DetailForm1** to `112`.

6. Select **DetailForm1** and using the properties pane, click on **Edit fields** and make sure only the **Title**, **Email**, and **Address** fields appear on the list. Remove any other fields if necessary.

7. Expand **DetailForm1** and, using the *Shift* key, select all the data cards and change its **Height** property to `130`.

8. Select **Title_DataCard1**, and from the properties pane, go to the **Advanced** tab and click **Unlock to change properties**, as seen in the following screenshot:

Figure 6.3 – Unlocking data card properties

9. Still in the **Advanced** tab, change the **DisplayName** property to uppercase, in this case, TITLE. Go to the **Properties** tab and set **Display mode** to **Edit**.

10. Expand **Title_DataCard1** and select **DataCardKey** to change these properties:

    Font to **Lato** and **Font size** to 14.

    Untick the **Auto height** property and set **Height** to 27.

    > **Tip**
    > If the height doesn't update, you might need to manually change the dimensions by expanding the control and then setting the value on the properties pane.

    Change **Color** to RGBA(149, 149, 149, 1).

11. Select **DataCardValue** and set these values:

    Font to **Lato** and **Font size** to 20.

    *   Using the formula bar, set the **Y** property to DataCardKey1.Y + DataCardKey1.Height + 10.

    *   Change **Height** to 60.

    Set all padding properties to 12.

    Change **Color** to RGBA(0, 0, 0, 0.8).

    Set **BorderThickness** to 1 and **BorderColor** to RGBA(237, 237, 237, 1).

12. Repeat *steps 7, 8, 9,* and *10* for the rest of the data card controls. Notice that you need to update the **Y** property formula on *step 10* to match each control name.

13. Select **DataCardValue** inside **Address_DataCard1** and set its **Height** property to App.Height - DetailForm1.Y - Address_DataCard1.Y - Self.Y - 30. Change **Vertical align** to Top.

14. Select **DetailScreen1** and set its **Fill** color to `ColorValue("#FBFAFB")`.

The detail screen should look as in the following screenshot:

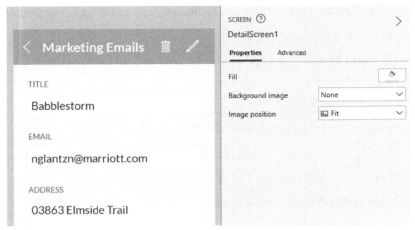

Figure 6.4 – Detail screen makeover

Setting the finishing touches for the Edit screen

1. Select **RectQuickActionBar3** and change its **Color** property to `ColorValue("#B4D2E9")`.

2. Using the *Shift* key, select the **IconCancel1** and **IconAccept1** icons to change all these properties at once:

   Y position to `12`

   Width and **Height** to `64`

   All padding properties to `16`

   Change the **X** property of **IconAccept1** to `Parent.Width - Self.Width - 20`.

3. Select **LblAppName3** and change its **Font** property to `Lato` and **Font size** to `24`.

4. Change the **Y** property of **EditForm1** to `112`.

5. Select **EditForm1** and using the properties pane, click on **Edit fields** and make sure only the **Title**, **Email**, **Address**, and **Attachments** fields appear on the list. Remove any other fields if necessary.

6. Expand **EditForm1**, select all data cards except for **Attachments_DataCard1** using the *Shift* key, and change its **Height** property to `130`.

7. Select **Title_DataCard2**, and from the properties pane, go to the **Advanced** tab and click **Unlock to change properties**.

8. Still in the **Advanced** tab, change the **DisplayName** property to uppercase, in this case, TITLE.

9. Expand **Title_DataCard2** and select **DataCardKey** and **StarVisible** to change these properties:

- **Font** to **Lato** and **Font size** to 14 (except for **StarVisible** next to the title label).

- Untick the **Auto height** property and set **Height** to 27.

- Change the **Color** property to RGBA(149, 149, 149, 1).

10. Select **DataCardValue** and set these values:

- **Font** to **Lato** and **Font size** to 20.

- Using the formula bar, set the **Y** property to DataCardKey4.Y + DataCardKey4.Height + 10.

- Change **Height** to 60.

- Set all padding properties to 12.

- Change **Color** to RGBA(0, 0, 0, 0.8).

- Set **BorderThickness** to 1 and **BorderColor** to If(IsBlank(Parent.Error), RGBA(237, 237, 237, 1), Color.Red).

11. Repeat *steps 7, 8, 9,* and *10* for the rest of the data card controls. Notice that you need to update the **Y** property formula on *step 11* to match each control name.

12. Select **DataCardValue** inside **Attachments_DataCard1** and set its **Height** property to App.Height - EditForm1.Y - Attachments_DataCard1.Y - Self.Y - 30.

13. Expand **Title_DataCard2** and select the **ErrorMessage1** label. Change the **Font** property to **Lato** and **Font size** to 14.

14. Select **EditScreen1** and set its **Fill** color to ColorValue("#FBFAFB").

After applying the previous steps, the makeover is now complete.

How it works...

Improving the user experience of an application involves many aspects, such as performance, rich features, and an appealing UI. Making the changes described in the previous steps enhances the UI by creating a unified design across the application. All screens follow the same pattern to create a seamless experience, as seen in the following screenshot:

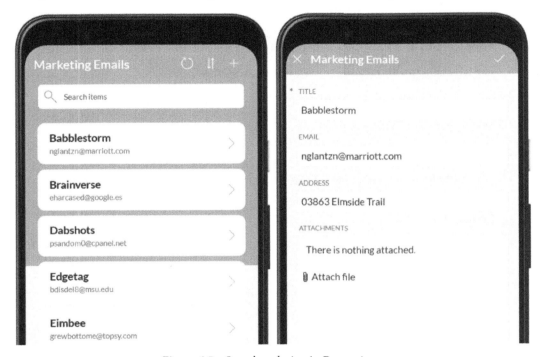

Figure 6.5 – Seamless design in Power Apps

The UI designs used for applications are always evolving. As a reference, you can review *Chapter 5*, *Extending the platform*, to take these rules into account when designing interfaces. For inspiration, you can also visit design websites such as Dribbble, `https://dribbble.com`, where designers showcase their work of website and application designs.

Building a responsive password manager in Power Apps – setting up the Azure Key Vault service

Password managers are tools to handle all your credentials from a central location, protecting them using a primary password and encryption. They can save both personal and work-related credentials for services we use every day.

We are going to leverage Microsoft Azure services to build our application. Azure is a platform that aims to help organizations meet their business needs with a wide range of cloud services.

Microsoft Azure offers a service that is called Azure Key Vault, which provides a "safe" to hold both credentials and certificates most securely by encrypting this information in hardware security modules. For more information, see `https://azure.microsoft.com/en-us/services/key-vault/`

Explanation and overview

To access our data source, we will use the Azure Key Vault connector, which is just one in the ever-growing list of connectors available for canvas apps. It will give us the ability to consume secrets stored in a vault.

This recipe will teach you how to set up Key Vault in your Azure subscription. For the most up-to-date quick start, please refer to `https://docs.microsoft.com/en-us/azure/key-vault/secrets/quick-create-portal`. You'll also find that there are many other ways to interact with Azure besides the portal.

How to do it...

1. Log in to your Azure subscription and select **Create a resource**. This action will open the Azure Marketplace, where you can browse all the resources available. Search for `Key Vault`, and when found, click on **Create**:

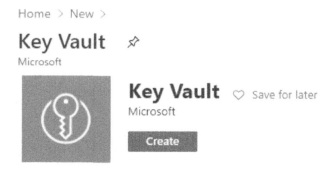

Figure 6.6 – Key Vault service

The next step is to gather all the required information to create your resource.

2. Select an existing resource group or create a new one. A resource group acts as a container for your resources.

3. Select a key vault name. Remember that this name must be unique across all of Azure because this will then be available through the REST API: `https://<key-vault-name>.vault.azure.net/`. As an example, I've used `PowerVault`.

4. Select the region that is closer to you to have better networking performance.

5. Select the **Standard** pricing tier.

6. Leave all other options as default and click **Review + create** and, after the validation is completed, click on **Create**.

7. After a while, the deployment of your resource will complete. Click on **Go to resource** to view your key vault.

How it works...

The current version of the connector only allows the consumption of secrets from a vault. We will add some credentials to our vault so that we can have them accessible from the app we are going to build in the next recipe.

While still in the Azure portal, go to your resource, and under **Settings**, go to **Secrets**:

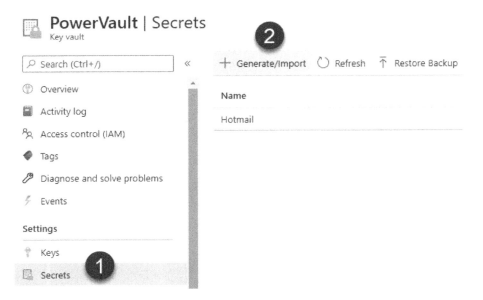

Figure 6.7 – Key vault secrets

Click on **Generate/Import** to start adding secrets. In the new window, please input the name of the secret and the value for it. Create as much as you want to have a set of data to shape your app.

Building a responsive password manager in Power Apps – designing an adaptive application

In the previous recipe, we completed an Azure Key Vault setup to hold the secrets we will consume from our app. This application's design will be responsive so that it can adapt when executing on desktops or mobile devices.

Explanation and overview

Building a responsive application in any platform requires some design principles to be evaluated before making the app. The different mediums in which our app is consumed need to be considered when designing the UI. You need to address the size and location of the controls for every device.

In Power Apps, there are many layout tools that can help you build these types of applications. Our goal is to create one application that works the same on desktop and mobile devices.

Getting ready

The complete application, as well as the resources needed to build it, can be found in our GitHub repo: `https://github.com/PacktPublishing/Microsoft-Power-Apps-Cookbook/tree/master/Chapter06`

How to do it...

1. Go to the Power Apps portal, `https://make.powerapps.com/`, and from the left pane, select **Create | Canvas app from blank**. In the dialog that opens, set the name to `Power Vault`. Keep the **Tablet** format.

2. Once the Studio opens, go to **File | Settings | Screen size + orientation**. Deactivate **Scale to fit** and **Lock orientation** and then click on **Apply**. Go back to the Studio by clicking the back arrow on the screen's top left.

3. From the left pane, select the **Data sources** option (represented by a database icon), and using the **Search** field, look for **Azure Key Vault**. Selecting this connection will open a configuration pane on the right. Enter the vault name used in the previous recipe, and then click on **Connect**.

4. Select the **App** element from the **Tree** view and, using the formula bar, change the **OnStart** property to the following:

```
Set(
    CurrentTheme,
    {
        Background: ColorValue("#E9E9E9"),
        TextPrimary: ColorValue("#292A2D"),
        TextSecondary: ColorValue("#A4A4A4"),
        TextFill: ColorValue("#F3F3F3"),
        Divider: ColorValue("#E9E9E9"),
        Font: Font: Font.'Segoe UI'
    }
)
```

Click on the ellipsis next to the **App** element and select **Run OnStart**.

5. On the left pane, select the **Media** option (represented by a movie reel with a music note) and click on **Upload**. Select the `safe.svg` file downloaded from our GitHub repository.

6. From the toolbar, expand **New screen** and select the **Split-screen** layout, as seen in the following screenshot:

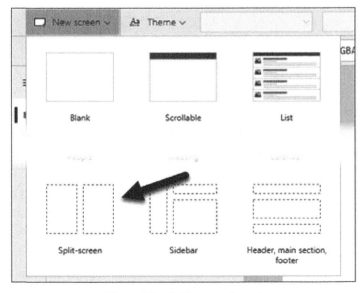

Figure 6.8 – Split-screen layout

This action will add a new screen called **Screen2**. Click the ellipsis next to this screen and rename it to `MainScreen`.

7. Using the formula bar, change the **OnVisible** property of **MainScreen** to the following:

```
UpdateContext({selected: false});
ClearCollect(
    Secrets,
    AzureKeyVault.ListSecrets().value
)
```

8. From the **Tree** view, select **Screen1**, and using the ellipsis next to it, click on **Delete**.

9. Expand **ScreenContainer1** and select **LeftSideContainer1**. Configure it as follows:

*   Using the properties pane on the right, select the last option in **Align (horizontal)** called **Stretch**, set all padding to 20, and disable **Flexible width**.

*   Using the formula bar, set the **Width** to the following:

```
If(MainScreen.Size = ScreenSize.Small, If(selected, 0,
Parent.Width), 280)
```

10. From the **Insert** panel located on the left, click on **Text label** under **Popular**. Set its properties as follows:

Using the properties pane, change the **Text** property to `Password Vault`, **Font size** to 14, and **Font weight** to **Bold**.

Using the formula bar, set the **Color** property to `CurrentTheme.TextPrimary` and **Font** to `CurrentTheme.Font`.

Rename this label as `ApplicationNameLbl`.

11. From the **Insert** panel, select **Text input** under **Popular**. Set its properties as follows:

Using the properties pane, clear the **Default** property and set **Hint text** to `Search`, **Font size** to 13, **Minimum width** to 32, **Border** to 0, and **Border radius** to 0.

Using the formula bar, set the **Color** property to `CurrentTheme.TextPrimary`, **Font** to `CurrentTheme.Font`, **Fill** to `CurrentTheme.TextFill`, **HoverFill** to `Self.Fill`, and **FocusedBorderThickness** to 1.

Rename this text input as `SearchTxt`.

12. From the **Insert** panel, click on **Text label** under **Popular**. Set its properties as follows:

    Using the properties pane, change **Text** to `Secrets`, **Font size** to `12`, **Font weight** to **SemiBold**, and **Top Padding** to `20`.

    Using the formula bar, set the **Color** property to `CurrentTheme.TextPrimary` and **Font** to `CurrentTheme.Font`.

    Rename this label as `SecretsLbl`.

13. From the **Insert** panel, click on **Vertical gallery** under **Popular**. On the properties pane, change **Layout** to **Image, title, and subtitle**.

    > **Positioning issue**
    >
    > Sometimes, when making a layout change in a gallery, the Studio moves the gallery inside the container. Ensure it is located at the end by clicking on its ellipsis and selecting **Reorder | Move to bottom**.

    Set the rest of the properties as follows:

    - Using the properties pane, disable **Show scrollbar** and enable **Show navigation**.

    - Using the formula bar, set the **Items** property to `Filter(Secrets, Find(SearchTxt.Text, name) > 0)`, **TemplateSize** to `84`, and **OnSelect** to the following:

    ```
    UpdateContext({selected: true, secret: Blank()});
    UpdateContext({secret: AzureKeyVault.GetSecret(This
    Item.name)})
    ```

    Rename this gallery as `SecretsGly`.

14. Expand **SecretsGly** and select **Separator4** (keep in mind that the names might change). Set the properties as follows:

    - Using the properties pane, change the **X** property to `48`.

    - Using the formula bar, set the **Fill** property to `CurrentTheme.Divider` and **Width** to `Parent.TemplateWidth - Self.X`.

    - Rename this rectangle as `SG_SeparatorRct`.

15. Select **NextArrow4** inside **SecretsGly** and set the properties as follows:

    Using the properties pane, change the **Width** and **Height** values to `48` and set all padding properties to `15` and **Focused border** to `0`.

Using the formula bar, set the **Color** property to `CurrentTheme.Divider`.

Rename this label as `SG_ArrowIcn`.

16. Select **Image4** inside **SecretsGly** and set the properties as follows:

Using the properties pane, change the **Image** property to **safe**, the **X** property to `0`, **Width** and **Height** to `48`, and all padding properties to `10`.

Rename this image as `SG_SafeImg`.

17. Select **Subtitle4** inside **SecretsGly** and set the properties as follows:

Using the properties pane, change the **Text** property to name, **Font size** to `10`, and **Font weight** to **Normal**.

Using the formula bar, set the **Color** property to `CurrentTheme.TextSecondary`, **Font** to `CurrentTheme.Font`, and the **Y** property to `Title4.Y - Self.Height - 5`.

Rename this label as `SG_NameLbl`.

18. Select **Title4** inside **SecretsGly** and set the properties as follows:

Using the properties pane, change **Font size** to `14`, **Font weight** to **Semibold**, and the **Y** property to `35`.

Using the formula bar, set the **Color** property to `CurrentTheme.TextPrimary`, the **X** property to `SG_SafeImg.X + SG_SafeImg.Width + 10`, **Font** to `CurrentTheme.Font`, and **Text** to `ThisItem.name`.

Rename this label as `SG_ValueLbl`.

The application, so far, should be like the following:

Figure 6.9 – Power Vault under construction

19. From the **Tree** view, select **RightSideContainer1**. Configure it by using the properties pane on the right. Select the last option in **Align (horizontal)** called **Stretch**, set the **Gap** property to 5 and all padding properties to 40, and disable **Flexible width**.

    Using the formula bar, set **Width** to `Parent.Width - LeftSideContainer1.Width` and the **Color** property to `CurrentTheme.Background`.

20. From the **Insert** panel located on the left, click on **Text label** under **Popular**. Set its properties as follows:

    Using the properties pane, change **Text** to `Name`, **Font size** to 14, and **Font weight** to **Semibold**.

    Using the formula bar, set the **Color** property to `CurrentTheme.TextPrimary` and **Font** to `CurrentTheme.Font`.

    Rename this label as `NameLbl`.

21. From the **Insert** panel located on the left, click on **Text label** under **Popular**. Set its properties as follows:

    • Using the properties pane, change **Font size** to 14 and all padding properties to 10.

    • Using the formula bar, set the **Color** property to `CurrentTheme.TextPrimary`, **Font** to `CurrentTheme.Font`, **Fill** to `CurrentTheme.TextFill`, and **Text** to `secret.name`.

    • Rename this label as `NameValueLbl`.

    • Select both `NameLbl` and `NameValueLbl`, copy them to the clipboard, and then paste them twice.

    • Select **NameLbl_1** and, using the properties pane, change **Text** to `Secret`. Rename this label as `SecretLbl`.

22. Select **NameValueLbl_1** and, using the formula bar, change the **Text** property to `secret.value`. Rename this label as `SecretValueLbl`.

    Select **NameLbl_2** and, using the properties pane, change **Text** to `Created`. Rename this label as `CreatedLbl`.

23. Select **NameValueLbl_2** and, using the formula bar, change the **Text** property to `secret.createdTime`. Rename this label as `CreatedValueLbl`.

24. From the **Insert** panel located on the left, click on **Button** under **Popular**. Set its properties as follows:

- Using the properties pane, change **Text** to `Go back`, **Align in container** to the first option called **Start, Border radius** to `0`, **Font size** to `12`, **Text alignment** to **Left**, and **Vertical align** to **Bottom**.

- Using the formula bar, set the **Color** property to `CurrentTheme.TextPrimary`, **Font** to `CurrentTheme.Font`, **Fill** to `Transparent`, **HoverColor** and **PressedColor** to `Self.Color`, **HoverFill** and **PressedFill** to `Self.Fill`, **OnSelect** to `UpdateContext({selected: false})`, and the **Visible** property to `MainScreen.Size = ScreenSize.Small`.

- Rename this button as `BackBtn`.

- Click **File | Save** on the main menu. Click on the **Save** button.

How it works...

After you have created the application, you can test the responsive design by running it from a browser on the desktop or the Power Apps application on a mobile device.

The application should look like this when it's viewed on a desktop browser:

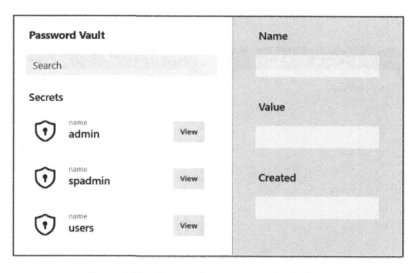

Figure 6.10 – Password manager on the desktop

When the application is running, the app should resize accordingly if you change the window's size. The controls resize and move thanks to the responsive containers:

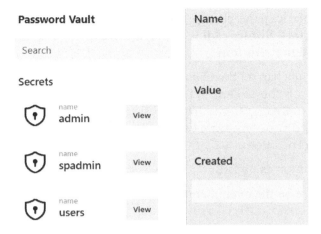

Figure 6.11 – Password manager on the resized desktop

Notice that the left section of the app remains unchanged when resizing the screen. That's intended because it's going to be the base form factor of mobile devices.

When running the app on a mobile device, the left section becomes the main screen, and the detail section will only appear when we select a secret from the gallery:

Figure 6.12 – Password manager on mobile

It might require some testing to get the desired design to work, mostly due to mobile devices' different device resolutions. Still, the new responsive screens available in Power Apps help to create a design template to build our apps.

7
Power Apps Everywhere

Throughout this book, we have seen how useful applications developed with Power Apps can be. Whether you are using multiple data sources or improving the application building process through components, Power Apps allows makers to create solutions quickly and reliably for the organization.

Keep in mind that applications created with this platform are not just accessible through the Power Apps portal. There are many ways to use them through embedding, desktop applications, mobile devices, and more.

This chapter will let you discover all the possible ways to interact with Power Apps through very different mediums with the help of the following recipes:

- Discovering Power Apps Mobile and the Windows desktop player
- Leveraging modern browsers for Power Apps
- Improving SharePoint document libraries with Power Apps
- Embedding Power Apps in SharePoint pages
- Making Power BI reports interactive with embedded power apps

- Working with Power Apps in Microsoft Teams channels
- Automating the integration of Power Apps inside Teams
- Building apps with Dataverse for Teams

Also refer to *Chapter 2, Building Model-Driven Apps* for another sample of application embedding.

Technical requirements

The licensing model for this platform depends on the type of connector needed for your data sources. Standard connectors such as the one used for SharePoint don't require an additional license besides Microsoft 365, but premium or custom connectors do require a Power Apps license.

For more information about the Power Apps licensing model, please refer to *Chapter 3, Choosing the right data source for your applications*. The complete version of this application is available from our GitHub repository at `https://github.com/PacktPublishing/ Microsoft-Power-Apps-Cookbook/tree/master/Chapter07`

Discovering Power Apps Mobile and the Windows desktop player

This recipe will help you discover how to interact with the applications created in Power Apps besides using the portal at `https://make.powerapps.com`

On mobile devices, the Power Apps application acts as a hub for all your solutions and is available on the most popular application stores:

- On Google Play: `https://play.google.com/store/apps/ details?id=com.microsoft.msapps`

- On Apple's App Store: `https://apps.apple.com/us/app/power-apps/ id1047318566`

- On Microsoft Store: `https://www.microsoft.com/store/ productId/9NBLGGH5Z8F3`

Once logged in, this hub will list all the applications the user has access to and is available on both phones and tablet devices.

These versions share a feature called **Pin to Home**, which creates an individual icon on the device's home screen to open a specific application.

How to do it...

1. Install the Power Apps application from your device's application store and sign in using your organizational account.

2. From the list of applications, select the ellipsis on the application you want to create an icon for and click **Pin to Home**. The following is the Power Apps application on each mobile device platform:

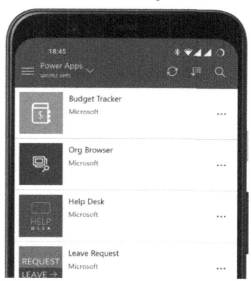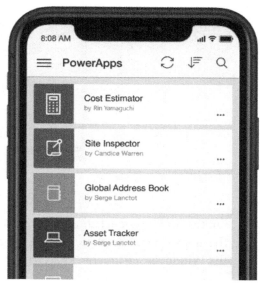

Figure 7.1 – Power Apps application on Android (left) and iPhone (right) devices

3. On Android devices, a dialog will open to place the icon automatically or manually in the location of choice by using drag and drop, as seen in the following screenshot:

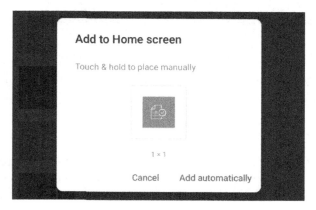

Figure 7.2 – Android's Pin to Home dialog

4. On Apple devices, a dialog will open with instructions to add the icon to the Home Screen as seen in the following screenshot:

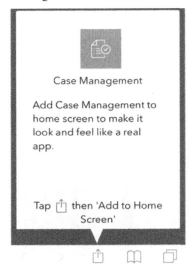

Figure 7.3 – Apple's Pin to Home dialog

5. On the desktop side, using the Microsoft Store version, selecting **Pin to Home** from the ellipsis menu displays a dialog asking whether you want to pin the application to the Windows Start menu, as seen in the following screenshot:

Figure 7.4 – Pin to Home in Microsoft Store version

We can apply this type of shortcut to any application available from the Power Apps application hub.

How it works...

Both the Apple and Google versions display the list of applications regardless of the deployed environment. In the Microsoft Store version, you need to select the environment to list the applications. However, the Microsoft Store version adds a new twist because it also makes this hub available for Windows desktop devices.

Using the **Pin to Home** feature helps user adoption by creating a shortcut for speedier access to your solutions. In the following screenshot, you can see how a power app looks like a standalone application on the Start menu:

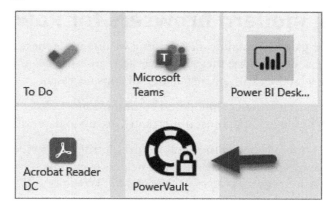

Figure 7.5 – PowerVault power app on the Start menu

The application also gets a standalone icon on mobile devices, which lets you bypass the Power Apps application by going directly to the desired app.

There's more...

The mobile versions of Power Apps offer the same capabilities as when running the applications from the browser. However, the Microsoft Store version cannot process some options, such as using the newest Dataverse connector.

Whenever an app requires a more recent feature, the hub displays a warning such as the one seen in the following screenshot:

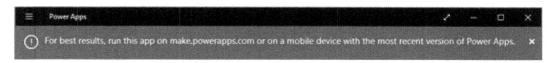

Figure 7.6 – Microsoft Store version warning

If you plan to target your apps for the Microsoft Store version, please test it thoroughly before deploying to production as this version lacks some features compared to the Power Apps portal player or the mobile versions.

Another limitation would be that this version only works with canvas apps. Model-driven solutions don't appear in the list of apps available.

Please refer to the *Leveraging modern browsers for Power Apps* recipe in this chapter for a more elegant workaround when using Power Apps on desktop systems.

Leveraging modern browsers for Power Apps

Web browsers are the gateway for almost everything we do online these days. They are not just for browsing websites anymore; they also serve apps and services and even help us to communicate with each other, with no installation of apps necessary.

That's why using a modern browser should be a common-sense rule for everyone; they use the latest web technologies and, most importantly, are up to date with security fixes.

In this recipe, we will leverage one of the latest features introduced in modern browsers to get faster access to the apps we create. This will help us overcome some of the issues mentioned in the *Discovering Power Apps Mobile and the Windows desktop player* recipe when working on desktop devices.

Getting ready

The workaround we are going to discover requires a Chromium-based browser such as Microsoft Edge or Google Chrome. For more information regarding which browsers use this technology in their core, please refer to `https://en.wikipedia.org/wiki/Chromium_(web_browser)`

How to do it...

1. Go to the Power Apps portal, `https://make.powerapps.com`, and from the left pane, click on **Apps** to view the list of applications in your environment of choice.

2. Click on the name of any application to execute it. This action will open a new window with the app running.

3. To improve the perception of your application as a standalone solution, click on the address section of the browser and include the following text, `&hidenavbar=true`, as seen in the following screenshot:

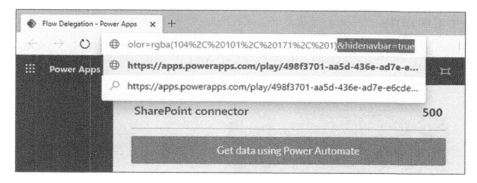

Figure 7.7 – Address parameters for the Power Apps player

Adding this parameter will remove all branding of Power Apps for your application. Now, let's see how to run our applications as standalone solutions on Microsoft Edge and Google Chrome.

Microsoft Edge

1. Click on the browser's ellipsis dropdown and then select **Apps | Install this site as an app** as seen in the following screenshot:

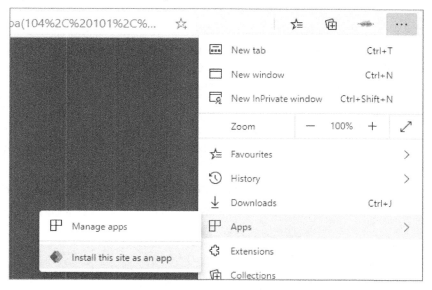

Figure 7.8 – Installing Power Apps as an app in Microsoft Edge

2. A dialog will open, asking for the name of this app. Leave it as default or rename it as desired, and then click **Install**. Immediately after this, a new window is created with the application running but without any browser decoration.

Google Chrome

1. Click on the browser's ellipsis dropdown and then select **More tools | Create shortcut…**, as seen in the following screenshot:

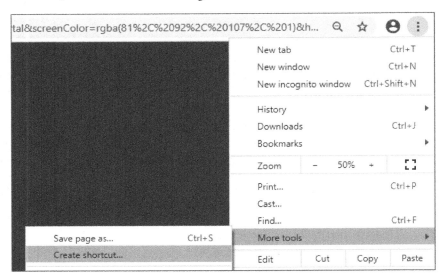

Figure 7.9 – Installing Power Apps as a shortcut in Google Chrome

2. A dialog will open, asking for the name of the shortcut. Leave it as default or rename it as desired, check **Open as window**, and click **Create**. Immediately after this, a new window is created with the application running but without any browser decoration.

On both browsers

1. Resize the window to the desired dimensions. The app window will remember the size for future executions.

2. As the app window appears in the Windows 10 taskbar, you can pin it for easier access, as seen in the following screenshot:

Figure 7.10 – App pinning on Windows 10

This action will make sure the icon stays on the taskbar even after the application closes.

How it works...

Access to your application is now easier than ever; no more going to the Power Apps portal or the Office 365 home page. The application can be executed directly as with any other on the system:

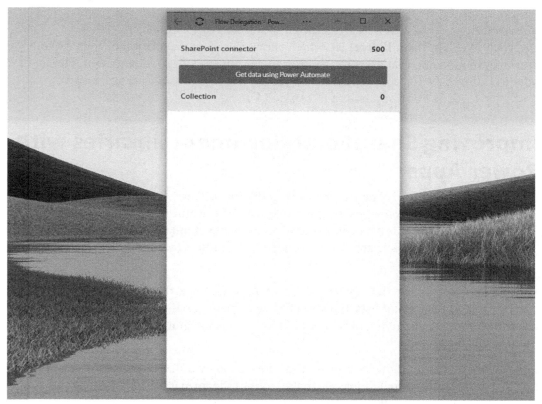

Figure 7.11 – A power app as a standalone application

You can reuse this technique with any other power app in your organization, giving your users faster access to your solutions. Also, notice that this method adds the apps to the list of apps from the Start menu in Windows 10.

There's more...

Google Chrome also creates a desktop shortcut for apps using this technique. It might be useful for other scenarios such as distributing these shortcuts using an org-wide **Group Policy (GPO)**. This solution could deploy the specified shortcut on the desktop of all devices of the organization. Please refer to this blog for an example of this: `https://www.prajwaldesai.com/create-desktop-shortcut-using-group-policy-gpo/`

Microsoft Edge can also benefit from the GPO solution by using specific policies, especially **WebAppInstallForceList**, which allows the silent installation of apps without user intervention and that users can't uninstall. For up-to-date documentation, please refer to `https://docs.microsoft.com/en-us/deployedge/microsoft-edge-policies#webappinstallforcelist`

Improving SharePoint document libraries with Power Apps

In *Chapter 1*, *Building pixel-perfect solutions with Canvas Power Apps*, we discovered the ability to embed Power Apps in SharePoint lists. This feature opens a wide range of possibilities to handle this data compared to SharePoint's standard forms by providing the ability to use a complete application using all the features that canvas Power Apps can provide.

We can also improve the SharePoint document libraries. Since they inherit the functionality of SharePoint lists, the same Power Apps integration applies. However, since the focus is on handling files instead of items, this integration lacks usability from a user perspective.

This recipe will explain how to improve this integration by utilizing a SharePoint feature called column formatting. Using code that describes the format we want to apply, we can change how columns are displayed. For more information, refer to `https://docs.microsoft.com/en-us/sharepoint/dev/declarative-customization/column-formatting`

Getting ready

Since we are using SharePoint as our data source, there are no licensing requirements for the app we are going to build. We will need a document library with metadata columns to improve the library's categorization. Then, we are going to create an application to handle this library.

The code needed for the column formatting is available in our GitHub repo at `https://github.com/PacktPublishing/Microsoft-Power-Apps-Cookbook/tree/master/Chapter07`

How to do it...

1. Go to the SharePoint site that will hold the document library, for example, `https://ampicurrents.sharepoint.com`. On the main site page, click on **+ New | Document library**, as seen in the following screenshot:

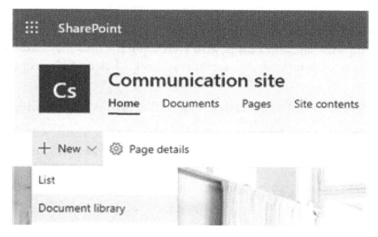

Figure 7.12 – Document library creation

This action will open a pane on the right asking for the name and description of the library. Enter `Book requests` for the name and leave the rest as default.

2. Once the library opens, click on the **+ Add column** link at the end of the column header, as seen in the following screenshot:

Figure 7.13 – Add column link

3. By selecting the data type from the dropdown, add the following columns:

Name	Type
Description	Multiple lines of text
ISBN	Single line of text
Available	Yes/No

Figure 7.14 – Library columns

4. Add files to the library by selecting **Upload | Files** from the toolbar. Once the upload completes, click on **Edit in grid view** to fill the file's metadata in bulk, just like when working with an Excel spreadsheet. Click on **Exit grid view** when finished.

5. Enter some test book data for each uploaded file, such as the following:

Description: 20,000 Leagues Under the Sea, also known under its more extended title, Twenty Thousand Leagues Under the Seas: An Underwater Tour of the World, is a classic science fiction novel written by Jules Verne published in 1870

ISBN: 0439227151

Available: Yes

6. From the toolbar, choose **Power Apps | Customize forms**. This action will send the data structure of the document library to Power Apps to build an app.

7. Once Power Apps Studio completes the app's creation, you will get a screen called **FormScreen1** to edit the library metadata. Select the **SharePointForm1** form control and, on the right pane, click on **Edit fields**.

8. On the **Fields** pane, leave only the **Description**, **ISBN**, and **Available** columns. Remove the rest by selecting the ellipsis icon on each field and selecting **Remove**, as seen in the following screenshot:

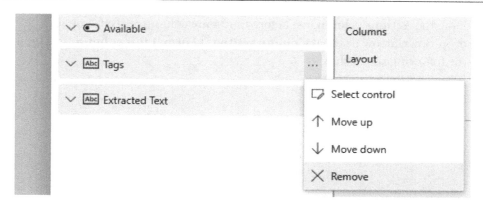

Figure 7.15 – Power Apps Fields pane

9. Drag the **Description** field to the end of the **Fields** list.

10. Select **Description_DataCard1** and, using the formula bar, change its **Height** property to `SharePointForm1.Height - Self.Y - 10`. Select the description text input control named **DataCardValue2** and change the **Height** property to `Description_DataCard1.Height - Self.Y - 20`, again using the formula bar. Lastly, change the **Mode** property to **Multiline**.

11. Expand **ISBN_DataCard1** and select **DataCardValue3** to change **Font size** to `12`. Change all **Padding** properties to `10`.

12. Repeat *step 11* on the **DataCardValue2** control inside **Description_DataCard1**.

13. Select **File** on Power Apps Studio's main menu, and from the **Save** section, click on **Save** and then **Publish to SharePoint**. On the dialog that appears, select **Publish to SharePoint** again.

14. Click on the back arrow at the top left of the screen, and then click on the **Back to SharePoint** link at the top left.

15. Back in the document library, click on the gear icon located at the upper right and then **Library settings**.

16. At the bottom of the **Columns** section, click on **Create column**. Name it `Actions`, and select **Calculated (calculation based on other columns)** as the type. In the **Formula** field, enter `=""` and click **OK** at the bottom of the screen.

17. Back in the library settings, click on the **Book requests** name to go back to the library.

18. Drag the **Actions** column just before the **Name** column and click on its drop-down arrow to select **Column settings | Format this column**, as seen in the following screenshot:

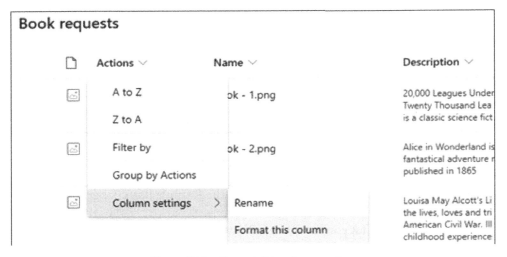

Figure 7.16 – Format this column option

19. On the pane that opens, click on **Advanced mode** near the bottom. Paste the code found in our GitHub repo from the `ColumnFormat.json` file.

How it works...

Working with Power Apps embedded in document libraries can help your users when they require more features besides what you get from the default SharePoint forms. However, the steps needed to use these apps are very awkward in the current SharePoint implementation.

To view the embedded app, you need to open the properties pane. Right now, there are two ways to achieve this:

- Click on the ellipsis of a particular file and select **More | Properties** (numbered steps in *Figure 7.17*).

- Choose a file, click on the details pane on the toolbar, and then look for the **Edit all** link (lettered steps in *Figure 7.17*).

The following screenshot describes the ways to open the properties pane:

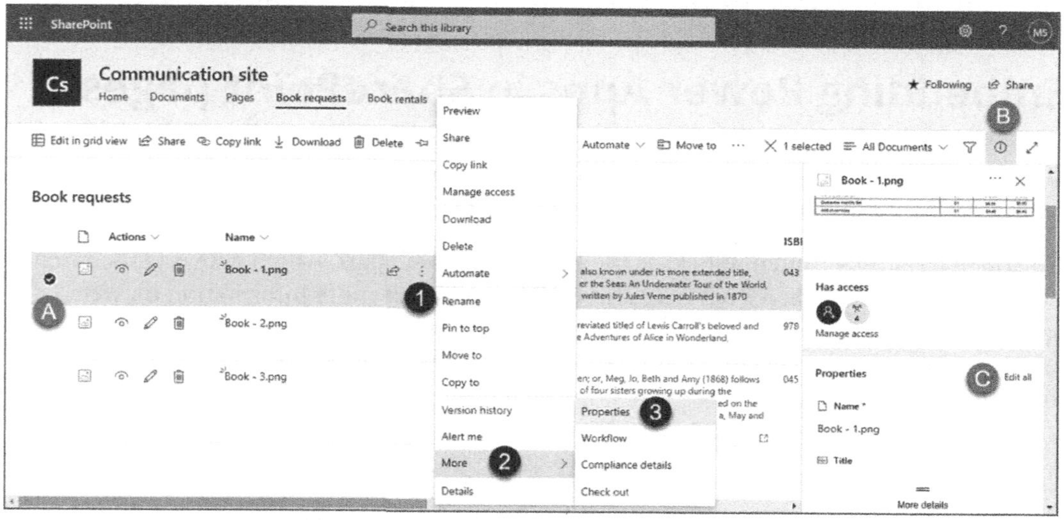

Figure 7.17 – Opening embedded power apps from the document library

With the help of SharePoint column formatting, we have added three action buttons to interact with the library's files:

- **Eye icon**: Default click to open (view) the files inside the library.
- **Pencil icon**: This action is a shortcut to open the properties pane and, therefore, the embedded power app.
- **Trash icon**: Clicking on this executes the delete action of the document library.

Now, we can edit the file properties faster by just clicking on the pencil icon.

There's more...

Using actions to improve the use of embedded power apps in document libraries is just an example of what you can achieve with column formatting. You can enhance the listing visualization, apply color rules depending on the columns' values, and even call a Power Automate cloud flow to interact with the file that triggered it.

For more examples of this feature, please refer to the SharePoint List Formatting Samples GitHub repository at `https://github.com/pnp/sp-dev-list-formatting`

Embedding Power Apps in SharePoint pages

SharePoint pages are the tool of choice when using SharePoint as a platform for content management. Using content blocks, called **web parts**, you can build pages with text, images, videos, and dynamic content.

One of SharePoint's content blocks is the Power Apps web part, which allows embedding a canvas app inside a SharePoint page for easier access. For more information on web parts, please refer to `https://support.microsoft.com/en-us/office/using-web-parts-on-sharepoint-pages-336e8e92-3e2d-4298-ae01-d404bbe751e0`

Getting ready

To use the Power Apps web part, we will need an existing application. The same rules for executing applications apply here:

- To be able to run the application, it needs to be shared with the users first.
- If there is a license requirement to use the app, it will be enforced on the users accessing the SharePoint page.
- The users must grant the use of any connectors inside the app.

For this recipe, we will use the same application designed in *Chapter 6, Improving User Experience*.

How to do it...

1. Navigate to the Power Apps portal, `https://make.powerapps.com`, and select the **Apps** section on the left pane. Locate the desired app from the list, and then click on its ellipsis dropdown and select **Details**.

2. When the **Details** page appears, look for **App ID** as seen in the following screenshot:

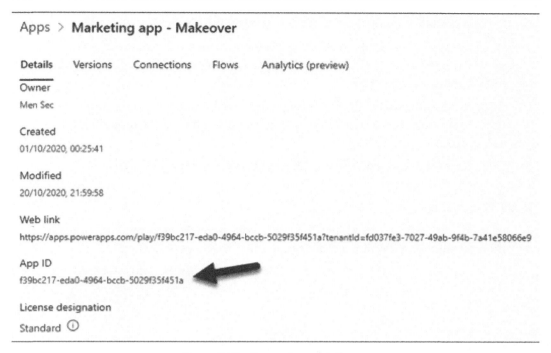

Figure 7.18 – Power Apps detail page

3. Copy the **App ID** GUID and save it to your clipboard.

4. Go to the desired SharePoint site and go to the page where you want to set up your app.

5. On the page's toolbar, click on **Edit**. Once the page is in edit mode, locate a space to embed the app and click the plus sign to add a web part, as seen in the following screenshot:

Figure 7.19 – Web parts in SharePoint pages

6. In the **Search** box, enter `PowerApps` and select it from the list.

7. Once inserted, click on the **Add an app** button to open the properties pane to the right. Paste the collected app ID in the **App web link or ID** field. The application should appear immediately.

8. Click on **Show border** if desired. Drag to extend the web part to the appropriate size. Depending on the layout and responsiveness of the app, it should fill the web part correctly.

9. Once the changes are complete, click **Republish** on the page's toolbar.

How it works...

After following the web part configuration steps, you should have a fully functional application on your SharePoint page, as seen in the following screenshot:

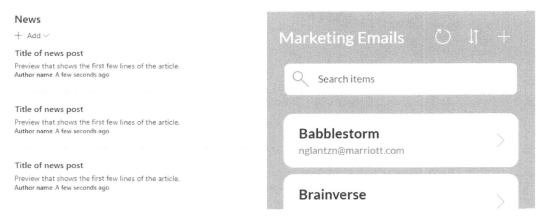

Figure 7.20 – Power App embedded in a SharePoint page

Embedding power apps on a SharePoint page can help your app discovery by placing them in the right location. For example, an ideal place for a vacation request app would be the HR department site.

There's more...

This feature has added value when using SharePoint with external users. Suppose your application doesn't need to be licensed by a Power Apps plan, and the application is embedded in a page of a site shared with external users. In this case, you are automatically creating a tool for external users to interact with the organizational assets defined in your application.

It is important to mention that there is also an improved version of the Power Apps web part that includes more features such as theme awareness, dynamic data handling, and more. Please refer to this repository to get the code, `https://github.com/pnp/sp-dev-fx-webparts/tree/master/samples/react-enhanced-powerapps`, and this instructional video on how to install it on your tenant, `https://www.youtube.com/watch?v=EFhP4uu0rlo`

Making Power BI reports interactive with embedded Power Apps

Power BI is a reporting tool for excellence. It allows the fusion of many data sources to build dashboards and reports that aid organizations in getting the knowledge they need from the insight received from this data.

Being part of the Power Platform, we can expect integrations from the other tools that compose this platform. For example, Power BI integrates with Power Automate via alerts. When an alert is triggered, a cloud flow can execute notifications depending on the trigger's data or also record these alerts into a data source for auditing purposes.

In the case of Power Apps, it allows the embedding of applications inside reports to extend the data visualization or processing of the information, thus improving the interaction with the analytics solution.

Getting ready

This recipe will make use of Power BI Desktop, the tool destined for designing reports and dashboards. Installing it from Microsoft Store is recommended because the system will update it automatically.

As for the data source, we will leverage Azure SQL Database as it gives you the ability to use a direct connection instead of importing the data into the report. Dataverse also provides this type of connection, but it is still in preview at the time of writing.

To have an Azure SQL database, you will need an Azure subscription. To apply for this and other services from the Microsoft cloud solution, sign up for a free account here: `https://azure.microsoft.com/en-us/free/`

Regarding Power Apps, since we are using a premium connector, please refer to the Preface section of this book to get more information about the licensing requirements.

How to do it...

The following steps will help you build this recipe sample, from creating the Azure SQL database to the Power BI report's design with the embedded power app.

Provisioning the data source

1. Go to the Azure portal, `https://portal.azure.com`, and click on **Create a resource**. This action will open Azure Marketplace. Using the search field, enter `SQL Database` and hit *Enter*.

2. From the list of services, select **SQL Database** and then click **Create**. This action will open the **Create SQL Database** page, as seen in the next screenshot:

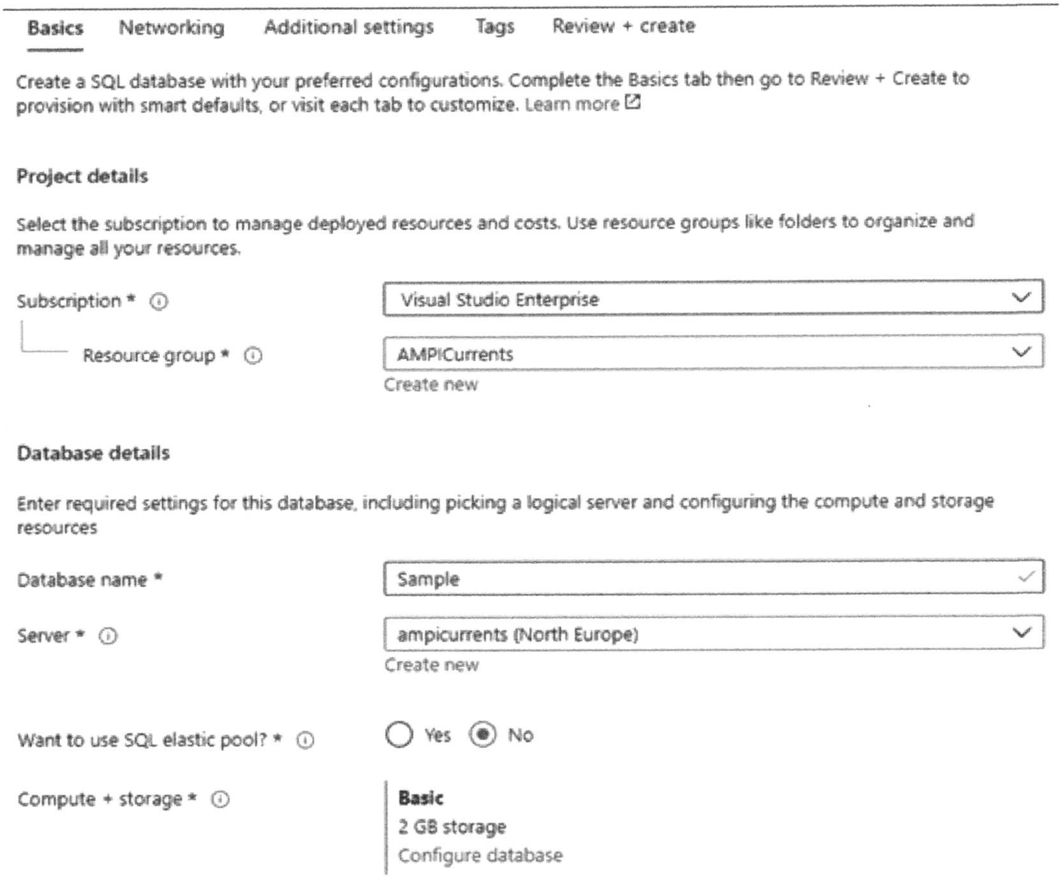

Basics   Networking   Additional settings   Tags   Review + create

Create a SQL database with your preferred configurations. Complete the Basics tab then go to Review + Create to provision with smart defaults, or visit each tab to customize. Learn more ☑

Project details

Select the subscription to manage deployed resources and costs. Use resource groups like folders to organize and manage all your resources.

Subscription * ⓘ | Visual Studio Enterprise   ⌄ |

└──── Resource group * ⓘ | AMPICurrents   ⌄ |
                                 Create new

Database details

Enter required settings for this database, including picking a logical server and configuring the compute and storage resources

Database name * | Sample   ✓ |

Server * ⓘ | ampicurrents (North Europe)   ⌄ |
                                 Create new

Want to use SQL elastic pool? * ⓘ   ◯ Yes ◉ No

Compute + storage * ⓘ | **Basic**
                                     2 GB storage
                                     Configure database

Figure 7.21 – Create SQL Database from the Azure portal

3. Select your subscription and resource group. Enter the name of the database in the **Database name** field and select a server. If you don't have an existing server, click on the **Create new** link just below the servers list and enter the required information: **Server name**, **Server admin login**, and **Password**. For the **Location** input, select one closest to your location for better response times.

4. Select **No** for the elastic pool setting and then click on **Configure database** in the **Compute + storage** setting. When the **Configure** page opens, select the pricing tier you want for your database. For testing purposes, click on the **Looking for basic, standard, premium?** link, then choose **Basic** for the lowest pricing tier, and then click on **Apply**.

5. Back on the **Create SQL Database** page, click on the **Networking** tab and select **Public endpoint** for **Connectivity method**. In the **Firewall rules** section, select **Yes** for both the **Allow Azure services and resources to access this server** and **Add current client IP address** options.

6. Click on the **Additional settings** tab and select **Sample** from the **Use existing data** setting.

7. Select the **Review + create** tab and then click on **Create**. This action will start the provisioning of the database. Once it finishes, you can continue to the next step.

Installing and configuring Power BI Desktop

1. The following link will open the Power BI Desktop page on Microsoft Store: `https://www.microsoft.com/store/productId/9NTXR16HNW1T`. Install the application and when it finishes, launch it. Log in using your organization's credentials by clicking **Sign In** on the app's title bar.

2. On the startup screen, click on **Get data**, and on the dialog that opens, look for **Azure SQL database** and click **Connect**. In the next dialog, enter the **Server** address and the **Database** name as entered in *step 3* of the previous task. Select **DirectQuery** for **Data Connectivity mode** and then click **OK**. These settings should appear as in the following screenshot:

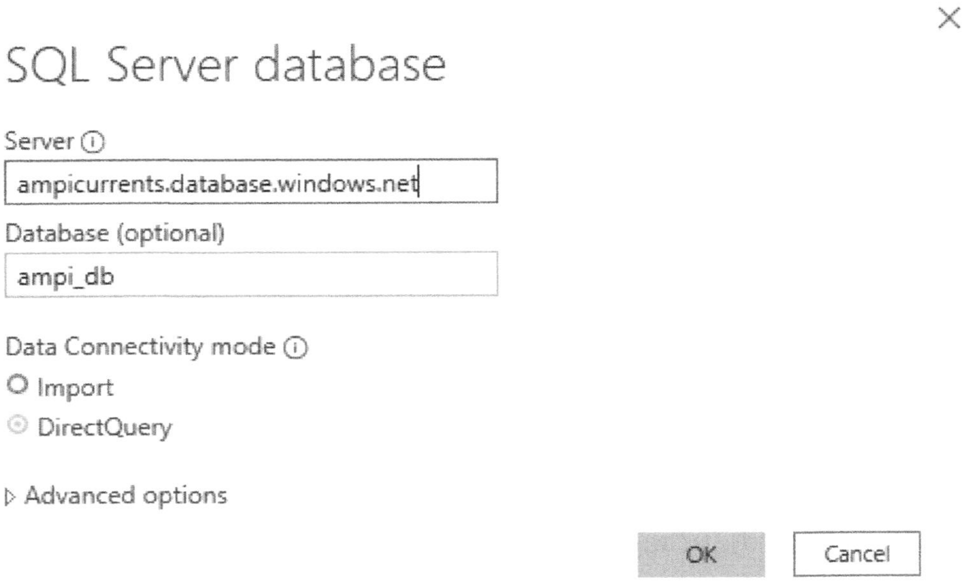

×

SQL Server database

Server ⓘ

ampicurrents.database.windows.net

Database (optional)

ampi_db

Data Connectivity mode ⓘ

◯ Import

◉ DirectQuery

▷ Advanced options

OK   Cancel

Figure 7.22 – Azure SQL Database configuration in Power BI

3. The next dialog is where you can set the authentication type. Select **Database** from the left pane and then enter the username and password defined for the database server in *step 3* of the *Provisioning the data source* section.

4. The **Navigator** dialog will open, displaying the contents of the database. Expand the database name and select the **SalesLT.Product** table, and then hit **Load**. The Power BI report now has the data source configured for the Azure SQL database, and now you can start designing your report.

5. From the **Fields** pane, located at the right, select the following fields: **ProductNumber**, **Name**, and **ListPrice**. These fields will appear in a table visualization as seen in the next screenshot:

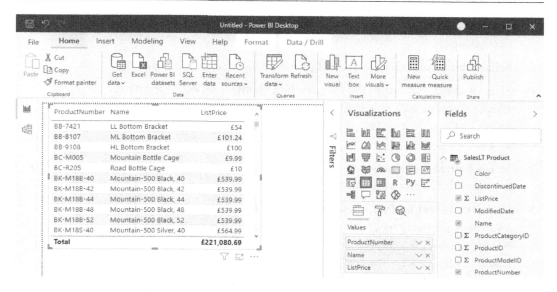

Figure 7.23 – Data source fields visualization in Power BI Desktop

6. Design the report to accommodate the values, and then select **Power Apps** from the main **Insert** tab. This action will add a particular visualization that will act as the container for the embedded power app. Select the same fields as in the previous step for this visualization.

7. Once the field configuration is complete, the visualization will change to embed the Power App. Click on **Create new**, and after a couple of seconds, a dialog will prompt you with a URL that will open the Power Apps Studio already connected to this report. Click **OK** and wait for the app to build.

Building the Power App

1. By default, the integration creates only one screen with a gallery beside the **PowerBIIntegration** control, which acts as a bridge between Power BI and Power Apps.

2. On the left pane, select the data icon, expand the **Connectors** section, and select **SQL Server**. On the fly-out menu, click on **Add a connection**. On the right pane that opens, choose **SQL Server Authentication**, and set the same parameters used to connect to the Azure SQL database from Power BI Desktop and click **Connect**.

3. Select **SalesLT.Product** from the list of tables and click **Connect**.

4. Select the **Gallery1** control and delete it. From the **Insert** toolbar, insert a label three times.

5. Select **Label1** and change its **Text** property to Product name.

6. Select **Label2** and, using the formula bar, change its **Text** property to First(PowerBIIntegration.Data).Name and the **Fill** property to RGBA(242, 242, 242, 0.5). Set the **Y** property to 120 and the **X** property to 40.

7. Select **Label3** and change its **Text** property to List price. Set the **Y** property to 240 and the **X** property to 40.

8. From the **Insert** toolbar, click on **Text | Text input**. Set the **Y** property to 320 and the **X** property to 40. Using the formula bar, change its **Default** property to First(PowerBIIntegration.Data).ListPrice and the **Fill** property to RGBA(242, 242, 242, 0.5). Change the **Format** property to Number.

9. Click on **Button** from the **Insert** toolbar and set the **Y** property to 440 and the **X** property to 40. Change the **Width** property to 560 and the **Text** property to Update list price. Using the formula bar, change the **OnSelect** property to the following:

```
Patch(
    '[SalesLT].[Product]',
    LookUp(
        '[SalesLT].[Product]',
        ProductNumber = First(PowerBIIntegration.Da
        ta).ProductNumber
    ),
    {ListPrice: Value(TextInput1.Text)}
);
Back();
PowerBIIntegration.Refresh()
```

10. Select all controls and change the **Font** property to **Lato** and **Font size** to 22.

11. On the main toolbar, click on **File** and then click on **Settings**. Select **Screen size + orientation**, disable **Scale to fit**, and click **Apply**.

12. Go to the **Save** section, give the app a name, and then click on the **Save** button located at the bottom right.

13. Once the app is saved, the Power BI Desktop application will update the report to reflect the embedded application, as seen in the following screenshot:

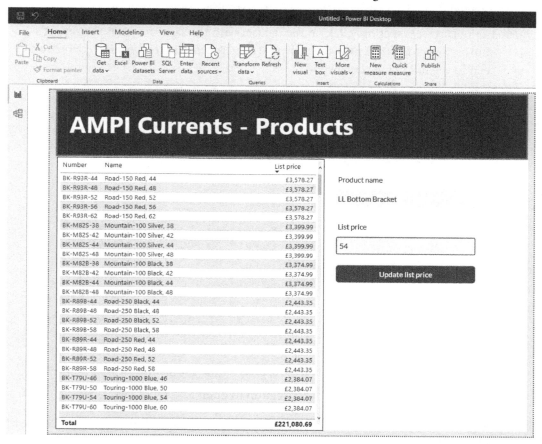

Figure 7.24 – Power app integrated into a Power BI report

14. For this integration to work, you need to publish the report to Power BI online. On the Power BI Desktop application, click on **Publish** from the **Home** toolbar. This action will prompt you to save the report to a location on your computer, and then a dialog will pop up, asking for the destination workspace. Pick the desired workspace or leave the default selection, **My workspace**, and then click **Select**.

15. Navigate to the Power BI website, https://www.powerbi.com, and log in using the same credentials as in Power BI Desktop, and then expand the previously selected workspace from the Power BI page's left pane.

16. In the **Datasets** section, click on the dataset with the same name as the report's ellipsis. Select **Refresh now** to verify that the credentials are working correctly, as seen in the following screenshot:

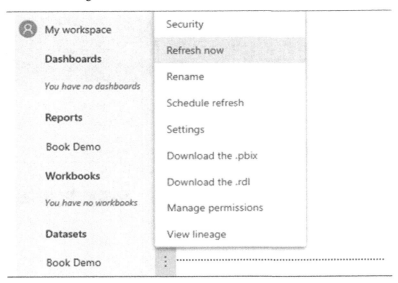

Figure 7.25 – Dataset options in Power BI online

17. Select the report from the **Reports** section to open it.

Now we have the app fully embedded with the report we designed locally on the Power BI online platform.

How it works...

There are two main factors in this recipe: **DirectQuery** and **PowerBIIntegration**:

- DirectQuery allows connectivity to the data source using a direct connection. When a data refresh is requested, Power BI queries the data directly on the data source instead of importing the data for processing.

- The Power BI integration control allows interaction between the data in Power BI and the Power App. The **Data** property of this control receives a table of records of the fields defined in the visualization, as seen in *step 5* from *Installing and configuring Power BI Desktop* section. For this reason, the code in Power Apps always uses the First function to get the first record of the **Data** property.

The published report will look as in the following screenshot:

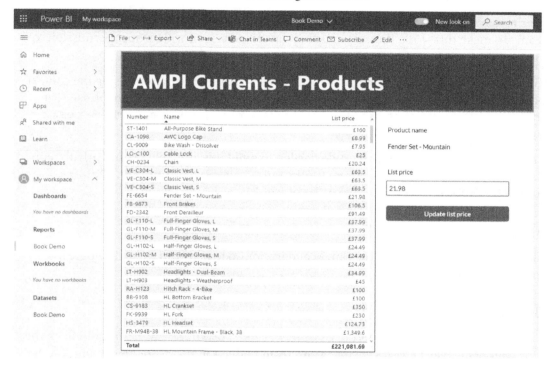

Figure 7.26 – Published report in Power BI online

This solution offers a way to update the data directly from the report using the embedded application. Using the **Refresh** method of the integration control, we can keep the data up to date in the report.

Working with Power Apps in Microsoft Teams channels

Microsoft Teams is the central hub of the organization's content. The variety of capabilities available in this platform range from communication and collaboration to content access and more.

One of the most valuable aspects is the opportunity to extend its features through customizations. For example, you can build custom applications, enhance messaging capabilities, build bots, and embed web content.

Power Apps allows the creation of applications integrated with this collaborative platform.

Getting ready

This recipe will build a Power App for Microsoft Teams to handle the channels in a given team. To make this work, the user must have access to a team with proper permission to add and remove apps.

The canvas app will take advantage of the Microsoft Teams integrations using the context parameters available when using an embedded app. For more information, please visit `https://docs.microsoft.com/en-us/powerapps/teams/embed-teams-app#use-context-from-teams`

The resulting application and the code needed to build it is available in our GitHub repo located at `https://github.com/PacktPublishing/Microsoft-Power-Apps-Cookbook/tree/master/Chapter07`

How to do it...

The first step will be creating the canvas application so that we can then distribute it through Teams channels.

Building the canvas app

1. Go to the Power Apps portal, `https://make.powerapps.com/`, and from the left pane, select **Create | Canvas app from blank**. On the dialog that opens, set the name to `Channel Manager`. Keep the **Tablet** format.

2. When the Studio opens, click on **File | Settings | Name + icon** and fill the **Description** field with `Microsoft Teams channel management system`. Still on **Settings**, select **Screen size + orientation**. Deactivate the **Scale to fit** option and click on **Apply**. Go back to the Studio by clicking the back arrow on the screen's top left.

3. On the **Tree** view, select the **App** element. Using the formula bar, select the **OnStart** property and paste the code downloaded from the GitHub repository located in the `App - OnStart.txt` file. Right-click on the **App** ellipsis to execute this code, as seen in the following screenshot:

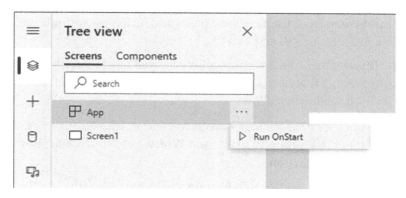

Figure 7.27 – OnStart execution

4. Rename the **Screen1** element to MainScreen by double-clicking on its name.

5. From the data sources panel located on the left (represented by a database icon), use the **Search** field to look for Microsoft Teams. Select this connector from the list and select **Connect** from the panel that opens on the right.

6. From the **Insert** panel located on the left (represented by a plus sign), click on **Text label** under **Popular**. Set the properties as follows.

    Using the properties pane, change the **Text** property to Channel Manager, **Font** to **Segoe UI**, **Font size** to 16, and **Font weight** to **Semibold**. For **Position**, set 0 for **X** and **Y**. Set the **Height** property to 60. For **Padding**, set 15 for **Top** and 20 for the rest.

    Using the formula bar, set **Width** to App.Width, **Color** to White, and **Fill** to CurrentTheme.MainColor.

    Name this label MainTitleLbl.

7. From the **Insert** panel, click on **Add icon** located under **Popular**. Set the properties as follows.

    Using the properties pane, change **Icon** to **Reload**, the **Y** property to 0, **Width** and **Height** to 60, and all **Padding** properties to 20.

    Using the formula bar, set the **X** property to App.Width - Self.Width, **Color** to White, and the **OnSelect** property to the code downloaded from the GitHub repository located in the RefreshIcn - OnSelect.txt file.

    Name this icon RefreshIcn.

8. Select **MainScreen** from the **Tree** view panel and, using the formula bar, change the **OnVisible** property to `Select(RefreshIcn)`.

9. From the **Insert** panel, add a vertical gallery located under **Popular**. On the **Select a data source** panel that opens next to the gallery, select **channelData**. Set the properties of the gallery as follows.

    Using the properties pane, change **Layout** to `Title and subtitle` and set the **X** property to 0, the **Y** property to 60, and **Width** to 350. Disable **Show scrollbar** and enable **Show navigation**.

    Using the formula bar, set the **Height** property to `App.Height - Self.Y`, **Fill** to `CurrentTheme.Background`, and **TemplateSize** to 100.

    Name this gallery `ChannelGly`.

10. From the **Tree** view, expand **ChannelGly** and follow these instructions, keeping in mind that some of the control numbers might change:

*   Select **Separator5** and, using the formula bar, set the **X** value to 20, **Fill** to `CurrentTheme.Divider`, and **Width** to `Parent.TemplateWidth - 40`.

*   Name this control `SeparatorRct`.

*   Select **NextArrow5** and, using the properties pane, set **Icon** to `Message`, the **Width** and **Height** values to 48, and all **Padding** to 10.

*   Using the formula bar, set **Color** to `CurrentTheme.TextSecondary` and the **X** property to `Parent.TemplateWidth - Self.Width - 20`.

*   Name this icon `MessageIcn`.

*   Select **Subtitle5** and, using the properties pane, change **Font** to **Segoe UI** and **Font size** to 10.

*   Using the formula bar, set the **Text** property to `Concatenate("Message count: ", Text(ThisItem.messageCount.'@odata.count'))` and **Color** to `CurrentTheme.TextSecondary`.

*   Name this label `MessageCountLbl`.

*   Select **Title5** and, using the properties pane, change **Font** to `Segoe UI`, **Font size** to 16, and the **Y** property to 25.

*   Using the formula bar, set the **Text** property to `ThisItem.displayName` and **Color** to `CurrentTheme.TextPrimary`.

*   Name this label `ChannelNameLbl`.

The application should look as in the following screenshot:

Figure 7.28 – Channel Manager application

11. From the **Tree** view, select **MainScreen** and from the **Insert** panel, expand **Layout**, and select **Container**. Set the properties as follows.

Using the formula bar, set the **Y** property to 60, the **X** property to 350, **Width** to App.Width - Self.X, **Height** to App.Height - Self.Y, and **Fill** to CurrentTheme.BackgroundAlt.

Name the container MessageCnt.

12. Select the **MessageCnt** container from the **Tree** view and then select the **Insert** panel. From the **Popular** section, add the following.

A **Text Label** control: Using the properties pane, change the **Text** property to Selected channel, **Font** to **Segoe UI**, and **Font size** to 12. Using the formula bar, set **Color** to CurrentTheme.TextPrimary.

Name this label ChannelLbl.

A **Text Label** control: Using the properties pane, change **Font** to **Segoe UI**, **Font size** to 12, the **X** property to 40, the **Y** property to 80, **Width** to 400, and the left padding to 10. Using the formula bar, set the **Text** property to ChannelGly. Selected.displayName, **Color** to CurrentTheme.TextPrimary, and **Fill** to CurrentTheme.Background.

Name this label ChannelDisplayNameLbl.

A **Text input** control: Using the properties pane, clear the **Default** property. Change **Font** to **Segoe UI**, **Font size** to 12, the **X** property to 40, the **Y** property to 182, **Width** to 400, **Border** to None, its width to 0, and **Border radius** to 0.

Using the formula bar, set the **Color** property to CurrentTheme.TextPrimary, **Fill** to CurrentTheme.Background, **HoverColor** to CurrentTheme.TextPrimary, and **HoverFill** to CurrentTheme.Background.

Name this text input MessageSubjectTxt.

An **Add icon** control: Using the properties pane, change **Icon** to **Send**, **Width** and **Height** to 48, and all **Padding** to 10. Using the formula bar, set the **Color** property to CurrentTheme.TextSecondary. We'll set the positioning properties later.

Name this icon SendIcn.

A **Text Label** control: Using the properties pane, change **Font** to **Segoe UI**, **Font size** to 10, **Text alignment** to Right, **Width** to 200, and the bottom padding to 7.

Using the formula bar, set the **Text** property to "Sent at " & Text(Now()), **Color** to CurrentTheme.TextSecondary, and the **Visible** property to confirmationVisible.

Name this label MessageSentLbl.

13. Right-click the **ChannelLbl** label to copy it. Select the **MessageCnt** container from the **Tree** view and paste the contents twice. Set the following properties for the new controls.

    Select the **ChannelLbl_1** control, and using the properties pane, change the **Text** property to Subject, the **X** property to 40, the **Y** property to 142, and **Width** to 150.

    Name this label MessageSubjectLbl.

    Select the **ChannelLbl_2** control, and using the properties pane, change the **Text** property to Message, the **X** property to 40, the **Y** property to 239, and **Width** to 150.

    Name this label MessageBodyLbl.

14. Right-click the **MessageSubjectTxt** text input to copy it. Select the **MessageCnt** container from the **Tree** view and paste the contents. Set the following properties.

    Select the **MessageSubjectTxt_1** control, and using the properties pane, change the **Mode** property to **Multiline**, the **X** property to 40, the **Y** property to 279, **Width** to 800, and all **Padding** properties to 10. Using the formula bar, set the **Height** property to App.Height - MessageCnt.Y - Self.Y - 60.

Name this text input `MessageBodyTxt`.

15. Select the **SendIcn** control inside the **MessageCnt** container and, using the formula bar, set the **X** property to `MessageBodyTxt.X + MessageBodyTxt.Width - Self.Width`, the **Y** property to `MessageBodyTxt.Y + MessageBodyTxt.Height`, and the **OnSelect** property to the code downloaded from the GitHub repository located in the `SendIcn - OnSelect.txt` file.

16. Select the **MessageSentLbl** control inside the **MessageCnt** container and, using the formula bar, set the **X** property to `SendIcn.X - Self.Width` and the **Y** property to `SendIcn.Y`.

17. Select **ChannelGly** and, using the formula bar, set the **OnSelect** property as follows:

```
Reset(MessageSubjectTxt);
Reset(MessageBodyTxt);
UpdateContext(
    {
        confirmationVisible: false,
        containerVisible: true
    }
)
```

The application should look as in the following screenshot by now:

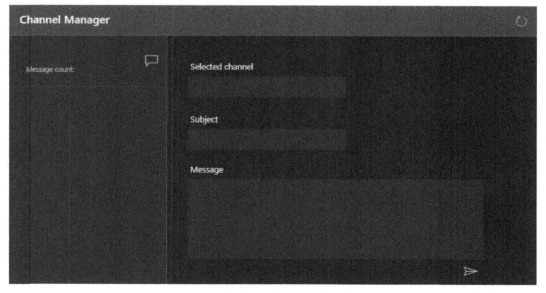

Figure 7.29 – Channel Manager application

18. Select the **MessageCnt** container and, using the formula bar, set the **Visible** property to `containerVisible`.

19. Add a text label from the **Insert** panel. Make sure this label is created outside the container and set the properties as follows.

    Using the properties pane, change the **Font** property to **Segoe UI**, **Font size** to 12, and **Text alignment** to **Center**. For **Position**, set 350 for **X** and 60 for **Y**.

    Using the formula bar, set the **Width** property to `App.Width - Self.X`, **Height** to `App.Height - Self.Y`, **Color** to `CurrentTheme.TextSecondary`, **Fill** to `CurrentTheme.BackgroundAlt`, **Visible** to `!containerVisible`, and the **Text** property as follows:

    ```
    If(IsBlank(Param("groupId")) || Param("groupId") =
    "{groupId}","This application only works when added to a
    Team","Select a channel to send a message")
    ```

    Name this label `InfoLbl`.

20. Click **File | Save** on the main menu. Click on the **Save** button and then click on **Close**, and then close the Studio tab on the browser.

Microsoft Teams integration

1. Back in the Power Apps portal, click on **Apps** on the left pane and click on the Channel Manager app's ellipsis. Select **Add to Teams**. This action will open a pane on the right to export the application file. Expand **Advanced settings** if you want to fill in the optional developer information. Click on **Download app** to get the application file to your device, and then click **Close** on the panel.

> **Error notice**
> On some occasions, you might receive an error when exporting the app to Teams: **Something went wrong. Your app was not exported**. This is a transient error. Simply try again until you receive the exported application.

2. Open the Microsoft Teams application or navigate to `https://teams.microsoft.com/`. Click on **Apps** on the lower section of the application's menu. An internal page of all available applications will open.

3. At the end of the list of categories, click on the **Upload a custom app** option and select **Upload for [your organization's name]**, as seen in the following screenshot:

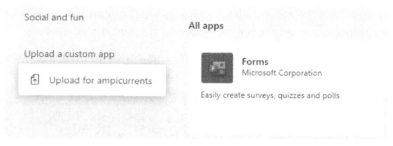

Figure 7.30 – Custom application upload

Upload the exported file to make the application available to the organization.

4. Go to any team you're part of and add a new tab on the **General** channel by clicking on the plus sign at the end of the tabs list. On the **Add a tab** dialog that opens, use the **Search** field to look for `Channel manager`. Select it from the list and then select **Add** from the application's details dialog. Finally, click **Save** on the application's information dialog.

How it works...

Using the Microsoft Teams context parameters, the application can integrate with any team to query all the channels it contains. With this information and the help of the Teams connector's built-in functions, it can query the number of messages each channel has, as seen in the following screenshot:

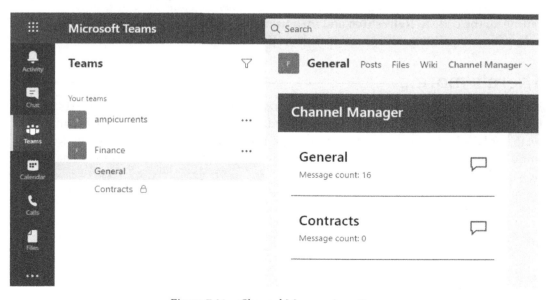

Figure 7.31 – Channel Manager in action

Selecting a channel from the gallery allows sending a message to this channel, for example, to let them know they're over the quota on the number of messages.

The context parameters also provide a way for the application to be theme-aware allowing the use of a theme to match, as seen in the following screenshot:

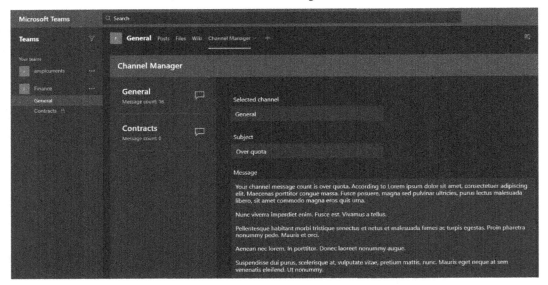

Figure 7.32 – Channel Manager using the dark theme

Besides using the Teams integration, this application uses a code reuse technique by setting all the code to **RefreshIcn** and then using it from several app locations using the **Select** function. This method improves the code maintainability of your applications.

There's more...

Using custom applications in Teams also extends to personal chats. Once a conversation has started, you can add a Power App deployed using the steps mentioned before in this recipe or by adding the Power App application itself and selecting an application. Keep in mind that if you choose one from the main Power Apps application, it has to be shared previously with all participants.

Automating the integration of Power Apps inside Teams

When a custom application gets deployed to the **Apps** section in Microsoft Teams, it becomes available to the whole platform. You can use them in channels, chats and even as a standalone application inside the Teams interface by pinning them to the main toolbar.

These methods allow you to configure Teams to match your needs. However, you might need to build an application for your entire organization that is quickly available for all users in the main toolbar without asking each user to pin it manually.

Using the Microsoft Teams admin portal, we can achieve this deployment requirement. We will also learn how to automate a team deployment with a power app included.

Getting ready

The resources needed to build this recipe are available on our GitHub repository located at `https://github.com/PacktPublishing/Microsoft-Power-Apps-Cookbook/tree/master/Chapter07`

To manage the Microsoft Teams admin portal, the user requires the Teams service admin role. An administrator can grant you this role through the Microsoft 365 admin center, `https://admin.microsoft.com/`, or using the Azure portal, `https://portal.azure.com/`

There is a license requirement for the team deployment automation section when using Power Automate actions that communicate with Microsoft Graph, which uses a premium connector. These two paid plans are available:

- For users: The **per user plan** or the **per user plan with attended RPA (Robotic Process Automation)**. Both let you access premium connectors, but the latter adds the RPA of legacy systems and includes AI Builder service credits.

- For the organization: The **per flow plan** allows the entire organization to use five flows without needing to license each user.

To communicate with Microsoft Graph, the Power Automate cloud flow will authenticate to Azure Active Directory through application permissions defined in an app registration. For more information about this, please refer to `https://docs.microsoft.com/en-us/azure/active-directory/develop/v2-permissions-and-consent#permission-types`

If you cannot access this admin resource, please ask your administrator to build the app registration using the provided steps.

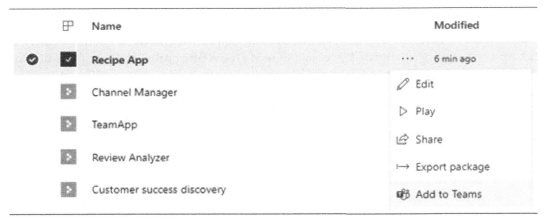

How to do it...

We will configure the organization's policies to pin a previously created power app in the Microsoft Teams main toolbar. Then, we will deploy a preconfigured team to the platform.

Importing the demo power app

1. Go to the Power Apps portal, `https://make.powerapps.com/`, and select **Apps** on the left pane. From the toolbar, click on **Import canvas app**.

    On the **Import package** page, click on **Upload** and select the `Recipe App.zip` file downloaded from our GitHub repository. Click on **Import** when ready.

2. Go back to the **Apps** page, select **Recipe App**, and expand the ellipsis menu to click on **Details**. Copy the app ID somewhere as we will use it in a Power Automate cloud flow. Return to the **Apps** page.

3. Select **Recipe App** and expand the ellipsis menu to click on **Add to Teams**. On the pane that opens on the right, click on **Download app** to get the application file to your device, and then click **Close**:

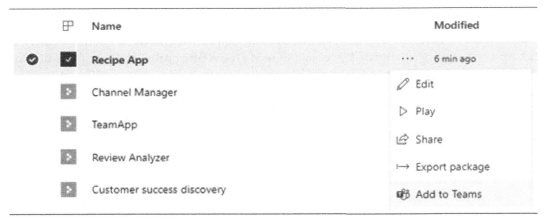

Figure 7.33 – Teams application export

Configuring Microsoft Teams policies

1. Go to the Microsoft Teams admin portal, `https://admin.teams.microsoft.com/`, and from the left pane, expand **Teams apps** and then click on **Manage apps**.

2. On the list toolbar, click on **+ Upload**, and on the dialog that opens, click on **Select a file**. Use the `Recipe App.zip` file exported from the **Add to Teams** option.

3. When the admin portal finishes uploading the application, look for it using the search field on the toolbar's right and click on its name. Copy the app ID as we are going to use it in the Power Automate cloud flow.

4. Go to the **Setup policies** option in the **Teams apps** section on the left pane. Click on **+ Add** on the toolbar to include a new policy. Name it `Recipe App`, and use the following as a description: `Demo app for policy testing`. Leave the rest of the options as default.

5. Click on **+ Add apps** under the **Pinned apps** section. On the pane that opens, use the **Search by name** field and look for `Recipe App`. When found, select it from the list by clicking on **Add**. Click on **Add** at the bottom of the pane.

6. Locate it on the list of pinned apps by using the **Move up** or **Move down** toolbar options. We will locate it under the Teams option as seen in the following screenshot:

Figure 7.34 – Recipe App pinned on Microsoft Teams

7. Click on **Save** at the bottom of the screen.

> **Policy configuration**
>
> It might take a while for the policy to be aware of the installed application. Until it does, it might throw an error. You can save the policy without adding the app and then try adding it again in a couple of hours.

8. Back in the list of policies, select the **Recipe App** policy and on the toolbar, click on **Manage users**. Using the **Search by display or username** field, add yourself to this policy. Click on **Apply** to finish this section.

Building a secure app registration

1. Go to the Azure Active Directory blade of the Azure portal, `https://portal.azure.com/#blade/Microsoft_AAD_IAM/ActiveDirectoryMenuBlade`. On the left pane, under **Manage**, select **App registrations**.

2. Click on **+ New registration**. On the **Register an application** page, enter `Team Access` as the name and leave **Accounts in this organizational directory only** selected. Leave the rest of the options as default and click on **Register**.

3. Once the registration finishes, click on **Certificates & secrets** on the left pane under **Manage**. Click on **+ New client secret**, and on the dialog that opens, add `Teams Access secret` as the description, select `Never` for the **Expires** section, and click on **Add**. Copy the secret's **Value** to a safe place, as you won't be able to see it again once leaving this page.

4. Click on **API permissions** on the left pane under **Manage**, and then click on **+ Add a permission**. On the pane that opens on the right, select **Microsoft Graph** and then **Application permissions**.

5. Using the search field, look for the following permissions and select the checkbox next to them:

- `Channel.ReadBasic.All`
- `TeamsAppInstallation.ReadWriteForTeam.All`
- `TeamsTab.ReadWrite.All`

Select these permissions as seen in the following screenshot:

Figure 7.35 – Microsoft Graph application permissions

> **Permissions search**
>
> There are some occasions where the **Search** field doesn't find the requested permission. For these cases, scroll to the permission and select it manually.

6. Once you have added all permissions, click on **Grant admin consent for your organization's name**. On the dialog that opens, select **Yes**.

7. Go back to the main page by clicking on **Overview** on the left pane. From the **Essentials** section, copy the **Application (client) ID** and **Directory (tenant) ID** values. We will use these, along with the secret, to help authenticate the Power Automate cloud flow.

Automatic deployment of Teams

1. Go to the Power Automate portal, `http://powerautomate.microsoft.com/`, and click on **+ Create** on the left pane. Select **Instant cloud flow** and, on the dialog that opens, enter `Team provisioning` for **Flow name** and select **Manually trigger a flow** from the trigger list.

2. When the Studio opens, click on **+ New step** and look for **Create a team** under **Microsoft Teams**. Enter `Demo Team` for **Team Name** and add a description.

3. Click on **+ New step** and look for **Delay** under **Schedule**. Set `15` for **Count** and `Second` for **Unit**.

4. Add a new step and look for **HTTP**. Configure it as follows:

- For **Method**, select `POST`.

   Set **URI** to:

   ```
   https://graph.microsoft.com/v1.0/teams/@
   {outputs('Create_a_team')?['body/newTeamId']}/
   installedApps.
   ```

   Set **Body** to the following:

   ```
   {
       "teamsApp@odata.bind": "https://graph.microsoft.com/
       v1.0/appCatalogs/teamsApps/<TEAMS_APP_ID>"
   }
   ```

   Replace `<TEAMS_APP_ID>` with the app ID collected in *step 3* of the *Configuring Microsoft Teams policies* section.

   Expand the **Show advanced options** section and for the **Authentication** field, choose `Active Directory OAuth`.

- For **Tenant**, set `Directory (tenant) ID` obtained in *step 7* of the *Building a secure app registration* section.

- For **Audience**, enter `https://graph.microsoft.com`

- For **Client ID**, set `Application (client) ID` obtained in *step 7* of the *Building a secure app registration* section.

- For **Secret**, enter the one collected in *step 3* of the *Building a secure app registration* section.

   The step configuration should look like the following:

Figure 7.36 – HTTP step configuration

5. Click on the ellipsis located on the right of this action and select **Rename**. Set its value as `Install Teams App`. Click on the ellipsis again and select **Copy to my clipboard**.

6. Click on **+ New step**, select the **My clipboard** tab, and click on **Install Teams App** from the list. Rename the new action as `Get Primary Channel` and set the following parameters:

•   Change **Method** to `GET`.

•   Set **URI** to the following:

```
https://graph.microsoft.com/v1.0/teams/@
{outputs('Create_a_team')?['body/newTeamId']}/
primaryChannel
```

•   Clear the **Body** field.

7. Click on **+ New step**, select the **My clipboard** tab, and click on **Install Teams App** from the list. Rename the new action as `Add Teams Tab` and set the following parameters:

    - Set the **URI** to the following:

    ```
    https://graph.microsoft.com/v1.0/teams/@
    {outputs('Create_a_team')?['body/newTeamId']}/channels/@
    {body('Get_Primary_Channel')?['id']}/tabs
    ```

    - For **Body**, insert the contents of the `Add Teams Tab.txt` file located in our GitHub repository. Replace <TEAMS_APP_ID> with the app ID collected in *step 2* of the *Configuring Microsoft Teams policies* section and replace <POWERAPPS_APP_ID> with the app ID collected in *step 2*.

8. Click on **Save** on the Power Automate toolbar.

How it works...

When you run the Power Automate cloud flow, it will create a **Demo Team** with **Recipe App** installed. Then, it will add a new tab to the **General** channel, making the application available to the users, as seen in the following screenshot:

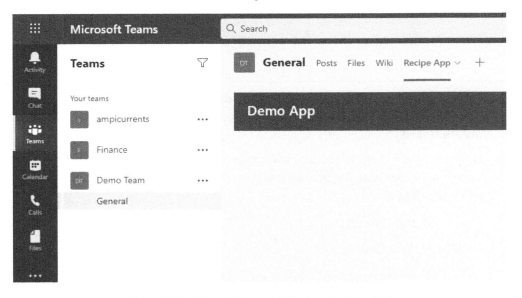

Figure 7.37 – Demo Team with Recipe App installed

The app registration is needed to be able to communicate with the Microsoft 365 API called **Graph**. This API allows handling resources and services programmatically in the Microsoft 365 ecosystem. For more information, please refer to `https://docs.microsoft.com/en-us/graph/overview`

The Teams policies allow setting rules for Microsoft Teams from a central location using configurations for specific users. To modify these rules for all users in the organization, you can edit the **Global (Org-wide default)** policy. Keep in mind that these policies take a few hours for changes to take effect. Once they are applied, users will get a notification on their Teams clients such as the one in the following screenshot:

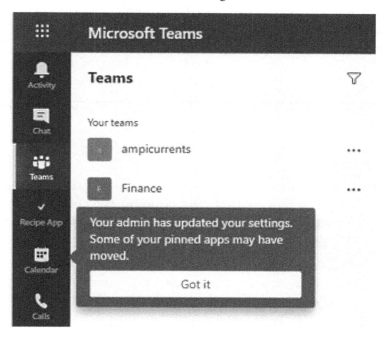

Figure 7.38 – Teams policies applied

The concepts explained in this recipe can be used as a template to build more complex solutions when automating Microsoft Teams' creation and configuration in your organization.

Building apps with Dataverse for Teams

Throughout this chapter, there have been many interactions with Microsoft Teams, from embedding tabs to integrating directly to the Teams interface.

Microsoft has released a new way to build apps for this platform by introducing Dataverse for Teams. This approach allows creating applications inside a team with the ability to use them through desktop devices and mobile devices. This team acts as a unique environment, just like the regular environments we have seen throughout the book.

Dataverse for Teams builds upon the idea of having several components that work together inside this Teams environment, including a built-in *light* version of Dataverse, Power Automate cloud flows, canvas apps, Virtual Agents chatbots, and more. More information regarding this topic can be found at `https://powerapps.microsoft.com/en-us/blog/a-closer-look-at-data-platform-capabilities-in-project-oakdale/`

This recipe will create an application using this new approach for building apps for Microsoft Teams.

Getting ready

The licensing model for Dataverse for Teams is as simple as: if the user has access to Teams, then they can access apps created by this platform. As it already includes the data source part, there is no actual need for premium connectors for data. In any case, this is also available with the standard licensing requirements.

There are some limitations regarding the data source compared to the regular version of Dataverse, such as storage capacity or integrations with other systems. To get more information regarding this, please refer to `https://docs.microsoft.com/en-us/powerapps/teams/data-platform-compare`

The resources needed to build this recipe are available at our GitHub repository located at `https://github.com/PacktPublishing/Microsoft-Power-Apps-Cookbook/tree/master/Chapter07`

How to do it...

1. Start your Teams desktop application or navigate, using a modern browser, to `https://teams.microsoft.com/`. From the platform's main toolbar, click on the ellipsis and, using the **Find an app** field, search for `Power Apps` as seen in the following screenshot:

Figure 7.39 – Power Apps application for Microsoft Teams

2. On the dialog that opens, click on **Add**. The application now appears on the main toolbar. For easier access, right-click on its icon and select **Pin**.

3. On the Power Apps application, click on **Create an app**. This action will prompt us to select a team where the application will be added. Select any of your teams and click on **Create**. If this is the first time creating an app for this team, the process might take a while because it needs to provision this team's environment.

4. When the environment completes its configuration, Power Apps Studio will open, asking for the app's name. Enter `Time Tracking` and click on **Save**.

5. On the left pane, the data source option is selected already. Click on **Create new table**. On the dialog that opens, enter `Time entry`, and click **Create**. On the table designer, click on the **Name** column, and from the drop-down menu, select **Edit column**. Enter `Title` for **Name** and click on **Save**.

6. From the toolbar, click on **+ Add column** or the plus sign at the end of the column's header, and include the following columns:

Name	Type	Advanced options
Description	Text	Max length: 500
Hours	Decimal	Max decimal places: 1
		Minimum value: 1
		Maximum value: 24
Billable	Yes/No	Default value: Yes

Figure 7.40 – Project table structure

7. Still on the data source panel, expand **Add data** and click on **Create new table**. On the dialog that opens, enter `Project`, and click **Create**. On the table designer, click on the **Name** column, and from the drop-down menu, select **Edit column**. Enter `Project name` for **Name** and click on **Save**.

8. Click on the plus sign at the end of the column's header and include the following columns:

Name	Type	Advanced options
Description	Text	Max length: 500
Project start	Date	
Project end	Date	

Figure 7.41 – Project table structure

9. Select the first row and enter random data, just like when entering data in Excel. Use the following screenshot as an example:

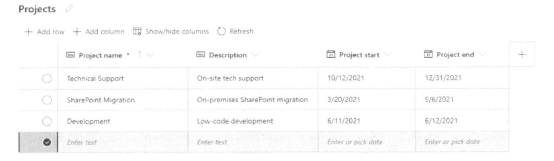

Figure 7.42 – Project table data

Click on **Close** when finished.

10. Click on the **Tree** view on the left pane and select the **App** element. Using the formula bar, select the **OnStart** property and add the code downloaded from the GitHub repository located in the `App - OnStart.txt` file. Right-click on the **App** element's ellipsis to execute this code, as seen in the following screenshot:

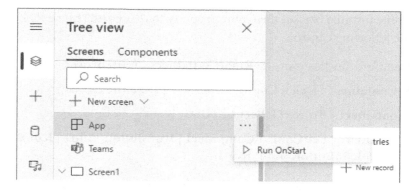

Figure 7.43 – OnStart execution

11. From the **Tree** view, select the ellipsis next to **Screen1** to rename it to
    `MainScreen`. You might notice that some screen elements disappear; this happens
    because the `varStyle` variable, located in the **OnVisible** property of **Screen1**, gets
    cleared when the screen is renamed, and this variable handles some default stylings.

    To solve this, add a temp screen using the **New screen** button from the toolbar and
    then delete it.

12. Expand **MainScreen | RightContainer1** and select **EditForm1**. On the properties
    pane on the right, set the following configuration.

    Click on **Edit fields** and, using the ellipsis option on each filed, reorder them to be
    as follows: **Title**, **Description**, **Billable**, and **Hours**. You can also use drag and drop.

    Change the **Columns** option to 2.

13. On the application canvas, select the **Title** card and drag its width to the screen's
    end. This action will expand the other cards as well.

14. Select the **Description** card and, using the formula bar, set the **Height** property to
    `(App.Height - Billable_DataCard1.Height) * 0.30`.

15. Select the **DataCardValue5** text box inside **Description_DataCard2** (keep in mind
    that the number might be different). Using the formula bar, change the **Height**
    property to `Parent.Height - Self.Y - 20`.

16. Expand each datacard and select each **DataCardValue** control to change its **Font
    size** property to `12` using the properties pane.

17. Select **MainScreen** from the **Tree** view, and using the formula bar, set the **Fill**
    property to `CurrentTheme.Background`.

18. Using the formula bar, set the **Color** property to `CurrentTheme.TextPrimary` for the following controls:

- All DataCardKey labels inside **RightContainer1 | EditForm1**
- **RightContainer1 | DeleteConfirmOverlay1 | DeleteText1**
- **LeftContainer1 | BrowseGallery1 | Title1**
- **LeftContainer1 | LeftControlContainer1 | IconButton_Add1 | IconButton_Add_Label1** and **IconButton_Add_Icon1**

19. Using the properties pane, change the **Color** property to `White` for the following controls:

- All icons inside **RightContainer1 | TopBar_RightContainer1**
- **LeftContainer1 | TopBar_LeftContainer1 | AppNameLabel1**

20. Using the formula bar, set the **HoverColor** property for all icons inside **RightContainer1 | TopBar_RightContainer1** to `ColorFade(Self.Color, -30%)`.

21. Using the formula bar, change the **Color** property of the **Subtitle1** label inside **LeftContainer1 | BrowseGallery1** to `CurrentTheme.TextSecondary`.

22. Using the formula bar, set the **Fill** property to `CurrentTheme.MainColor` for the following controls:

- **RightContainer1 | TopBar_RightContainer1**
- **LeftContainer1 | TopBar_LeftContainer1**

23. Select the **TopBottomDivider1** rectangle inside **RightContainer1** and delete it.

24. Select the **LeftRightDivider1** rectangle and, using the formula bar, change the **Fill** property to `CurrentTheme.Divider`, set the **Y** property to `TopBar_LeftContainer1.Height`, and set the **Height** property to `Parent.Height - Self.Y`.

25. Select **Image1** inside **BrowseGallery1** and, using the formula bar, paste the contents of the `Icon.txt` file downloaded from our GitHub repository.

After adding some test data, the application should look as in the following screenshot:

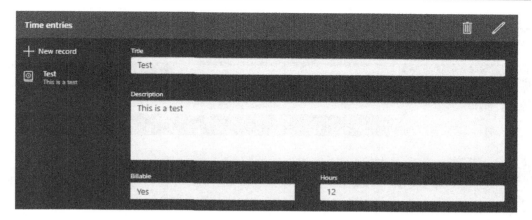

Figure 7.44 – Time tracking app using Teams' dark mode

Let's see how to modify the data source now that the application design is complete.

26. Go to the data source section on the left pane and click on the ellipsis next to the **Time entries** table and select **Edit data**.

27. Click on the plus sign at the end of the column headers. Set the name of the new column to `Project` and the type to **Lookup**. On the **Related table** dropdown, choose the **Project** table and then click **Create**. Click **Close** to finish the table edits.

28. Go back to the **Tree** view and select **EditForm1**. On the properties pane, click on **Edit fields** and then on **+ Add field** located at the top of the **Fields** panel. Click on the check next to the **Project** field and then click on **Add**.

29. Using drag and drop, move the **Project** field until it is below the **Title** field. Close the **Fields** panel.

30. Inside **Project_DataCard1**, select **DataCardKey** and, using the formula bar, set the **Color** property to `CurrentTheme.TextPrimary`. Now, select **DataCardValue** and set **Font size** to `12` using the properties pane.

31. On the top toolbar, click on **Save** and then **Publish to Teams**. On the dialog that opens, click on **Next**. The next dialog will display a list of the current team's channels to add the application as a tab. Click on the plus sign next to **General**, and then click on **Save and close**.

How it works...

The Dataverse for Teams apps template is responsive by default, so it eases the application building process by giving us a canvas preconfigured for both desktop and mobile devices. Besides this, because we added the **Time entries** table initially, the template also takes care of linking the gallery and form controls to this data source.

Adding more data sources or applying some design to the application is all it takes to have a complete solution like the one seen in the following screenshot:

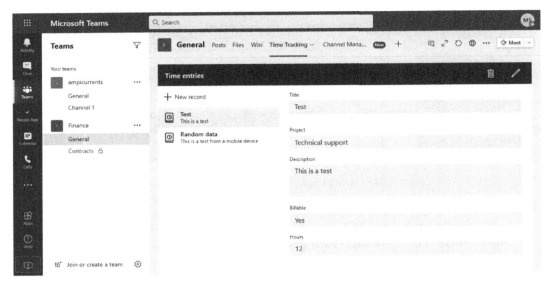

Figure 7.45 – Dataverse for Teams as a tab

Using this application on mobile clients of Microsoft Teams only requires navigating to the Teams channel and then clicking on the **MORE** tab to see the application in the list of tabs available. The following is the application as seen on a mobile device with the dark mode enabled:

Figure 7.46 – Dataverse for Teams on a mobile client

If you need to build a responsive solution that works on every device that can exist on the boundaries of the Dataverse for Teams limitations, such as 1 million rows or the lack of some column data types, this type of canvas app is a great solution.

There's more...

Dataverse for Teams also incorporates the ability to include Power Automate cloud flows and Power Virtual Agents chatbots, so when you build a solution, you can add more enhancements to it.

Also, when working on this platform, you can get more configuration options by clicking on the **Build** tab, and then inside the list of items for a team, click on **See all**. You will see the whole list of elements to build applications as seen in the following screenshot:

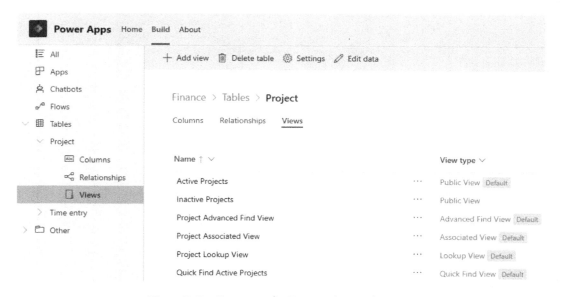

Figure 7.47 – Dataverse for Teams solution elements

Going down this route allows you to, for example, configure the views or relationships of a table. These options are not available from the data source editor inside the canvas Studio of Dataverse for Teams.

8

Empowering your applications with no code Artificial Intelligence

Artificial Intelligence (**AI**) applies when computers perform tasks such as learning or problem-solving using capabilities commonly found in intelligent beings. When working with the Power Platform, improving business processes has become our primary task. Using the skills found in AI, we can significantly enhance these processes.

AI Builder is a Power Platform add-on that brings these skills to the low-code platform with custom models such as form processing and object detection, or prebuilt models such as text recognition and language detection. These model types are used depending on the business scenario they aim to solve.

This chapter will use some of these models to solve specific business needs using the following recipes:

- Creating a customer success solution using sentiment analysis
- Building a text recognition system using canvas apps
- Using Power Automate to create an invoice classification system

Technical requirements

Working with AI Builder requires a different licensing model than the one we have been using. An administrator needs to purchase the capacity add-on and allocate it to the environment where AI Builder is required. This add-on includes 1 million service credits. To get a better estimate on the use of these credits, Microsoft provides the AI Builder calculator with some usage scenarios that can help you understand the costs: `https://powerapps.microsoft.com/en-us/ai-builder-calculator/`

There is also a 30-day trial license that allows the use of these features without requiring the capacity add-on. For more information, please refer to `https://docs.microsoft.com/en-us/ai-builder/administer-licensing`

The complete version of this application is available from our GitHub repository at `https://github.com/PacktPublishing/Microsoft-Power-Apps-Cookbook/tree/master/Chapter08`

Creating a customer success solution using sentiment analysis

Building solutions for business departments is an essential task for Power Platform makers. Finding manual procedures that can be automated is our goal.

This recipe will help the marketing department discover customer success stories using AI Builder's sentiment analysis by examining the company's Twitter feed to find positive comments using built-in canvas functions.

Getting ready

The connection that the application will use is Twitter. You can authorize this connection using credentials (shared application) or using an authenticated application created on Twitter. For more information regarding this, please visit `https://developer.twitter.com/en/docs/authentication/oauth-1-0a`

The application created in this recipe is available from our GitHub repo at `https://github.com/PacktPublishing/Microsoft-Power-Apps-Cookbook/tree/master/Chapter08`

How to do it...

This recipe will use a SharePoint list to store the customer success content and a canvas app using Twitter's connector.

Creating the SharePoint list

1. Go to your desired SharePoint site. Click on the gear icon located at the top right, and then select **Site contents**.

2. Below the site title, you will find a toolbar; click on **New | List**. In the dialog that opens, select **Blank list**. Name it Customer stories, leave **Description** empty, and click on **Create**.

3. On the new list, click on the **Add column** indicator at the end of the column titles. From the dropdown, select the column type, fill in the required properties on the pane that opens on the right, and then hit **Save**. Add each of the following columns:

Column name	Column data type
Date	Date and time
Message	Multiple lines of text
Link	Single line of text

Figure 8.1 – Customer stories list columns

4. Rename the **Title** column Twitter handle by clicking on it and then **Columns settings | Rename**.

The new list should look like the following:

Customer stories

Twitter handle ∨   Date ∨   Message ∨   Link ∨

Welcome to your new list
Select the New button to get started.

Figure 8.2 – Customer stories list columns

The SharePoint data source is already complete. Let's continue with the app.

Building the canvas app

1. Go to the Power Apps portal, `https://make.powerapps.com/`, and from the left pane, select **Create | Canvas app from blank**. On the dialog that opens, set the name to `Customer success discovery`. Keep the **Tablet** format.

2. When the Studio opens, click on the database icon on the left and look for `Twitter` using the **Search** field. Select this connection and, on the right pane, select the desired authentication type. Once authorized, continue to the next step.

3. Using the **Search** field again, look for `SharePoint`, and select an already configured connection.

   If you don't have one, click **New connection**, and this will open a pane on the right. Select **Connect directly (cloud services)** and then click **Connect**.

4. Select the site where you created the `Customer stories` list. If it's not on the list, enter the URL manually in the **Enter the SharePoint URL for the location of your list** field. Choose the list and then click **Connect**.

5. Click on the plus sign on the left pane and, under **Popular**, select **Text label**. Leave the **X** and **Y** properties as `40`. Change **Width** to `330` and the **Text** property to `Enter the number of tweets to analyze`. Name this label `InfoLbl`.

6. Go to the **Insert** pane on the left and select **Text input**. Set the **Y** property to `40` and, using the formula bar, set the **X** property to `InfoLbl.X + InfoLbl.Width`. Change **Default** to `20`, **Width** to `40`, **Format** to **Number**, and **Border radius** to `0`. Name this control `TweetsAmountTxt`.

7. From the **Insert** pane, select **Button**. Set the **Y** property to `40` and, using the formula bar, set the **X** property to `TweetsAmountTxt.X + TweetsAmountTxt.Width + 20`. Change the **Width** property to `100`, **Text** to `Load`, and **Border radius** to `0`. Name this button `LoadBtn`.

8. From the **Insert** pane, under **Layout**, select **Flexible height gallery**. Set the **X** property to `40` and the **Y** property to `100`. Using the formula bar, change the **Width** property to `App.Width - Self.X - 40`, **Height** to `App.Height - Self.Y - 40-`, **BorderThickness** to `1`, and **BorderColor** to `RGBA(237, 237, 237, 1)`. Change the **Layout** property to **News feed** and name this gallery `TimelineGly`.

9. Select the **LoadBtn** control and, using the formula bar, change the **OnSelect** property to the following:

```
ClearCollect(
    timeline,
```

```
ForAll(
        Twitter.HomeTimeline({maxResults:
            TweetsAmountTxt.Text}),
        {
                Handle: TweetedBy,
                Date: CreatedAt,
                Message: TweetText,
                Image: First(MediaUrls).Value,
                Sentiment: AIBuilder.AnalyzeSentiment
                (TweetText).sentiment,
                Link: "https://twitter.com/" & TweetedBy &
                "/status/" & TweetId
        }
    )
)
```

10. Press the play button on the screen's top right and then click **LoadBtn** to create the collection.

11. Select the **TimelineGly** control and select the collection we just created, as seen in the following screenshot:

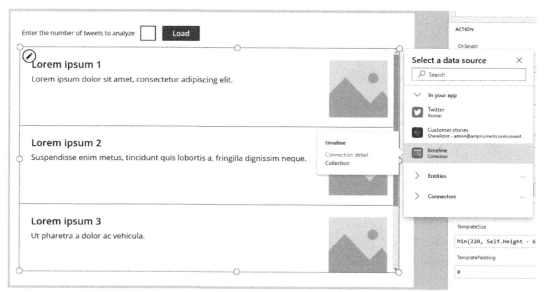

Figure 8.3 – Associating the timeline collection

12. Go to the **Tree** view on the left pane and expand **TimelineGly**.

    Select the **Image9** control (keep in mind that some of the numbers might change), and using the formula bar, change the **Image** property to `ThisItem.Image`, **BorderThickness** to 1, and **BorderColor** to `RGBA(237, 237, 237, 1)`. Set the **Y** property to 32 and name this control `TimelineImg`.

    Click on the **Separator5** control and, using the formula bar, change its **Fill** color to `RGBA(237, 237, 237, 1)`. Name this control `TimelineRct`.

    Select the **Body8** control and, using the formula bar, change its **Text** property to `ThisItem.Message`. Name this label `TimelineBodyLbl`.

    Click on the **Title10** control and, using the formula bar, change its **Text** property to `DateTimeValue(ThisItem.Date)`. Set **Font size** to 12 and the **Y** property to 60. Name this label `TimelineDateLbl`.

13. With the gallery still expanded, go to the **Insert** pane on the left and select **Text label**.

    Using the formula bar, change the **X** property to `TimelineDateLbl.X`, the **Y** property to `TimelineDateLbl.Y`, **Width** to `TimelineDateLbl.Width`, **Height** to `TimelineDateLbl.Height`, the **Text** property to `ThisItem.Sentiment`, and the **Color** property to the following:

    ```
    Switch(ThisItem.Sentiment, "positive", DarkGreen,
    "negative", DarkRed, Black)
    ```

    Using the property pane, change **Font size** to 12, **Text alignment** to `Right`, and **Font weight** to **SemiBold**. Name this control `TimelineSentimentLbl`.

14. Go to the **Insert** pane on the left and select **Button**.

    Using the property pane, change the **Y** property to 15, **Width** to 180, **Height** to 30, the **Text** property to `Save to SharePoint`, and **Font size** to 12. Name this button `SaveBtn`.

    Using the formula bar, change the **X** property to `TimelineDateLbl.X` and the **Visible** property to `CountRows(timeline) > 0`. Change the **OnSelect** property to the following:

    ```
    Patch(
        'Customer stories',
        Defaults('Customer stories'),
        {
            Title: ThisItem.Handle,
            Date: DateTimeValue(ThisItem.Date),
    ```

```
                Message: ThisItem.Message,
                Link: ThisItem.Link
        }
    )
```

15. Select **SaveBtn** and press *Ctrl + C, Ctrl + V* to copy and paste it inside the **TimelineGly** control. Rename the new button `ViewBtn`.

    Using the property pane, change the **Y** property to `15`, the **Text** property to `View on Twitter`, and **Width** to `160`.

    Using the formula bar, change the **X** property to `SaveBtn.X + SaveBtn.Width + 20`, the **Fill** property to `RGBA(153, 207, 236, 1)`, and the **OnSelect** property to `Launch(ThisItem.Link, {}, LaunchTarget.New)`.

How it works...

With the help of this canvas app, the integration between Twitter and SharePoint becomes an easy task.

The application loads the tweets into a collection while analyzing the tweet messages' sentiment using built-in AI Builder functions. The use of collections allows further handling of Twitter's data without overloading the API.

The designed application should look as in the following screenshot:

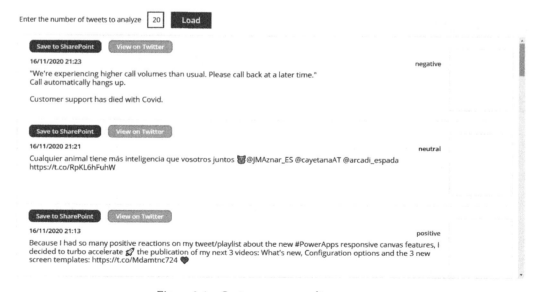

Figure 8.4 – Customer success discovery app

Depending on the sentiment, the marketing personnel can quickly discover which tweets are good material for customer success stories while also monitoring for bad reviews that could arise.

Building a text recognition system using canvas apps

Form Recognizer is an excellent tool for the data extraction of structured documents using a trained model; such documents can be forms, invoices, quotes, and the like. However, there are some cases where the information needed has no structure.

Text recognition is one of the features available in AI Builder. It processes text from images and PDF documents.

This recipe will create a solution to analyze photos taken from handwritten records and then include this information in a Dataverse table for archiving or further analysis.

Getting ready

This recipe will use some sample images using handwritten text. You can get them from our GitHub repo at `https://github.com/PacktPublishing/PowerApps-Cookbook/tree/master/Chapter08` along with the Power Platform solution created in this recipe.

How to do it...

This recipe will use a solution to package the table needed to store the sample images' information, and the canvas app used to extract it.

Creating the solution

1. Go to the Power Apps portal, `https://make.powerapps.com/`, and from the left pane, select **Solutions**. Click on the **+ New solution** link in the top toolbar. This action will open a pane on the right. Set the display name as `Review Analysis` and the name as `ReviewAnalysis`.

2. From the **Publisher** dropdown, select **+ Publisher** to add a new one. This action will open a new window, so be aware of pop-up blockers.

    On the new window, set the following values:

    *   Set **Display name** as `AMPI Currents` and **Name** as `ampicurrents`.

- Set **Prefix** to apc and leave **Option Value Prefix** as default.

- Enter the contact details, especially if you plan to use this publisher in the marketplace.

3. Click **Save and close** and then click on **Done** on the **Currently creating a new publisher** dialog. Select your newly created publisher from the list.

4. Leave the rest of the fields as default and click on **Create**. Once the solution is created, select it from the list of solutions to start working with it.

Defining the table

1. From the toolbar, click on **+ New | Table**. On the pane that opens on the right, set the following values:

- For the **New table** section, set **Display name** as Review, **Plural display name** as Reviews, and **Name** as review.

- For the **Primary Name Column** section, set **Display name** as Full Name and **Name** as fullname.

   Click **Create** to start building the table.

2. Once the table has finished provisioning, click on **+ Add column** in the toolbar and, on the pane that opens on the right, set **Display name** as Review Photo and **Name** as reviewphoto. Set **Data type** as **Image** and click on **Done**.

3. Click on **+ Add column** again and, on the pane that opens on the right, set **Display name** as Review content and **Name** as reviewcontent. Set **Data type** to **Text Area** and by expanding **Advanced options**, set **Max length** to 1000. Click on **Done** afterward.

4. Click on **Save Table** at the bottom of the screen.

5. Go to the **Forms** tab and click on the **Information** form of the main **Form type**.

   From **Table columns**, drag **Review content** to the form canvas under the **Full name** column. Then, on the properties pane located on the right, expand **Formatting**, and check **Automatically expand to use available space**.

   Drag **Review Photo** just below the **Review content** column in the form canvas.

6. Click on the **Publish** button located on the screen's top right. Once it finishes publishing, click on the **Back** button located on the screen's top left.

7. Go back to the solution by clicking on **Review Analysis** on the **Solutions** breadcrumb trail located at the top, as seen in the following screenshot:

Figure 8.5 – Solutions breadcrumb trail

Now that we have our data source configured, let's build the application.

Building the app

1. From the **Solutions** toolbar, click on **+ New | App | Canvas app | Tablet form factor**.

2. When Power Apps Studio opens, click on the database icon located on the left pane. Using the **Search** field, enter Reviews, and select the table from the list.

3. From the main menu, click on **File | Save**. Set the app's name to Review Analyzer and click on **Save** at the bottom of the screen. Click the back arrow at the top left of the screen to go back to the Studio.

4. Click on the plus sign on the left pane, expand **AI Builder**, and select **Text recognizer**.

5. On the properties pane located on the right, click on **TextRecognizer1** to rename the control to ReviewRecognizer. Using the formula bar, set **Width** to App. Width / 2.5 and **Height** to App.Height - Self.Y * 2.

6. From the **Insert** pane on the left, click on **Text label** under **Popular**. Using the formula bar, set its **X** value to App.Width / 2.5 + 80. Leave the **Y** property as 40. Set the **Text** property to Full Name, **Font** to **Lato**, and **Font size** to 12. Change the left padding to 0. Name this label FullNameLbl.

7. From the **Insert** pane on the left, click on **Text input** under **Popular**.

   Using the properties pane, clear the **Default** property, then change the **Y** property to 80 and **Hint text** to Select the field, then the recognized content. Set **Font** to Lato and **Font size** to 16. Change the **Border** width to 1, **Border radius** to 0, and the **Hover** fill color to White.

Using the formula bar, set the **X** value to `App.Width / 2.5 + 80`, **Width** to `App.Width - Self.X - 40`, **BorderColor** to `RGBA(202, 202, 202, 1)`, **FocusedBorderThickness** to `2`, and **FocusedBorderColor** to `DarkBlue`.

Name this input `FullNameTxt`.

8. Right-click **FullNameLbl** and click on **Copy**. Right-click anywhere on the canvas and click on **Paste**. Rename the copied label to `ReviewLbl`. Set the **Y** property to `140` and change the **Text** property to `Review`.

9. Perform the same copy procedure with the `FullNameTxt` control. Rename the copied text input `ReviewTxt`. Set the **Y** property to `180` and change **Mode** to **Multiline**. Using the formula bar, set **Height** to `App.Height - Self.Y - 100`. Change all padding to `10`.

10. From the **Insert** pane on the left, click on **Button** under **Popular**. Using the formula bar, set its **X** value to `App.Width / 2.5 + 80`, its **Y** value to `App.Height - 40 * 2`, and **Width** to `App.Width - Self.X - 40`. Set **Font** to **Lato**, **Font size** to `14`, **Border** width to `1`, and **Border radius** to `0`. Change the **Text** property to `Save review` and name this button `SaveBtn`.

The designed interface should look like the following:

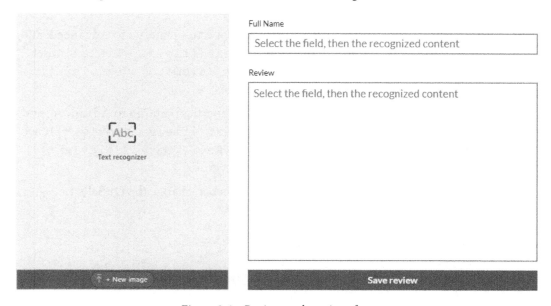

Figure 8.6 – Review analyzer interface

11. Click on the plus sign on the left pane, and under **Media**, select **Image**. Name the control `ReviewImg` and set its **Visible** property to `Off`. Using the formula bar, change its **Image** property to `ReviewRecognizer.OriginalImage`.

12. On the **Tree** view, click on **Screen1** and rename it to `MainScreen`. On the properties pane, go to **Advanced**, and set the **OnVisible** property to `UpdateContext({field: "Title"})`.

13. Click the **ReviewRecognizer** control and using the formula bar, set the **OnChange** property to the following:

```
If(
    !IsBlank(ReviewRecognizer.Selected),
    If(
        field = "Title",
        UpdateContext({TitleData: TitleData & " " &
        ReviewRecognizer.Selected.Text}),
        UpdateContext({ReviewData: ReviewData & " " &
        ReviewRecognizer.Selected.Text})
    )
)
```

14. Select the **FullNameTxt** control and from the properties pane, go to **Advanced**, and change the **OnSelect** property to `UpdateContext({field: "Title"})`, set the **OnChange** property to `UpdateContext({TitleData: Self.Text})`, and change the **Default** property to `TitleData`.

15. Click on the **ReviewTxt** control and from the properties pane, go to **Advanced**, and change the **OnSelect** property to `UpdateContext({field: "Review"})`, set the **OnChange** property to `UpdateContext({ReviewData: Self.Text})`, and change the **Default** property to `ReviewData`.

16. Select the **SaveBtn** control and, using the formula bar, change the **OnSelect** property to the following:

```
Patch(
    Reviews,
    Defaults(Reviews),
    {
        'Full Name': FullNameTxt.Text,
        'Review content': ReviewTxt.Text,
```

```
          'Review Photo': {Value: ReviewImg.Image}
     }
)
```

17. Click **File | Save** on the main menu. Click on the **Save** button and then **Publish**. Select **Publish this version** on the dialog that opens. Finally, click on **Close** and then close the Studio tab on the browser.

18. Back on the **Solutions** page, click on **Done** on the **Currently creating a new canvas app** dialog.

The solution is now ready to recognize documents.

How it works...

This application allows the text recognition of images or PDF files. You can use the sample images found in the GitHub repository along with the exported solution.

First, select the field that will receive the recognized contents and then start clicking on the bounding boxes of the image to insert its text. The user can edit the received contents to fix spelling errors or add more content.

Once the content is verified, they can click on **Save review** to store the data, along with the image, to the Reviews table:

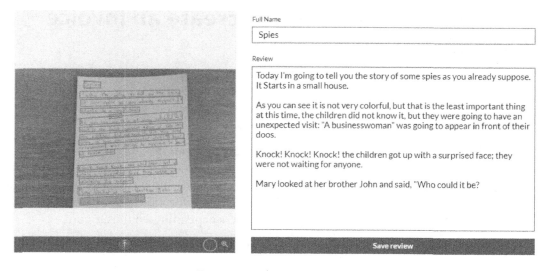

Figure 8.7 – Short story review

The **OnChange** and **OnSelect** properties play a significant role in the application logic by dictating which field needs to be updated and keep track of the user changes. The invisible image control allows the conversion from the Base64 content used in the **Text Recognizer** control to an actual image format needed for the **Review Photo** data type.

The stored review can be seen in the Reviews table as follows:

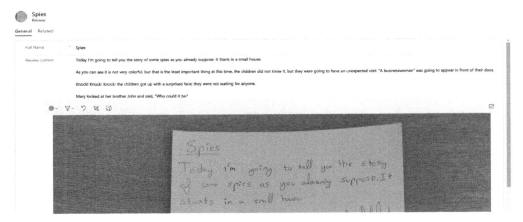

Figure 8.8 – Short story review stored in the Reviews table

The stored information can be categorized or further analyzed by trained personnel.

Using Power Automate to create an invoice classification system

Dealing with the invoice classification process is a tedious task for the financial department. Invoices usually come via email with little to no information regarding the provider, the amount, or the products involved, leaving no option for the financial staff but to open each invoice to categorize them manually.

We will demonstrate one way to improve this process by creating a SharePoint document library where the staff can upload invoices without opening and reviewing them manually. A Power Automate cloud flow will monitor this library. When a new invoice is uploaded, a trained Form Recognizer model will extract the required information from these invoices to enrich its metadata and trigger an approval process depending on the amount.

Other approaches to enhance this process include the following:

- Monitoring an email account with a Power Automate cloud flow that analyzes the invoices attached to emails to store them in a specific location with the proper metadata.

- Using the Power Platform data gateways, connect to the on-premises network folder where the local financial system drops the invoices that need classification and cloud storage.

These are just some sample scenarios that could be improved by using Power Platform solutions.

Getting ready

This recipe will use some sample invoices to train the AI Builder model. You can get them from our GitHub repo at `https://github.com/PacktPublishing/Microsoft-Power-Apps-Cookbook/tree/master/Chapter08` along with the Power Automate cloud flow created in this recipe.

How to do it...

Let's implement this recipe by configuring the AI Builder model, creating the SharePoint document library, and finally, building the cloud flow.

Configuring the model

1. Go to the Power Automate portal, `http://powerautomate.microsoft.com/`, and from the left pane, click on **AI Builder | Build**.

2. If you plan to use a trial account, click on the **Start free trial** button on the ribbon at the top of the screen. If your environment already has the capacity add-on, continue to the next step.

3. Select the **Form Processing** option and, in the dialog that opens, name the AI model `Invoice model`, and click on **Create**. Once the model is created, the **Choose information to extract** page will open.

4. Add the following fields by entering them and hitting *Enter*:

   Invoice number

   Customer name

   Invoice date

   Department

   Amount

In the following screenshot, you can see the fields added:

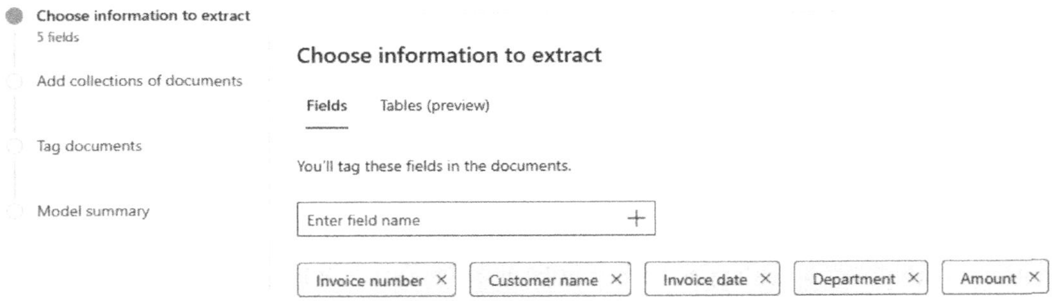

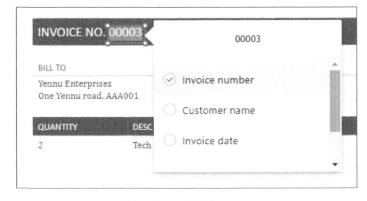

Figure 8.9 – Fields configured for extraction

Click on **Next** when finished.

5. On the **Add collections of documents** page, click on **New collection** to add a new one. Click on the **Collection 1** label to rename it as AMPI Currents invoices, and then click on the plus sign.

6. On the pane that opens on the right, click on **Add documents | Upload from local storage** and select the five PDF files downloaded from the GitHub repo named Invoice_0001.pdf through Invoice_0005.pdf. Once selected, click on **Upload 5 documents**. When the upload process finishes, click on **Close**.

7. Back in the **Add collections of documents** page, click on **Analyze**.

8. Once it finishes, you will land on the **Tag documents** page. Click on the **AMPI Currents invoices** collection on the right to start tagging the fields created in *step 4*.

9. Click on each area of the invoice to tag the corresponding field as seen in the following screenshot:

Figure 8.10 – Field tagging

10. Draw a selection box to highlight several words such as the sample `Yennu Enterprises` as **Customer name**.

11. When all fields are tagged in one invoice, it appears with a checkmark indicating that the tagging process is complete. Repeat the same tagging procedure with all the uploaded documents. Notice that some fields will get automatically tagged based on previous selections. Once the tagging process is complete, click on **Next** to continue.

12. On the **Model summary** page, click on **Train** to start training the model with the provided files. This process will take a while, so click on **Go to models** to go to the **Models** page. Keep an eye on the **Status** column to monitor the training process of **Invoice model**. Once it finishes, the status will change to **Trained**.

13. When the training process completes, click on **Invoice model** from the list to open its property page. To perform a test on the model, click on **Quick test**, and then **Upload from my device**. Select `Invoice_Test.pdf` from the files downloaded from the repository. If the test is successful, all the fields should get recognized on the test file. Click on **Close** to finish.

14. Back on the **Invoice model** property page, click on **Publish** to make this model available to the platform.

Creating the SharePoint document library

1. Go to your desired SharePoint site, click on the gear icon located at the top right, and then select **Site contents**.

2. Below the site title, you will find a toolbar; click on **New | Document library**. A panel will open on the right side where you can input the name of your library. Name it `Invoices`, leave **Description** empty, and click on **Create**.

3. On the new library, click on the **Add column** indicator at the end of the column titles. From the dropdown, select the column type, fill the required properties on the pane that opens on the right, and then hit **Save**. Add each of the following columns:

Column name	Column data type
Invoice number	Single line of text
Customer name	Single line of text
Invoice date	Date and time
Department	Single line of text
Amount	Currency
Status	Choice [Pending Approval, Approved, Rejected]
Comments	Multiple lines of text

Figure 8.11 – Invoices library columns

4. Reorder the columns by dragging them to get the desired order. The following screenshot displays the **Invoices** library using the order of the previous columns:

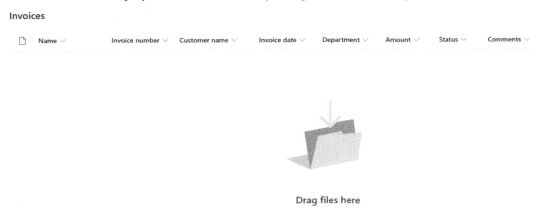

Invoices

| □ | Name ∨ | Invoice number ∨ | Customer name ∨ | Invoice date ∨ | Department ∨ | Amount ∨ | Status ∨ | Comments ∨ |

Drag files here

Figure 8.12 – Invoices document library

Now that we have created the document library, let's build a cloud flow.

Building the cloud flow

1. From the library toolbar, select **Automate | Power Automate | Create a flow**. This action will display a panel with ready-made templates to create a flow. Click on **See your flows** to build your own. Please note that this cloud flow needs to be created in the default environment for it to work.

2. Once in the Power Automate portal, go to **My flows** on the left pane and then click on **New flow | Automated cloud flow** to build a triggered flow. On the dialog that opens, enter `Invoice recognizer` for **Flow name** and choose **When a file is created in a folder** from the list of triggers and then click **Create**.

3. When the cloud flow gets created, the first action that appears is the trigger action. Enter the SharePoint location of the `Invoices` folder in **Site Address** and select it from the folder dropdown.

4. Click on **New step** and look for **Get file metadata using path** under **SharePoint**. Enter the same site address used for the trigger action. As for **File Path**, use the following expression:

```
base64ToString(triggerOutputs()?['headers/x-ms-file-path-
encoded'])
```

5. Click on **New step** and look for **Process and save information from forms** under **AI Builder**. From the **AI model** dropdown, select **Invoice model**, select **PDF Document** from the **Form type** field, and select **File Content** from the previous step as seen in the following screenshot:

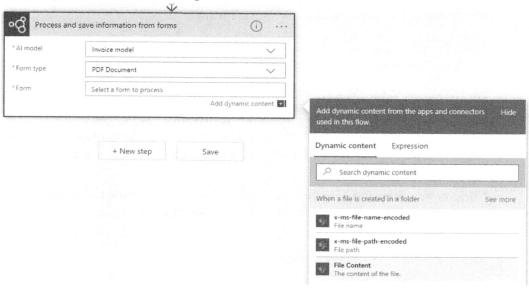

Figure 8.13 – File content selection

6. Add a new step and look for **Update file properties**. Set the same **Site Address** and **Library Name** as in the trigger action. For **Id**, look for **ItemId** on the **Dynamic content** pane.

From the **Dynamic content** pane, select **Invoice number value** for **Invoice number**, **Customer name value** for **Customer name**, and **Department value** for **Department**.

Select the **Invoice date** field and from the **Expression** tab in the **Dynamic content** pane, enter the following: formatDateTime(. Go to the **Dynamic content** tab and look for **Invoice date value**. Delete the closing parenthesis and enter this content: , 'MMM dd yyyy'). Then, click **OK**.

The complete formula should look similar to the following:

```
formatDateTime(outputs('Process_and_save_information_
from_forms')?['body/responsev2/predictionOutput/labels/
Invoice_2d2b151ab11da7f1fe4e154b2d3d7d6d/value'], 'MMM DD
YYYY')
```

Click on the **Amount** field and from the **Expression** tab in the **Dynamic content** pane, enter the following: `replace(`. Go to the **Dynamic content** tab and look for **Amount value**. Delete the closing parenthesis and enter this content: `, '$', ''`). Then, click **OK**.

The complete formula should be like the following:

```
replace(outputs('Process_and_save_information_from_
forms')?['body/responsev2/predictionOutput/labels/Amount/
value'], '$', '')
```

For the **Status Value** field, select **Pending Approval**.

7. Add a new step and look for **Create a sharing link for a file or folder** under **SharePoint**. Set the same **Site Address**, **Library Name**, and **Item Id** as the previous step. For **Link Type**, select **View only** and choose **People in your organization** for the **Link Scope** field.

8. Click on **New Step** and look for **Approvals**. Select to add the **Start and wait for an approval** action. For **Approval type**, select **Approve/Reject – First to respond**. Set the following parameters:

- **Title**: `Invoice approval request`.

- **Assigned to**: Enter the email of any user in your tenant to receive the approval request. You can add several accounts separated by a semicolon.

- **Details**: This field is the body of the approval message. Use the following code as a template:

```
# Invoice approval
Invoice:
Customer name:
Date:
Amount: ****

[Click here to open the invoice]()
```

9. Complete the **Details** field template using the **Dynamic content** pane, selecting the following values for each field:

- Invoice: **Invoice number value**.

- Customer name: **Customer name value**.

- Date: Use the following expression:

```
formatDateTime(outputs('Process_and_save_information_
from_forms')?['body/responsev2/predictionOutput/labels/
Invoice_2d2b151ab11da7f1fe4e154b2d3d7d6d/value'], 'MMM DD
YYYY')
```

Amount: **Amount value** (leaving two asterisks before and after).

Between the parentheses: **Sharing Link**.

The complete action should look like the following:

Figure 8.14 – Approval step configuration

10. Select the ellipsis from the **Update file properties** action and select **Copy to my clipboard**. Click on **New step** and go to the **My clipboard** tab, and select the previously copied step.

11. Use the ellipsis on the new action and click **Rename**. Set the label to **Update file properties on response** and hit *Enter*.

Expand the **Status Value** dropdown and select **Enter custom value**. From the **Expression** tab in the **Dynamic content** pane, enter the following: if (equals (. Go to the **Dynamic content** tab and select **Outcome**. Delete both closing parentheses and enter this content: , 'Approve'), 'Approved', 'Rejected'). Then, click on **OK**.

The complete formula should be like the following:

```
if(equals(outputs('Start_and_wait_for_an_
approval')?['body/outcome'], 'Approve'), 'Approved',
'Rejected')
```

Click on the **Comments** field and using the **Dynamic content** pane, go to the **Expression** tab and enter the following: first (. Go to the **Dynamic content** tab and select **body** from the **Start and wait for an approval** action. Delete the closing parenthesis and enter this content: ?['responses'])?['comments']. Then, click on **OK**.

The complete formula should be like the following:

```
first(outputs('Start_and_wait_for_an_
approval')?['body']?['responses'])?['comments']
```

Now that we have completed the cloud flow that handles the approval, let's see how it works.

How it works...

As we mentioned at the beginning of this recipe, this cloud flow gets activated whenever a user uploads a file to the Invoices document library. It then analyzes the content of the file with the help of the previously trained AI Builder model. The resulting data helps to update the document metadata of the file in the document library.

Using the Power Automate approval feature, we create an approval request with the extracted invoice data, giving the approver upfront information to streamline the approval process.

The approval request sent to the approver is interactive and permits an immediate response, as seen in the following screenshot:

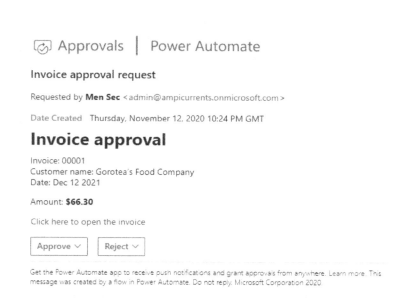

Figure 8.15 – Approval request in Outlook on the web

The cloud flow pauses until the response gets collected through the approval process and finally updates the status metadata with the result.

Along with the invoice files needed to train the model, the GitHub repo also includes an Invoice_Test.pdf file, which can help you test the cloud flow.

There's more...

Having extracted the data from the invoice permits a more complex cloud flow in which you could deal with conditions depending on this data. For example, if the invoice's amount is less than $300, no approval is required; or if the department is finance, then the approval process would require several approvers, and they all need to respond.

Using AI Builder collections (defined in *step 5* of the *Configuring the model* section) allows using several invoice formats per model. This new feature permits creating one model for all the invoice recognition needs instead of building one model per invoice format.

Recently, the platform released a new prebuilt model for invoices. This model allows the detection of standard fields from invoices helping us with the model configuration effort. Keep in mind that it's still in preview. Learn more from the announcement here: https://emea.flow.microsoft.com/en-us/blog/process-invoices-with-ai-builder/

9
Discovering the Power Platform admin center

Building solutions with the Power Platform unleashes opportunities for business users to solve their needs, whether creating a supporting app, orchestrating an automation, designing a business intelligence report, or even designing an AI-infused solution using Power Virtual Agents.

All of these platform solutions need a robust backend to support their functionality while also providing the supporting tools and configurations required to manage the platform correctly.

The Power Platform admin center is the central location to manage the backend of all platforms. It integrates all the functionality from the previous Power Apps admin center and the Dynamics 365 admin center.

This chapter will let you discover the essential tools and configurations available from the Power Platform admin center through the following recipes:

- Managing Power Platform environments
- Gathering Power Platform analytics
- Synchronizing data using data integration
- Managing connectors through data policies

Technical requirements

From a security perspective, managing the Power Platform admin center requires at least the Power Platform admin role. If your organization includes Dynamics 365, this admin access role also gives you access to the admin center.

However, in Microsoft Teams, when a team gets provisioned with Dataverse for Teams, it creates an environment. Users included in the owners group of this team can access the environment's configuration in the Power Platform admin center.

Managing Power Platform environments

Environments are containers of Power Platform components. They include all your solution components, such as applications, flows, and data. They also serve as a medium to isolate these components, whether for security reasons or to have independent development environments.

There are different types of environments. Each serves a particular functionality as explained next:

- **Production**: As the name implies, this environment is the one your end users will use when executing your solutions.
- **Sandbox**: This type of environment is a testing ground for your solutions. You can reset it to start from scratch.
- **Trial**: You can use these environments for rapid feature testing as they get deleted after 30 days. There is also a subscription-based type focused on enterprise delivery. More info here: `https://docs.microsoft.com/en-gb/power-platform/admin/trial-environments`

- **Developer**: This type of environment is the one that is created when a user of the organization applies for Power Apps Community Plan. More info here: `https://powerapps.microsoft.com/en-us/communityplan/`

- **Microsoft Teams**: This type of environment is the one that gets provisioned when a user creates a solution using the Power Apps application inside a team using Dataverse for Teams.

There is also the `(default)` environment that gets created automatically for each tenant with no Dataverse database. More information is available here: `https://docs.microsoft.com/en-us/power-platform/admin/environments-overview`

Managing these environments depends mainly on the capacity available in your organization, which by default is 1 GB of database capacity. Organizations can increase this by acquiring add-ons or Power Platform licenses. Regarding the licenses, this increment can vary depending on the number and their type.

For a more up-to-date increment definition, please refer to the *Subscription capacity* section of the Microsoft Power Apps and Power Automate Licensing Guide available at `https://go.microsoft.com/fwlink/?linkid=2085130`

How to do it...

Provisioning an environment can be done with or without a database. In this recipe, we will learn the differences between these two regarding security.

As a shared step for the following sections, go to the Power Platform admin center by opening this URL, `https://admin.powerplatform.microsoft.com`, or `https://aka.ms/ppac` for short. Once in the admin center, select **Environments** on the left panel.

Creating an environment without a database

1. From the toolbar, click **New** and, on the panel that opens on the right, enter `NoDatabase` for **Name**.

2. For **Type**, choose **Production**, and then select a region closest to your location.

3. Leave **Purpose** as default and leave the **Create a database for this environment?** option unchecked. Your settings should look like the following:

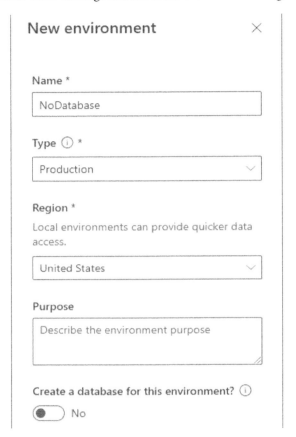

Figure 9.1 – Environment settings without database

Click **Save** when finished. After a couple of seconds, the environment provisioning process will complete.

Creating an environment with a database

1. Back on the toolbar, click on **New**. On the panel that opens on the right, enter DatabaseEnv for **Name**. For **Type**, choose **Production**, and then select a region closest to your location. Leave **Purpose** as default and this time, check the **Create a database for this environment?** option, and then click **Next**.

2. On the **Add database** panel, choose the desired language, and enter `packt-cb` as the **URL** prefix for this environment. This prefix needs to be unique. Choose the required currency and disable the **Deploy sample apps and data** option.

3. Selecting whether you want to **Enable Dynamics 365 apps** is only available for the default region. Leave the **Security group** section unchanged and then click on **Save**.

    Building this environment will take longer because it needs to provision the Dataverse database as well.

How it works...

When you create an environment without a Dataverse database, the security is handled at the environment level. Selecting **NoDatabase** from the list displays a detail page where you can add users as an **Environment admin** or an **Environment maker**, as seen in the following screenshot:

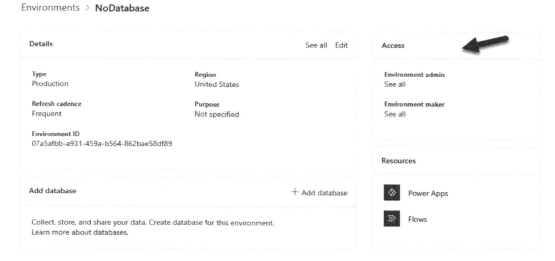

Figure 9.2 – Database-less environment

In a nutshell, the admin can perform administrative tasks such as adding users while the maker can add resources to the environment. For more information on this regard, follow this link: `https://docs.microsoft.com/en-us/power-platform/admin/environments-overview#environment-permissions`

When an environment gets a database, Security roles control the access to this database, including more granularity on the access levels down to the record-level security. To configure these roles, click on **Security roles** in the **Access** section, as seen in the following screenshot:

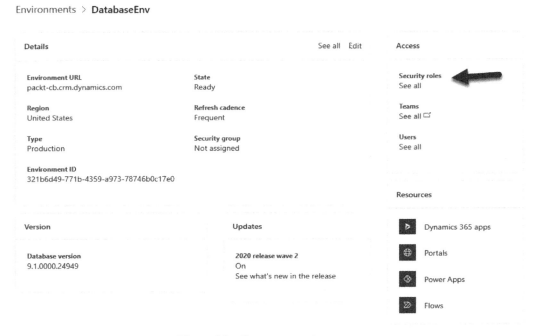

Figure 9.3 – Dataverse environment

For an overview of these roles, please navigate to: `https://docs.microsoft.com/en-us/power-platform/admin/database-security`

To take advantage of these improved security roles, you will need to know how to configure them properly. For a complete definition of the scope and privileges of the security roles, please open: `https://docs.microsoft.com/en-us/power-platform/admin/security-roles-privileges`

Gathering Power Platform analytics

Analytics is a vital tool to measure the performance of a given process. These measures can vary depending on their target. For example, website analytics offer info on visitors for a given site, their location, and the like. This information provides website owners with clear evidence that they might need to improve their infrastructure to handle the number of visitors or add another server near the location of visitors from a given country.

Similarly, for the Power Platform, this kind of information is vital because we could learn about essential indicators such as the devices our applications are running on, how many runs of a given flow, and most importantly, how many errors our users are getting.

In this recipe, we will learn about all the ways we could get this information.

Getting ready

To gather the analytics information, you will need administrative access such as Environment admin or the Power Platform admin role.

How to do it...

Gathering analytics data can be done from various locations depending on the specific platform you wish to review. Let's have a look at each of them.

Power Platform admin center

1. Go to the Power Platform admin center by opening this URL, `https://admin.powerplatform.microsoft.com`, and then expand **Analytics** from the left panel.

2. Select **Common Data Service** (or **Dataverse** when updated), and from the **Home** tab, click on **Change filters**, as seen in the following screenshot:

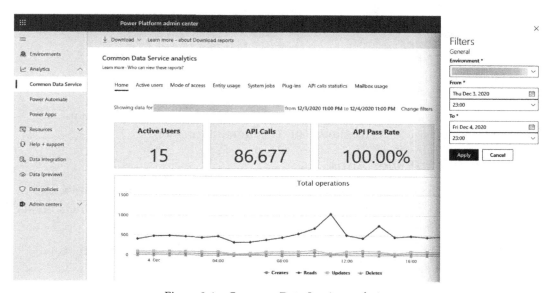

Figure 9.4 – Common Data Service analytics

Select the environment from which you want to view the reports and the time frame.

3. Select **Power Automate** from the left pane to view the **Runs** tab of the selected environment. Click on **Change filters** to choose the environment and time period.

4. Click on **Power Apps** to get to the **Usage** tab. Click on **Change filters** to choose the environment and time period.

Power Apps portal

1. Go to the Power Apps portal, `https://make.powerapps.com`, and click on **Apps** on the left pane.

2. Select an app from the list and, using its ellipsis dropdown, select **Analytics (preview)**, as seen in the following screenshot:

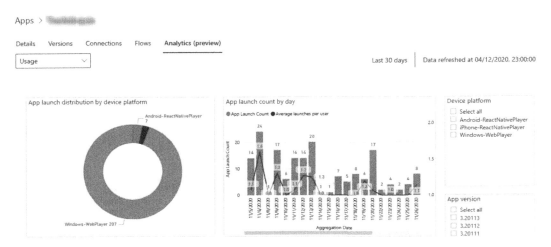

Figure 9.5 – Power Apps analytics

App-specific analytics will open, displaying **Usage** information. You can use the dropdown to view **Performance** and **Location** information.

SharePoint list Power Apps

1. Go to the SharePoint site holding the list or document library customized with a power app. For this example, we will use the `Book requests` document library created in *Chapter 7, PowerApps Everywhere*.

2. Open the library and then click on the gear located at the screen's top right and select **Library settings**.

3. From the **Settings** page, click on **Form settings** and then click on **See versions and usage**. This action will open the embedded power app's **Details** tab. Click on the **Analytics (preview)** tab to review its data.

> **Embedded Power Apps analytics**
> This feature is undocumented and might not work under some scenarios.

Power Automate

1. Go to the Power Automate portal, `https://powerautomate.microsoft.com`, and click on **My flows** on the left pane.

2. Select a flow from the list and, using its ellipsis dropdown, select **Analytics**. This action will open the flow-specific analytics, as seen in the following screenshot:

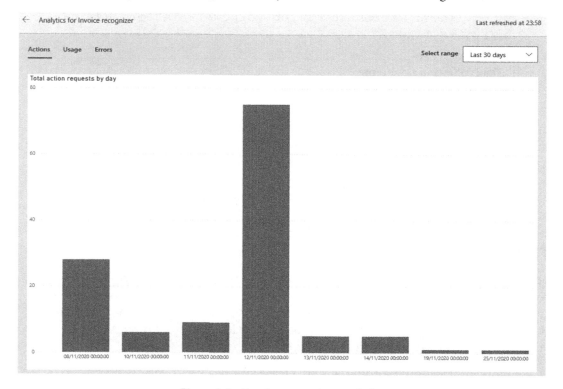

Figure 9.6 – Invoice recognizer analytics

These are the current options to gather analytics from the Power Platform.

How it works...

Each analytic option displays specific information regarding each platform. While Power Apps and Power Automate provide data about the execution of each app or flow, the admin center provides a complete overview of each environment as a whole. The following links provide insight into the data available in the Power Apps admin center regarding the following:

- Dataverse (also known as Common Data Service):
  `https://docs.microsoft.com/en-us/power-platform/admin/analytics-common-data-service`

- Power Apps:
  `https://docs.microsoft.com/en-us/power-platform/admin/analytics-powerapps`

- Power Automate:
  `https://docs.microsoft.com/en-us/power-platform/admin/analytics-flow`

> **Data collection timeframe**
> Keep in mind that this data is collected for the last 30 days only.

In Power Apps, there is another approach to gathering analytics data by manually submitting statistics with the help of Azure's Application Insights. By provisioning this Azure resource, you can use it to store events collected from your application. Follow this documentation to configure it:
`https://docs.microsoft.com/en-us/powerapps/maker/canvas-apps/application-insights`

There's more...

Besides the tools available from the Power Platform itself, Microsoft has released a set of components that collect data across all the environments to help in your organization's governance and compliance rules: the Microsoft Power Platform **Center of Excellence (CoE)** Starter Kit, using Power Platform tools such as Power Apps, Power Automate, and Power BI, all working together from a Dataverse database.

To get more information regarding this kit, please visit `https://docs.microsoft.com/en-us/power-platform/guidance/coe/starter-kit`

There is also a third-party solution that digs deeper into the analytics information gathered from Power Apps and Power Automate. Power Studio enhances analytics data manipulation while also adding tools such as flow versioning, migration, and monitoring. Visit the following link to find out more: `https://flowstudio.app/about`

Synchronizing data using data integration

When building solutions, one of the essential tasks is to keep track of the data sources. You need to ensure that data comes from the proper sources and that this data's integrity will remain intact.

Because of this, there are scenarios where you might need to build a synchronization structure to keep your work tables up to date. Examples of these are as follows:

- Keeping the most up-to-date data in your development environments from production
- Syncing tables from an external organization into your environments

There are many tools to achieve this, such as Power Automate or Dataflows. The Power Platform admin center provides one called data integration.

Getting ready

This recipe will require building a table in two different Dataverse environments to which you need to have access. The data from these tables will get synced between the two.

How to do it...

First, we will create the same Dataverse table in each environment, and then we will configure the integration project.

Building the tables

1. Go to the Power Apps portal, `https://make.powerapps.com/`, and select the source environment from the **Environments** selector at the screen's top right.

2. On the left pane, expand **Data** and select **Tables**. From the toolbar, click on **+ New table** and, on the pane that opens on the right, set the following values:

   In the **New table** section, set **Display name** as `Objective`, **Plural display name** as `Objectives`, and **Name** as `objective`.

For the **Primary Name Column** section, set **Display name** as Company Name and **Name** as companyname.

Click **Create** to start building the table.

3. Once the table has finished provisioning, click on **+ Add column** in the toolbar. On the pane that opens on the right, set **Display name** as Year and **Name** as year. Set **Data type** to Whole number and then expand **Advanced options** to set **Minimum value** to 2000 and **Maximum value** to 2050. Click on **Done** when finished.

4. Click on **+ Add column** again and set **Display name** as Goal and **Name** as goal. Set **Data type** to Decimal Number and then click **Done**.

5. Click on **Save Table** at the bottom of the screen.

6. Go to the **Forms** tab and click on the **Information** form of the main **Form type**.

7. From **Table columns**, drag the **Year** column to the form canvas under the **Company name** column and then drag **Goal** just below the **Year** column.

The form should look as in the following screenshot:

Figure 9.7 – Objective main form

8. Click on the **Publish** button located on the screen's top right. Once it finishes publishing, click on the **Back** button located on the screen's top left. If this button is missing, simply navigate back in your browser.

9. Go to the **Data** tab and click **+ Add record** from the toolbar. This action will open a new tab with the information form. Enter some sample data and then hit **Save**. Click **New** to add more data, three or four records to sync later. When finished, close the browser tab.

10. Back in the `Objective` table definition, click on the **Environments** selector on the screen's top right, and select the destination environment. Repeat *steps 2* through *8* to create the destination table.

Setting up the connection

1. Still on the destination environment, from the left pane, expand **Data** and then click on **Connections**. Check whether you already have a Common Data Service connection such as the one in the following screenshot:

Figure 9.8 – Common Data Service connection (soon Dataverse)

If you don't have this connection, click **+ New connection** from the toolbar and then, using the search field at the top right of the screen, look for Common Data Service.

Select this connection and on the dialog that appears, click on **Create**. You will need to enter the organizational credentials that will grant you access to this environment.

2. If you need different credentials to connect to the source environment, use the **Environments** selector at the screen's top right, select the source environment, and repeat *step 1* to create the connection on this environment.

Configuring the data integration project

1. Go to the Power Platform admin center, `https://aka.ms/ppac`, and then click **Data integration** from the left panel.

2. On the toolbar, click on **New project** and, on the pane that opens, enter `Objective synchronization` for **Project name**.

3. Click on **Create connection set** and input `Sync connection` in the **Connection set name** field.

4. From the **First app connection** dropdown, select the source connection we created in the previous section. You will see it listed as Common Data Service with the email from your credentials on top. Next to this dropdown, choose your source environment from the drop-down list.

5. Select the destination connection from the **Second app connection** dropdown, and next to it, select the destination environment. The connection set should look like the following:

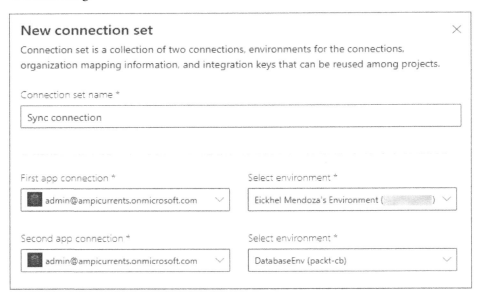

Figure 9.9 – Connection set configuration

If you used different credentials to access each environment, then choose the correct one for each.

6. In the **Select organization** section, choose the source and destination business units from each dropdown, and then click **Save**.

7. Back in the project configuration, click on **Choose template**, select **Common Data Service to Common Data Service** from the list, and then click **Ok**.

8. From the **Organizations** dropdown, select the business units match as configured in `Sync connection` and then click on **Create**.

9. When the project finishes its configuration, it will appear in the list of **Projects** on the **Data integration** page. Click on its name to configure it.

10. From the toolbar, click on **+ Add task**. On the panel that opens on the right, enter `Objectives table` into the **Task name** field and then select the **Objectives** table on each environment using the **Table** dropdowns. Select the business units match from the **Select organization** dropdown and then click on **Save**.

11. When the task finishes saving, click on its name from the list of **Tasks** to configure it.

12. Use the search field to look for the `ownerid` column, and then click on this column's **Actions** ellipsis and select **Delete**.

13. From the toolbar, click on **Add mapping**. This action will add a record with the text `[None]` to both the **Source** and **Destination** columns. Click on this text to select the **Year** column for both columns. Repeat this action to add **Company Name** and the **Goal** column.

14. Click **Save** on the toolbar and then go back by clicking **Objective synchronization** on the breadcrumb trail.

15. From the toolbar, click on **Run project**. This action will start the integration process. Go to the **Execution history** tab to monitor the execution. When the synchronization completes, you will see a **Completed** status, as seen in the following screenshot:

▷ Run project

Data integration > **Objective synchronization**

Tasks   Connections   Scheduling   **Execution history**

Filter executions by keyword

Name		Last update	Submitted	Status
7ca5d800-37f9-11eb-aef8-e3c8bb37123d 2020-12-06T22:07:58.8000035+00:00 Immediate	...	12/06/2020 10:08:20 PM	2 minutes ago	⊘ Completed

Figure 9.10 – The completed process in the execution history

16. Go to the Power Apps portal, `https://make.powerapps.com/`, and select the destination environment using the **Environments** selector.

17. On the left pane, expand **Data** and select **Tables**. Look for the **Objective** table using the search field on the screen's top right. Remember to select **All** or **Custom** on the dropdown next to it.

18. Select the table from the list and then go to the **Data** tab to verify the copied records.

How to do it...

Using the created project, you can transfer data between two tables from two environments. Adding more tasks allows the inclusion of more tables to keep them in sync.

You can also schedule this process to match your needs or even restart the integration from scratch by selecting **Run project with all data** from the project ellipsis menu, as seen in the following screenshot:

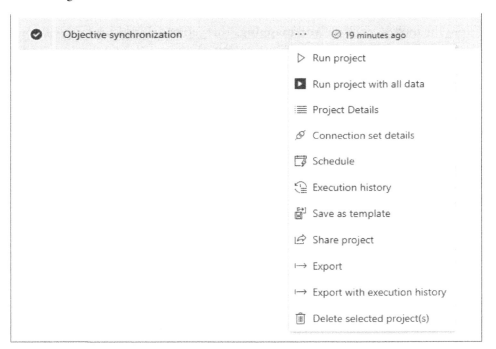

Figure 9.11 – Integration project options

The proper execution of these integration processes relies on the defined table mappings. Keep an eye on this configuration for data that can't be mapped directly, for example, the owner of the record, because it would need to exist in both environments with the same ID.

There's more...

The connection sets serve as a bridge between environments, but they don't need to exist on the same tenant. If you create a Common Data Service connection using credentials that permit access to another tenant, you can use them in a data integration process. This configuration will allow the transfer of data between different organizations.

Data integration also includes a more granular way to filter and process data when configuring its mappings. Advanced query allows the use of Power Query to improve the data manipulation process when integrating data. More information on how to use this technique can be found here: `https://docs.microsoft.com/en-us/power-platform/admin/data-integrator#advanced-data-transformation-and-filtering`

Managing connectors through data policies

The Power Platform has an ever-growing list of connectors available from different vendors. These connectors perform various tasks, such as handling files on cloud services or communicating data through APIs.

Keeping track of these communications would be extremely difficult without the use of data policies.

These policies control sensitive data by using three groups: Business, Non-Business, and Blocked. Placing connectors in these groups builds a fence between them: if you place a connector such as SharePoint in the Business group and then add Dropbox to Non-Business, then your users won't be able to create an app or a flow that uses both connectors. For more detailed information on these policies, please refer to `https://docs.microsoft.com/en-us/power-platform/admin/wp-data-loss-prevention`

This recipe will create a policy to block popular social media connectors and block any new connector added to the Power Platform.

Getting ready

To build this policy, you will need access to the Power Platform admin center via the Power Platform/Dynamics 365 admin role or the tenant admin role.

How to do it...

1. Go to the Power Platform admin center, `https://aka.ms/ppac`, and then click **Data policies** from the left pane. From the toolbar, click on the **New Policy** button.

2. Enter `Block social media` in the **Name your policy** field and then click **Next**.

3. On the **Assign connectors** screen, use the search field to look for the Twitter connector. When found, using the ellipsis next to it, choose **Block**.

   Repeat this step for Facebook, Instagram, Pinterest, and YouTube. The list of blocked connectors should look like the following:

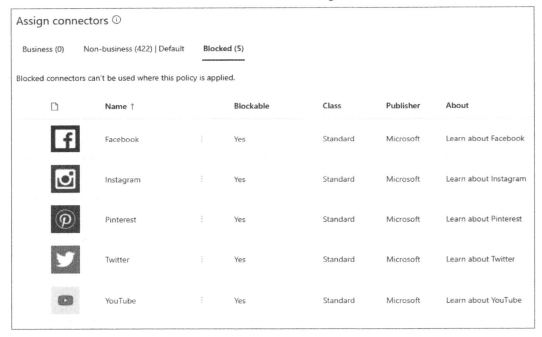

Figure 9.12 – Blocked connectors list

4. Click on **Set default group** on the screen's top right. On the dialog that opens, select **Blocked**, and click **Apply**.

5. Click on **Next** on the **Assign connectors** screen.

6. On the **Define scope** screen, leave **Add all environments** selected and then click **Next**.

7. Click **Create policy** on the **Review and create policy** screen to finish the guided process.

How it works...

When the policy comes into action, the connectors' use is blocked when a power app or a Power Automate solution tries to use it.

For example, if a maker goes to the Power Apps portal, `https://make.powerapps.com/`, and creates a canvas app from blank named `Twitter feed` using the **Phone** layout and then tries to add the Twitter connector, the platform will block its use with the following dialog:

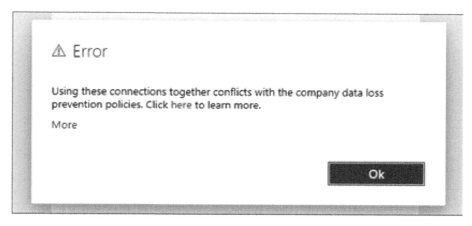

Figure 9.13 – Twitter connector blocked

This policy will also include any new connectors added to the Power Platform to the Blocked group until a user with an administrative role unblocks it by adding it to the Business or Non-Business group.

10
Tips, Tricks, and Troubleshooting

When building applications, Power Apps provides a robust platform filled with features for rapid application building. Examples of these features include a responsive UI designer, connectors for data source handling, and a full deployment toolset.

However, as on every development platform, not all features are included, or some are still a work-in-progress. Maybe some of these features have limitations or run in a different scope of what we want to accomplish. For situations like these, developers often look for out-of-the-box solutions or workarounds to meet their goals.

In this chapter, we will present a series of workarounds that help solve some of the platform's limitations or improve the use of a particular feature already available. The following recipes are examples of these workarounds:

- Sharing OneDrive data between tenants
- Playing with vectors: SVGs in canvas apps
- Transferring SharePoint list Power Apps from one site to another
- Troubleshooting using the Power Apps canvas Monitor
- Extending screen real estate using a canvas control

- Handling image resources in components
- Changing Azure SQL Server connections in Power Apps with ease
- Renaming files in SharePoint document libraries

Technical requirements

Depending on your solution's needs, if your data source requires a premium connector, you will require a license. For more information about the Power Platform licensing model, please refer to *Chapter 3, Choosing the right data source for your applications*. The complete version of this application is available from our GitHub repository at `https://github.com/PacktPublishing/Microsoft-Power-Apps-Cookbook/tree/master/Chapter10`

Sharing OneDrive data between tenants

Sharing applications with internal users is a pretty straightforward task. Build the canvas app, publish it, and then share it with specific users, groups, or the entire organization. If your app uses a data source, it might require more steps. For example, for Dataverse, you will need to configure the security for the tables used in your application.

There is also another form of sharing: **guest access**. You can invite users to your organization by making them guest users in the organization's Azure Active Directory. For more information in this regard, go to `https://docs.microsoft.com/en-us/powerapps/maker/canvas-apps/share-app#share-with-guests`

Once the guest user gets included in the organization, you can share your app using the standard method. However, not all connectors support guest access regarding data sources because some work by requesting access to the user's own tenant.

Let's take the following scenario as an example:

A user of tenant A shares a canvas app using OneDrive with a guest user of tenant B. When the user of tenant B opens the canvas app, the application will request access to the OneDrive of the guest user in tenant B. The file used as a data source in tenant A won't exist on tenant B.

This recipe will help you discover a workaround to solve the limitation presented in the previous example. You can extrapolate this solution to use it with other connectors that don't support guest access. The following link provides a list of connectors and their guest access support: `https://docs.microsoft.com/en-us/powerapps/maker/canvas-apps/share-app#what-connectors-support-guest-access`

Getting ready

When sharing an app with guest users, the licensing model depends on the app's connectors. Microsoft provides a table with specific sharing scenarios here: `https://docs.microsoft.com/en-us/powerapps/maker/canvas-apps/share-app#what-license-must-be-assigned-to-my-guest-so-they-can-run-an-app-shared-with-them`

To test this recipe, we will need a guest user of another organization to share this app. Add this user if you have the admin role or request this from an administrator using the steps described here: `https://docs.microsoft.com/en-us/powerapps/maker/canvas-apps/share-app#steps-to-grant-guest-access`

The resources needed to build this recipe as well as the app and the cloud flows are available at our GitHub repository located at `https://github.com/PacktPublishing/Microsoft-Power-Apps-Cookbook/tree/master/Chapter10`

How to do it

To solve this particular limitation of sharing access presented in the example of this recipe, we will use Power Automate's help to get the app's data.

Uploading the data

1. Go to the Microsoft 365 portal, `https://www.office.com/`, and from the list of applications available on the left, look for **OneDrive** and open it.

2. Upload the `Sample Data.xlsx` file downloaded from our GitHub repository.

Building the cloud flow to get Excel data

1. Navigate to the Power Automate portal, `http://powerautomate.microsoft.com/`, and from the left pane, select **+ Create**. Click on **Automated cloud flow**, enter `Get Excel data` for **Flow name**, and click on **Skip**.

2. In the **Search connectors and triggers** field, enter `When an HTTP request is received`. When found, click on it from the list.

3. Click on **+ New step** and look for **List rows present in a table** under **Excel Online (Business)**. Set the following properties:

   Location: OneDrive for Business

   Document Library: OneDrive

File: Use the file picker to select **Sample Data.xlsx**

Table: **DataTable1**

Select Query: Expand **Show advanced options** and enter `first_name, last_name, email`

4. Click on **+ New step** and look for **Select** under **Data Operation**. From the **Dynamic content** pane, select **Value / List of Items** in the **From** field.

   In the **Map** section, do the following.

   Enter `fullName` for the **key** and pick **first_name, last_name** from the **Dynamic content** pane for the **value** field.

   Enter `email` for the **key** and pick **email** from the **Dynamic content** pane for the **value** field.

   This step should look like the following:

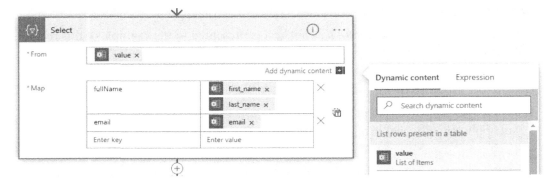

Figure 10.1 – Flow Select action

5. Click on **+ New step**, and look for **Response** under **Request**. Using the **Dynamic Content** pane, select the output of the **Select** action in the **Body** field.

6. Hit **Save**. Open the trigger action card and copy the **HTTP POST** URL. We are going to use it in another flow.

Building the flow to communicate with Power Apps

1. From the left pane, click **+ Create** and then click on **Instant cloud flow**. Enter `Get data from Flow` for **Flow name**, select **PowerApps** from the list of **Choose how to trigger this flow**, and then click **Create**.

2. Click on **+ New step**, and look for **HTTP**. Change the **Method** to **POST** and paste the **HTTP POST URL** from *step 6* of the previous section in the **URI** field.

   Click on **+ New step** and look for **Respond to a PowerApp or flow** under **PowerApps**. Click on **+ Add an output** and choose **Text**. In the **Enter title** field, enter `data`. Click on **Enter a value to respond** and, using the **Expression** tab next to the **Dynamic content** pane, enter `join(body('HTTP'), ';')`.

3. Hit **Save** and close the **Power Automate** tab.

Building the app

1. Go to the Power Apps portal, `https://make.powerapps.com/`, and on the home page, click on **Canvas app from blank**. Enter `OneDrive Shared` for **App name**, set the **Format** as **Phone**, and click **Create**.

2. Once the Studio opens, go to the **Insert** pane on the left (represented by a plus sign) and click on **Button** under **Popular**.

   Go to the **Action** toolbar and select **Power Automate**. A list of flows will appear on a pane on the right. Click on **Get data from Flow** and then delete the button. We are only using this to associate the flow with the app.

3. Go to the **Tree view** pane on the left and select the **App** element. Using the formula bar, set the **OnStart** property to the contents of the `App - OnStart.txt` file downloaded from our GitHub repository. Click the ellipsis next to the **App** control and click on **Run OnStart**.

4. Go to the **Insert** pane on the left and click on **Text label** under **Popular**. Set its properties as follows:

   Using the **Properties** pane on the right, set the **Text** property to `Excel data`, **Font** to **Open Sans Condensed**, **Font size** to `32`, **Font weight** to **Semibold**, the **X** and **Y** properties to `0`, **Height** to `100`, and the left **Padding** to `20`.

   Using the formula bar, set **Width** to `App.Width`, **Color** to `White`, and **Fill** to `ColorValue("#1D455F")`.

   Name this label `HeaderLbl`.

5. Back on the **Insert** panel, click on **Vertical gallery** under **Popular**. From the panel that opens next to the gallery, select **ExcelDataCol**. Set its properties as follows:

Using the **Properties** pane, set **Layout** to **Title and subtitle**, **Template padding** to 15, disable **Show scrollbar**, and enable **Show navigation**.

Using the formula bar, set **Width** to App.Width, **Y** to HeaderLbl.Y + HeaderLbl.Height, and **Height** to App.Height - Self.Y.

Name this gallery DataGly.

Expand **DataGly** and select the **Separator2** control (keep in mind that these numbers might change). Using the formula bar, set its **Fill** color to RGBA(235, 237, 242, 1) and name this rectangle SeparatorRct.

6. Now select the **NextArrow2** control and delete it.

7. Select the **Subtitle2** control and change **Font** to **Segoe UI** and **Font size** to 16. Using the formula bar, change **Color** to RGBA(150, 153, 162, 1) and the **Text** property to ThisItem.Email. Name this label SubtitleLbl.

8. Select the **Title2** control and change **Font** to **Segoe UI**. Using the formula bar, change **Color** to RGBA(63, 64, 71, 1) and the **Text** property to ThisItem.FullName. Name this label TitleLbl.

The design of your application should follow the one shown here:

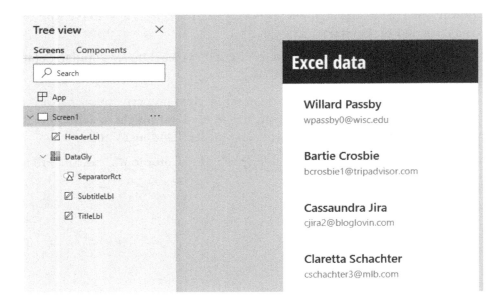

Figure 10.2 – Power Apps application design

9. Click on **File | Save** and then click on the **Save** button located at the screen's bottom right. After it completes this process, click on the **Share** button.

10. Enter the guest user's name or email and then click on the **Share** button at the bottom. The guest user should receive an email like the following:

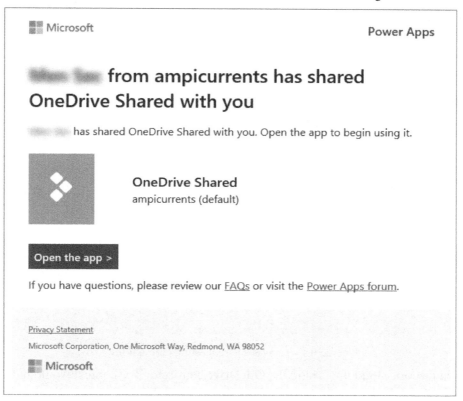

Figure 10.3 – Shared app email

The guest user can then click on **Open the app >** to execute the canvas app from their tenant.

How it works

The application gets the Excel data from OneDrive using two cloud flows:

- Get Excel data requests the data from Excel using the regular connectors, but an HTTP request triggers it. An HTTP response handles the output.

- Get data from Flow gets the data from the previous cloud flow. It gets activated by the app, and the output gets sent back to the app.

The reason for doing this is that the context of the connectors used in an app or cloud flow comes from the running user. That's why when a user executes an app that uses a connector, the platform requests that the user grants permission to use this connector, as seen in the following screenshot:

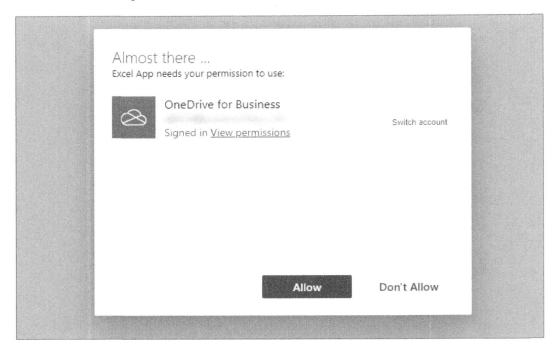

Figure 10.4 – Canvas app requesting permissions

If we used just one cloud flow using the OneDrive connector, the context would have gone to the app and then to the user, making this impossible to share, as we discussed at the beginning of this recipe. Using two cloud flows breaks the context as we use HTTP requests and responses to communicate with each other.

Using this approach also serves a scenario where you want to share only some of the Excel file contents and not the complete file. The file owner can still work on the file, and only a particular table gets shared with guest users.

Playing with vectors – SVGs in canvas apps

Scalable Vector Graphics, also known as **SVG**, is a vector image format that uses an **Extensible Markup Language (XML)** structure. This means that it's a text-based file format composed of coordinates that together draw an image.

One particular advantage of this format is that the quality is not affected when you change its dimensions. Being a vector format, it draws the image according to its dimensions. One usage example is a company logo, where you need to maintain quality, no matter the size, in places such as on business cards, websites, and document templates.

This format provides even more features, such as animation or HTML content styling. For the complete documentation, please refer to `https://developer.mozilla.org/en-US/docs/Web/SVG`

Getting ready

The resources needed to build this recipe, as well as the canvas app, are available in our GitHub repository located at `https://github.com/PacktPublishing/Microsoft-Power-Apps-Cookbook/tree/master/Chapter10`

How to do it

1. Go to the Power Apps portal, `https://make.powerapps.com/`, and on the home page, click on **Canvas app from blank**. Enter `SVG Demo` for **App name**, keep the **Tablet Format**, and click **Create**.

2. Go to the **Insert** pane on the left (represented by a plus sign), expand **Media**, and click on **Image**.

   Using the **Properties** pane located on the right, set the **X** and **Y** properties to `0` and **Image position** to **Fill**.

   Using the formula bar, set **Width** to `App.Width`, **Height** to `App.Height`, and **Image** to the following code:

```
"data:image/svg+xml," & EncodeUrl("<svg xmlns='http://
www.w3.org/2000/svg' width='100%' height='100%'
viewBox='0 0 1600 800'>
    <rect fill='#0f0f0f' width='1600' height='800'/>
    <g >
        <polygon fill='#1d1e2e' points='1600 160 0 460 0
        350 1600 50'/>
        <polygon fill='#2c2e4d' points='1600 260 0 560 0
        450 1600 150'/>
        <polygon fill='#3a3d6c' points='1600 360 0 660 0
        550 1600 250'/>
        <polygon fill='#494d8b' points='1600 460 0 760 0
```

```
              650 1600 350'/>
              <polygon fill='#575caa' points='1600 800 0 800 0
              750 1600 450'/>
        </g>
    </svg>")
```

3. From the **Insert** panel, click on **Text label** under **Popular**. Using the **Properties** pane, set the **Text** property to Power Apps Cookbook, **Font** to **Segoe UI**, **Font size** to 48, **Font weight** to **Semibold**, the **X** and **Y** properties to 28, **Width** to 390, and **Height** to 160. Change the color to White.

The screen should look like the following:

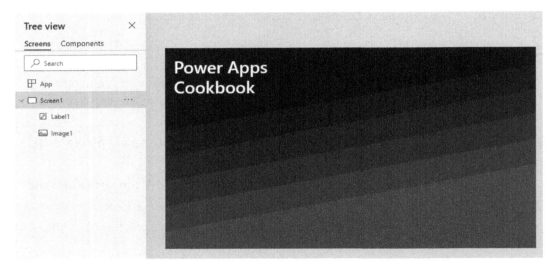

Figure 10.5 – SVG background image

4. Try resizing the image manually.

5. From the main toolbar, click on **New screen | Blank**. Using the formula bar, set the **Fill** property to RGBA(39, 67, 125, 1).

6. Go to the **Insert** pane on the left, expand **Media**, and click on **Image**.

Using the formula bar, set the **X** property to (App.Width - Self.Width) / 2, the **Y** property to (App.Height - Self.Height) / 2, and the **Image** property to the contents of the Image2 - Image.txt file downloaded from our GitHub repository.

You should see a ring loader animation as seen in the following screenshot:

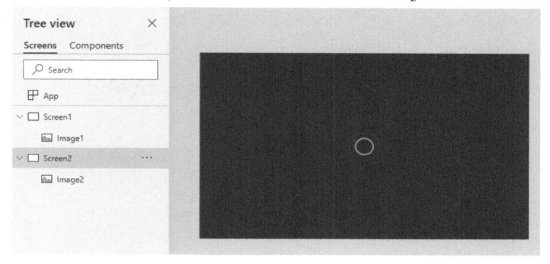

Figure 10.6 – Ring loader animation

7. From the main toolbar, click on **New screen | Blank**. Using the formula bar, set the **Fill** property to RGBA(237, 237, 237, 1).

8. Go to the **Insert** pane on the left, expand **Media**, and click on **Image**.

    Using the **Properties** pane, set **Width** to 790 and **Height** to 100.

    Using the formula bar, set the **X** property to (App.Width - Self.Width) / 2, the **Y** property to (App.Height - Self.Height) / 2, and the **Image** property to the contents of the Image3 - Image.txt file downloaded from our GitHub repository.

You should see SVG shadow effects as in the following screenshot:

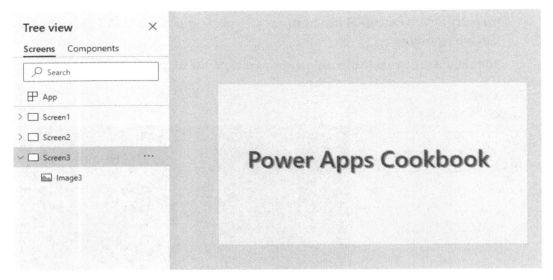

Figure 10.7 – Text using CSS shadow effects

9.   From the main toolbar, click on **File** | **Save**.

Now that we have used several SVG features inside Power Apps, let's see how it works.

How it works

SVG images act as a container of many components such as **Cascading Style Sheets** (**CSS**) styles, vector drawings, and text elements.

By adding the `"data:image/svg+xml,"` prefix to the **Image** properties, we let the control know the type of image format it will display. Encapsulating the SVG code inside the `EncodeUrl` function ensures that the encoding is correct. For more info on this, please visit `https://docs.microsoft.com/en-us/powerapps/maker/canvas-apps/functions/function-encode-decode`

Keep in mind that we can introduce control properties or variables inside the SVG code to make it work for us. For example, on **Image3**, we are referencing `Label1.Text` to be the text to display. The following is an extract from that code:

```
<text x='20' y='70' style='font-family: Segoe UI; font-size:
72; font-weight: 600; text-shadow: 4px 4px 0px #511B5190; fill:
#511B51AA;'>" & Label1.Text & "</text>
```

Another added value of using SVG images is the file size. Being composed of only text content, the file size is minimal. For comparison purposes, the background image used on **Screen1** occupies just 474 bytes. If we used regular formats such as JPG images, the file size would increment to 10,717 bytes. In the end, the less our applications take up resources, the better.

There's more

There are many SVG resources freely available on the internet, just like the loading animation used on **Screen2**, which was found here: `http://samherbert.net/svg-loaders/`. Just make sure to replace double-quotes with single-quotes before wrapping the code inside the `EncodeUrl` function.

Transferring SharePoint List Power Apps from one site to another

SharePoint List Power Apps improves the standard SharePoint forms by embedding canvas apps into SharePoint lists or document libraries, taking advantage of Power Apps' full potential to handle SharePoint data. However, even though this makes life easier for users, it doesn't for developers.

By default, you can only customize the form using Power Apps Studio. To get the full Power Apps portal experience, you have to fiddle through the list or document library settings to get there. These embedded apps are not visible on the Power Apps portal's list of apps.

To make matters worse, you can't take advantage of the Export/Import feature. If you build the application on a development site and then plan to export it to a production site, it won't work.

With PowerShell's help, we will learn how to take an exported application package and modify it so we can import it to the destination site.

Getting ready

This recipe uses PowerShell to transform the exported package. Windows 10 already comes with Windows PowerShell preinstalled, but there is also a newer version called **PowerShell Core**, which is multiplatform and is available on Windows, macOS, and Linux. For more information on how to install it, please refer to `https://docs.microsoft.com/en-us/powershell/scripting/install/installing-powershell?view=powershell-7.1`

The PowerShell script is available in our GitHub repository located at `https://github.com/PacktPublishing/Microsoft-Power-Apps-Cookbook/tree/master/Chapter10`

How to do it

In this recipe, we will customize a list on the source site (development) with a canvas app, and then we will export this app to the destination site (production).

Building and customizing the list on the source site

1. Go to the development SharePoint site and then click on the gear at the top right of the screen and select **Site contents**.

2. From the toolbar, click on **+ New**, and select **List**. For the sake of simplicity, click on **Blank list**. On the dialog that opens, enter `Power Platform` as the **Name**, disable **Show in site navigation**, and then click **Create**.

3. Once in the list, from the toolbar, select **Power Apps | Customize forms**. This process will start building the app from the list structure.

4. The app gets created with a **SharePointForm1** control, and a **Fields** pane opened on the right of Power Apps Studio. From the list of fields, click on the ellipsis next to **Attachments** and select **Remove**.

5. Go to the **Insert** pane on the left (represented by a plus sign) and click on **Text label** under **Popular**. Set its properties as follows:

   Using the **Properties** pane on the right, set the **Text** property to `Power Platform`, **Font size** to `24`, **Font weight** to **Semibold**, the **X** and **Y** properties to `0`, **Height** to `60`, and the left and bottom **Padding** to `10`.

   Using the formula bar, set **Width** to `App.Width`, **Color** to `White`, and **Fill** to `RGBA(0, 84, 148, 1)`.

   Name this label `HeaderLbl`.

6. From **Tree view**, select the **SharePointForm1** control and, using the formula bar, set the **Y** property to `HeaderLbl.Height` and change the **Item** property to `SharePointIntegration.Selected`.

The application should look like the following:

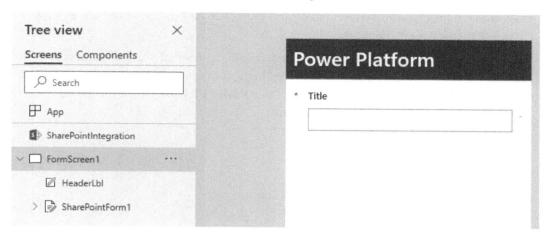

Figure 10.8 – SharePoint list app

7. On the main toolbar, click on **File | Save** and then **Publish to SharePoint**. Click on **Publish to SharePoint** again on the dialog that opens, and then click on the back arrow at the screen's top left. Finally, click on the **Back to SharePoint** link at the screen's top left.

8. Refresh the browser a couple of times on the list to get the changes. From the list's toolbar, click on **+ New** to verify it is using the embedded app.

Exporting the app

1. Still on the source list, click on the gear located at the screen's top right and select **List settings**. Once there, click on **Form settings** and then click on the **See versions and usage** link. The **Details** page of the embedded canvas app will appear on the Power Apps portal.

2. From the toolbar, click on **Export package**, and on the page that opens, set **Name** to `Power Platform Dev`. Leave the rest of the fields as the default.

3. From the **Review Package Content** section, click on the wrench icon next to the app. On the pane that opens, select **Create as new** and then click on **Save**.

4. When finished, click the **Export** button on the **Export package** page. After a while, it will download the package for this app. Save it to your computer and place `SPListTransform.ps1` from our GitHub repository in the same folder.

Configuring the destination site

1. Go to the production SharePoint site and then click on the gear at the screen's top right and select **Site contents**.

2. From the toolbar, click on **+ New** and select **List**. Given that you have access to both sites, click on **From existing list**. On the dialog that opens, select your development site from the list on the left and then choose **Power Platform** from the list on the right, as seen in the following screenshot:

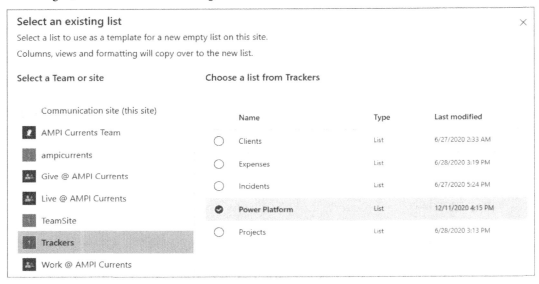

Figure 10.9 – Existing list dialog

Click on **Next** and, on the dialog that opens, uncheck **Show in site navigation** and click **Create**.

If you don't have access to the development site from the production site, please create the list again as we mentioned in *step 2* of the *Building and customizing the list on the source site* section.

3. Once the list gets created, go back to **Site contents** using the gear at the screen's top right. On the **Contents** list, click on the ellipsis next to the **Power Platform** list and select **Settings**.

4. Grab the following information:

- **siteUrl**: From the browser's address bar, copy the SharePoint site address. In our example, it is `https://ampicurrents.sharepoint.com/sites/Production`. If you are working on the root site, then it should be something like `https://ampicurrents.sharepoint.com`

- **listId**: From the browser's address bar, copy the GUID at the end of the URL. In our example, it is `6ddcd69c-9eb2-4a71-8924-1f392570fe5d`.

- **listUrl**: From the **Settings** page, copy the **Web Address**. In our example, it is `https://ampicurrents.sharepoint.com/sites/Production/Lists/Power Platform/AllItems.aspx`

- The data gets gathered from these locations:

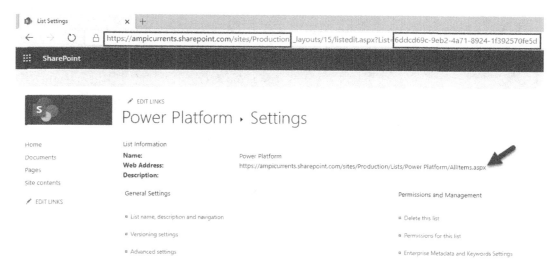

Figure 10.10 – Transformation parameters

Keep this data safe, as we will use it later on in the package transformation.

Transforming the exported package

1. On Windows devices, use File Explorer to navigate to the folder where both files are located. From the **Menu** bar, click on **File | Open Windows PowerShell** as seen in the following screenshot:

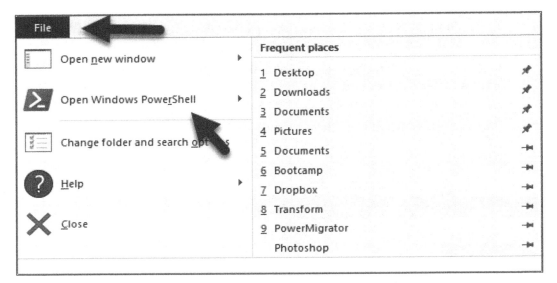

Figure 10.11 – Windows PowerShell from File Explorer

2. When the Windows PowerShell console opens, enter the following command:

```
.\SPListTransform.ps1 -fileName "<package_filename>"
-siteUrl "<siteUrl>" -listId "<listId>" -listUrl
"<listUrl>"
```

Replacing the < > placeholder parameters with the values from your production site. Make sure not to forget the double-quotes, especially with URLs that might contain spaces. Using our example data, the command looks like the following:

```
.\SPListTransform.ps1 -fileName ".\
PowerPlatform_20201211225221.zip" -siteUrl "https://
ampicurrents.sharepoint.com/sites/Production" -listId
"6ddcd69c-9eb2-4a71-8924-1f392570fe5d" -listUrl "https://
ampicurrents.sharepoint.com/sites/Production/Lists/Power
Platform/AllItems.aspx"
```

After entering the corresponding parameters, press *Enter*.

> **PowerShell execution policy**
>
> If you receive a security error about running scripts disabled on the system, you might need to change the execution policy. Use the following command for a quick bypass:
>
> `Set-ExecutionPolicy -ExecutionPolicy Bypass`
>
> For more information regarding these policies, please visit `https:/go.microsoft.com/fwlink/?LinkID=135170`

3. When the script completes, a new compressed file will appear with the name of `Result.zip`.

Importing the new package

1. Go to the Power Apps portal, `https://make.powerapps.com/`, and select **Apps** from the left pane.

2. From the toolbar, click on **Import canvas app**. On the **Import package** page, click on **Upload** and browse for the `Result.zip` file.

3. In the **Review Package Content** section, click on the wrench action next to the app element.

    In the **Resource name** field, enter `Power Platform Prod` and click on **Save**.

4. Back on the **Import package** page, click on **Import**. After a couple of seconds, a message will appear letting you know that the import process has been successful, as seen in the following screenshot:

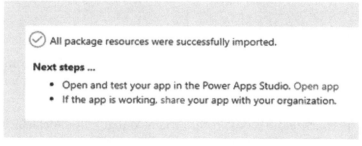

Figure 10.12 – Successful package import

Click on the **Open app** link to complete the app configuration.

5. Once Power App Studio opens, go to the **Data sources** pane located on the left. Click on the ellipsis near the existing SharePoint connection and select **Remove**.

6. Using the search field located at the top of the **Data sources** pane, enter `SharePoint`. Once found, select it from the list and use one of the active connections given that this connection has access to the production site, or click on **Add a connection** to configure it to the production site.

7. After setting up the connection, select the production site from the list of sites that appear on the right pane, and then select the **Power Platform** list. Click on **Connect** when finished.

8. Click on **File | Save | Publish to SharePoint**. Click **Publish to SharePoint** again on the dialog that opens and then click on the back arrow at the screen's top left.

9. Finally, click on the **Back to SharePoint** link at the screen's top left.

10. Once in the SharePoint list, refresh a couple of times until you get the embedded canvas app when you click on **+ New** to enter data as seen in the following screenshot:

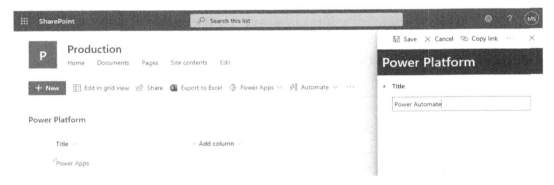

Figure 10.13 – SharePoint list Power App

Now let's discover how the script works.

How it works

When you export a canvas app using the Power Apps portal, it creates a compressed .zip file with all the configuration and resources needed. It contains elements such as connections, components, and image resources.

The script takes this package and looks for the main configuration file, which connects the app with the given list. Using the production parameters with the script, changes this link to the production list.

You can use this technique to replicate embedded apps on different sites or different lists on the same site.

These lists can have different structures, and when you change the connection at the end of the import procedure, you can adapt the app to the list changes.

Troubleshooting using the Power Apps canvas Monitor

Monitoring application performance is a must for business solutions built for an enterprise. As a Power Platform maker, you need to take care of application slowdowns, connectivity issues, or any other incident that might arise.

As we mentioned in *Chapter 9, Discovering the Power Platform admin center*, you can use the **Performance** page from the **Analytics** metrics to measure execution variables for a specific Power App.

However, the Power Apps portal provides a monitoring tool that gathers performance indicators in real time. In this recipe, we will learn how to take advantage of this tool.

Getting ready

To build this recipe, we will need a SharePoint list with data already loaded. We provide an Excel file to create this list as well as the completed app in our GitHub repository located at `https://github.com/PacktPublishing/Microsoft-Power-Apps-Cookbook/tree/master/Chapter10`

How to do it

In this recipe, we will need to provision test data into a SharePoint list, and then we will use this list as the data source for the canvas app.

Provisioning the SharePoint list

1. Go to the desired SharePoint site and then click on the gear at the screen's top right and select **Site contents**.

2. From the toolbar, click on **+ New**, and select **List**. Select **From Excel** and then click on the **Upload file** button. Browse to select `MonitorData.xlsx` downloaded from our GitHub repository.

3. On the **Customize** dialog, leave the default settings and click on **Next**. SharePoint will provide a name for the list, change the **Name** field to `Monitor Data` and uncheck **Show in site navigation**. Click **Create** when finished.

4. Wait a couple of seconds until the list gets created before moving to the next step.

Building the app

1. Go to the Power Apps portal, `https://make.powerapps.com/`, and click on **Canvas app from blank**.

    On the dialog that opens, enter `Monitor test` for **App name**, set **Format** as **Phone**, and click on **Create**.

2. Once the Studio opens, go to the **Data sources** pane on the left (represented by a database icon) and look for `SharePoint`. Configure the connection using your credentials or use an existing one. Select the site and the list from the right pane and click **Connect**.

3. Go to the **Insert** pane on the left (represented by a plus sign) and select **Button** under **Popular**.

    Using the **Properties** pane on the right, set the **Text** property to `Non-Delegable` and the **Y** property to `100`.

    Using the formula bar, set the **Width** property to `App.Width - Self.X * 2`, and the **OnSelect** property as follows:

    ```
    UpdateContext({result: First(Filter('Monitor data', name
    = "Ilse Burch")).name})
    ```

4. Right-click **Button1** on the canvas, select **Copy**, and then right-click anywhere on the canvas and choose **Paste**. Set the new button's properties, **Button1_1**, as follows:

    Using the **Properties** pane, set the **Text** property to `Collection`, the **X** to `40`, and the **Y** to `200`.

    Using the formula bar, set the **OnSelect** property to the following:

    ```
    ClearCollect(dataCol, 'Monitor data');
    UpdateContext({result: First(Filter(dataCol, name = "Ilse
    Burch")).name})
    ```

5. Right-click anywhere on the canvas again and select **Paste**. Set the **Button1_2** properties as follows:

    Using the properties pane, set the **Text** property to LookUp, the **X** to 40, and the **Y** to 300.

    Using the formula bar, set the **OnSelect** property to the following:

    ```
    UpdateContext({result: LookUp('Monitor data', name =
    "Ilse Burch").name})
    ```

6. Go to the **Insert** pane on the left and select **Text label** under **Popular**. Set its properties as follows:

    Using the **Properties** pane, set **Text alignment** to **center**, the **X** to 40, and the **Y** to 400.

    Using the formula bar, set the **Text** property to result.

7. The completed application should look like the following:

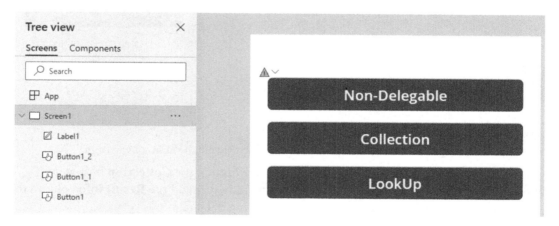

Figure 10.14 – Canvas app ready to monitor

8. From the main toolbar, click on **File | Save**. Go back using the back arrow at the screen's top left.

9. Click on **Advanced Tools** on the left (represented by a wrench and a screwdriver) and click on **Open monitor**. This action will open a new window with Monitor connected to this Power Apps session.

Now that we have everything set up, let's see how the Monitor tool helps discover how the Power Apps backend works.

How it works

When Monitor opens, it connects to the Power Apps backend to observe every interaction with the application, from button clicks to the screen's **OnVisible** executions.

Press the play button on Power Apps Studio, and for best results, place each window next to each other as seen in the following screenshot, or better yet, use two computer monitors if available.

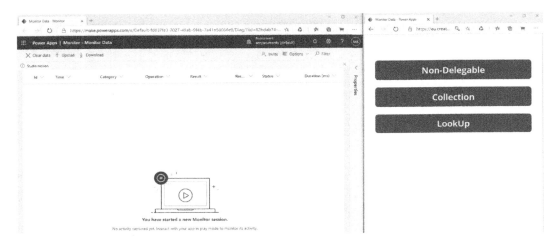

Image 10.15 – Power Apps Monitor side by side with the Monitor Data app

Press the buttons in this order: the **Non-Delegable** button, the **Collection** button, and finally, the **LookUp** button. From the Monitor window, expand the **Result info** column to see what happens behind the scenes when requesting data.

The following is the result of this execution:

Id ∨	Time ∨	Category ∨	Operation ∨	Result ∨	Result info ∨
1	13:35:03.195	UserAction	Select	Success	
2	13:35:04.261	Network	getRows	Success	
3	13:35:04.263	Network	getRowsCount	Success	Requested 500 rows. Received 500 rows.
▲ 4	13:35:04.265	Delegation	First	Warning	Formula not delegated. 1 rows scanned.
5	13:35:15.183	UserAction	Select	Success	
6	13:35:15.702	Network	getRows	Success	
7	13:35:15.772	Network	getRowsCount	Success	Requested 500 rows. Received 500 rows.
▲ 8	13:35:15.805	Function	ClearCollect	Warning	Partial dataset. 500 rows collected.
9	13:35:22.021	UserAction	Select	Success	
10	13:35:22.177	Network	getRows	Success	
11	13:35:22.177	Network	getRowsCount	Success	Requested 1 rows. Received 1 rows.

Image 10.16 – Power Apps Monitor session

The execution shows the following result:

- The lines with an **Id** of **1** to **4** represent the request using `First (Filter` code. As you can see, even though we are requesting the first element, the data source gets scanned to the default delegation limit of 500, thus sending the warning.

- Lines **5** to **8** represent one common workaround many makers tend to do to avoid delegation warnings: using collections to get the data to apply the filter. However, as you can see, it hits the delegation limit and also throws a warning.

- Finally, lines **9** to **11** get the requested record directly, thus improving the app's performance, especially when using mobile networks to access the data.

As you can see, these are vital indicators of how performant your app can be.

You can also use this tool on applications already published by going to the Power Apps portal and, from the list of apps, clicking on the ellipsis menu of any given app, and selecting **Monitor**. When it opens, click **Play published app** from the toolbar to analyze it.

For more information regarding the capabilities of this tool, please refer to `https://docs.microsoft.com/en-us/powerapps/maker/monitor-canvasapps`

There's more

Canvas apps are not the only ones that can benefit from the Monitor tool. Model-driven apps can also take advantage of it to review events gathered from an app. For more information on how to use this tool on these types of Power Apps, please refer to `https://powerapps.microsoft.com/en-us/blog/monitor-now-supports-model-driven-apps/`

Extending screen real estate using the canvas control

When building apps, you need to take into account the specific user interface needs for your app. You can design many screens, use tabbed menus, or use forms to organize the input data.

One control remains hidden from both **Insert** methods in Power Apps Studio, which only appears when a specific type of screen gets created: **the canvas**. This control generates a container that scrolls vertically to the dimensions you specify, just like a website on the internet. This recipe will show you how to use it.

Getting ready

The completed app, as well as the image resources, are available in our GitHub repository located at `https://github.com/PacktPublishing/Microsoft-Power-Apps-Cookbook/tree/master/Chapter10`

How to do it...

The following steps will use the canvas control to replicate a website:

1. Go to the Power Apps portal, `https://make.powerapps.com/`, and click on **Canvas app from blank**.

2. On the dialog that opens, enter `Power Apps homepage` for **App name**, keep the **Tablet Format**, and click on **Create**.

3. Click on **File | Settings | Screen size + orientation**, disable **Scale to fit**, and click **Apply**. Go back using the back arrow located at the screen's top left.

4. Click on the **Media** panel on the left (represented by a movie reel) and then click on **Upload**. Browse to select both the `hero.jpg` and the `Microsoft.svg` files downloaded from our GitHub repository.

5. From the toolbar, click on **New screen** and select **Scrollable**.

6. From the list of screens, click the ellipsis next to **Screen1** and select **Delete**.

7. Click the ellipsis next to **Screen2** and click **Rename**. Set the name as `HomepageScreen`.

8. From the **Tree view** pane, select **LblAppName1**, and using the ellipsis menu next to it, choose **Delete**.

9. From the **Tree view** pane, select **RectQuickActionBar1** and rename it to `HeaderRct`. Right-click on this control and choose **Reorder | Bring to front**.

    Using the **Properties** pane on the right, change **Height** to `60` and **Color** to `White`.

10. From the **Insert** panel on the left (represented by a plus sign), click on **Container** under **Layout**. Set its properties as follows:

    Using the **Properties** pane, set the **Y** property to `0` and **Height** to `60`.

    Using the formula bar, set the **Width** property to `App.Width * 0.85` and the **X** property to `(App.Width - Self.Width) / 2`.

    Name this container `HeaderCnt`.

11. Keep **HeaderCnt** selected and, using the **Insert** panel, click on **Image** under **Media**.

    Using the **Properties** pane, set the **Image** property to **Microsoft**, **X** to `0`, and **Width** to `120`.

    Name this image `MicrosoftLogoImg`.

12. Keep **HeaderCnt** selected and, using the **Insert** panel, click on **Text label** under **Popular**. Set its properties as follows:

    Using the **Properties** pane, set the **Text** property to `Power Apps`, **Font** to **Segoe UI**, **Font size** to `14`, **Font weight** to **Semibold**, **X** to `120`, **Y** to `0`, **Width** to `120`, and **Height** to `60`.

    Using the formula bar, set the **Color** property to `ColorValue("#742774")`.

    Name this label `PowerAppsLbl`.

13. Right-click **PowerAppsLbl** and choose **Copy**. Right-click anywhere inside **HeaderCnt** and select **Paste**. Select **PowerAppsLbl_1** and set the properties as follows:

    Using the **Properties** pane, set the **Text** property to `Overview    Pricing Partners    Learn    Community` (maintain the spaces), **Font size** to `12`, **X** to `270`, **Width** to `400`, and **Height** to `60`.

    Name this label `MenuLbl`.

14. Right-click **MenuLbl** and choose **Copy**. Right-click anywhere inside **HeaderCnt** and select **Paste**. Select **MenuLbl_1** and set the properties as follows:

    Using the **Properties** pane, set the **Text** property to `Sign in    Try free` (maintain the spaces), and **Width** to `140`.

    Using the formula bar, set the **X** property to `Parent.Width - Self.Width - 100`.

    Name this label `OptionsLbl`.

15. Keep **HeaderCnt** selected and, using the **Insert** panel, click on **Button** under **Popular**. Set its properties as follows:

    Using the **Properties** pane, set the **Text** property to `Buy now    >`, **Y** to `10`, **Width** to `100`, **Border radius** to `2`, **Font** to **Segoe UI**, and **Font size** to `12`.

    Using the formula bar, set the **X** property to `Parent.Width - Self.Width`, and the **Fill** property to `ColorValue("#742774")`.

    Name this button `BuyNowBtn`.

16. Now that we have completed the header of the home page, your app should look like the following:

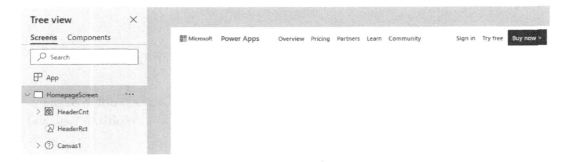

Figure 10.17 – Header component complete

17. From **Tree view**, select the **Canvas1** control and rename it to `HomeCvs`. Expand it, select **DataCard1**, and rename it to `HeroDtc`.

    Using the formula bar, set **Height** to `1200`.

18. To insert the following controls, always keep **HeroDtc** selected.

19. Using the **Insert** panel, click on **Image** under **Media**. Set its properties as follows:

    Using the **Properties** pane, set the **Image** property to **hero**, change **Image position** to **Fill**, and **X** and **Y** to `0`.

Using the formula bar, set **Width** to `Parent.Width` and **Height** to `Parent.Height`.

Name this image `HeroImg`.

20. Using the **Insert** panel, click on **HTML text** under **Display**. Set its properties as follows:

Using the **Properties** pane, set **X** and **Y** to `0`.

Using the formula bar, set **Width** to `Parent.Width`, **Height** to `Parent.Height`, and **HtmlText** as follows:

```
"<div style='background: linear-gradient(to bottom,
#000000 0%, rgba(0, 0, 0, 0.98) 1%, rgba(255, 255, 255,
0.02) 54%, rgba(255, 255, 255, 0) 55%); width: 100%;
height: 100%; position: absolute; left: 0; top: 0;'></
div>"
```

Name this control `HeroShadowHtml`.

21. Using the **Insert** panel, click on **Text label** under **Popular**. Set its properties as follows:

Using the **Properties** pane, set **Font** to **Segoe UI**, **Font size** to `28`, **Font weight** to **Semibold**, **Text alignment** to **center**, **Y** to `40`, **Width** to `730`, **Height** to `120`, and **Color** to `White`.

Using the formula bar, set the **X** property to `(App.Width - Self.Width) / 2`, and the **Text** property to (maintain the line feeds):

```
"The world needs great solutions.
Build yours faster."
```

Name this label `HeroLbl`.

22. Right-click **HeroLbl** and choose **Copy**. Right-click anywhere inside **HeroDtc** and select **Paste**. Select **HeroLbl_1** and set the properties as follows:

Using the **Properties** pane, set **Font size** to `12`, **Font weight** to **Normal**, **Y** to `165`, **Width** to `535`, and **Height** to `50`.

Using the formula bar, set the **Text** property to the following:

```
"Now everyone can quickly build and share low-code apps
with Microsoft Power Apps."
```

Name this label `HeroSubLbl`.

23. Right-click **BuyNowBtn** on **HeaderCnt** and choose **Copy**. Right-click anywhere inside **HeroDtc**, and select **Paste**. Select **BuyNowBtn_1** and set the **properties** as follows:

    Using the **Properties** pane, set **Text** to `Start free    >`, **Y** to `240`, and **Width** to `120`.

    Using the formula bar, set the **X** property to `(App.Width - Self.Width) / 2`.

    Name this button `StartBtn`.

24. From the main toolbar, click on **File | Save**. When the saving finishes, click on **Close** and close the browser tab.

These steps complete the first section of the Power Apps home page simulation.

How it works

We have created a replica of the first section of the Power Apps home page (December 2020 edition). Using the canvas control, we can imitate the scrolling effect websites have when they have more content, as you can see in the following screenshot:

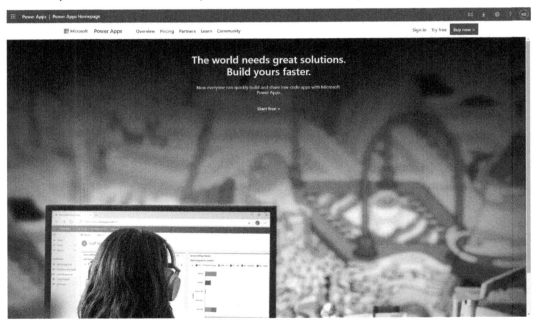

Figure 10.18 – Power Apps home page replicated on a canvas app

Back in the Power Apps portal, click on **Apps**, and look for **Power Apps Homepage**. Click on its name to run it.

In the new browser tab, you will see the application acting as the Power Apps home page. If you scroll, the header will remain on top, and the rest of the contents will move accordingly. For best results, add &hidenavbar=true at the end of the URL in the browser's address bar.

You can use the provided app to continue replicating the Power Apps home page as an exercise.

Handling image resources in components

In *Chapter 5*, *Extending the Platform*, we learned about the Power Apps **components** feature – small building blocks that encapsulate a set of controls to be reused across an application.

These components isolate themselves from the applications so they can get used anywhere, no matter their purpose. This behavior means that a component can't access variables or resources from an application unless passed through custom properties.

It also means that resources included in components won't be available from the applications loading those components.

Let's use the following example: You create a component to display an **About** dialog for all your solutions. This dialog includes the logo of your company. When you build it, everything works correctly, but the logo doesn't show when you use it, as a component, in your solutions.

This happens because the component only packs its definition and doesn't include resources. Let's discover how to deal with these situations using this recipe.

Getting ready

The completed app and its resources are available in our GitHub repository located at https://github.com/PacktPublishing/Microsoft-Power-Apps-Cookbook/tree/master/Chapter10

To accomplish our solution, we need to convert the resources to **Base64** encoding. You can use the provided PowerShell script or use a website that offers these types of conversions. We will use the Base64.Guru website for our recipe.

How to do it

To make this work, we need to prepare our resources before using them in our components.

Prepare the resources

1. Navigate to `https://base64.guru/converter/encode/image`. Under the **Local File** section, click on **Choose File**. Browse to find the `AMPI logo.png` file downloaded from our GitHub repository. You can also use any logo of your own.

2. Click on **Encode image to Base64**, and in the **Base64** section, click on the **Copy** link located on the right. This action will save this data on your clipboard.

Build the component

1. Go to the Power Apps portal, `https://make.powerapps.com/`, and click on **Apps** on the left pane.

2. Click on the **Component libraries** tab. Use an existing component library or click on **New component library** if you don't have one already.

3. From **Tree view**, click on the **Components** tab and click on the **New component** link under the tab.

4. From the **Insert** panel located on the left (represented by a plus sign), click on **Rectangle** under **Popular**. Set its properties as follows:

   Using the **Properties** pane on the right, set the **X** and **Y** properties to 0.

   Using the formula bar, set **Width** to `Parent.Width`, **Height** to `Parent.Height`, **Fill** to `White`, **BorderThickness** to 1, and **BorderColor** to `ColorValue("#757070")`.

   Name this rectangle `BorderRct`.

5. From the **Insert** panel, expand **Media** and select **Image**. Set its properties as follows:

   Using the **Properties** pane, set **Width** to 500 and **Height** to 250. If you used your logo, set these proportions accordingly.

   Using the formula bar, set **X** to `(Parent.Width - Self.Width) / 2`, **Y** to `(Parent.Height - Self.Height) / 2 - 60`, and set the **Image** property as follows:

   ```
   "data:image/png;base64," & ""
   ```

Paste the contents of the conversion performed in the previous section inside the last double-quotes. The logo should appear inside the image control, as seen in the following screenshot:

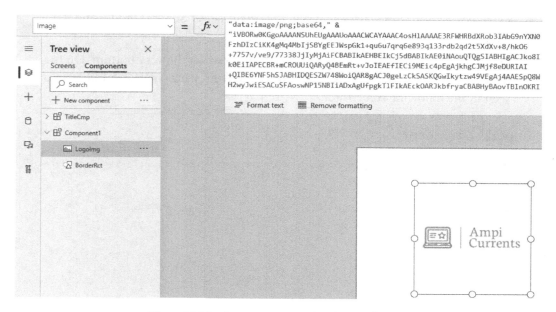

Figure 10.19 – Image represented in Base64 format

Name this image LogoImg.

6. From the **Insert** panel, click on **Text label** under **Popular**. Set its properties as follows:

   Using the **Properties** pane, set **Text** to ® 2020 - AMPI Currents, **Font** to **Segoe UI**, **Font size** to 24, **Font weight** to **Semibold**, **Text alignment** to Center, and **Width** to 500.

   Using the formula bar, set **X** to (Parent.Width - Self.Width) / 2, **Y** to (Parent.Height - Self.Height) / 2 + 60, and **Color** to RGBA(116, 116, 116, 1).

   Name this label CopyrightLbl.

7. From **Tree view**, double-click on the **Component1** name to rename it to AboutCmp.

8. From the main toolbar, click on **File | Save**. If you were editing an existing one, click on **Publish**. Click on **Close** and close the browser tab.

Building the app

1. Back in the Power Apps portal, click on **Canvas app from blank**. On the dialog that opens, set the app name as `Component Test` and click on **Create**.

2. Once Power Apps Studio opens, from **Tree view**, select **Screen1**, and using the formula bar, set the **Fill** color to `RGBA(130, 141, 158, 1)`.

3. On the **Insert** panel, click on **Get more components** at the very bottom. On the pane that opens on the right, select **AboutCmp** from your component library, as seen in the following screenshot:

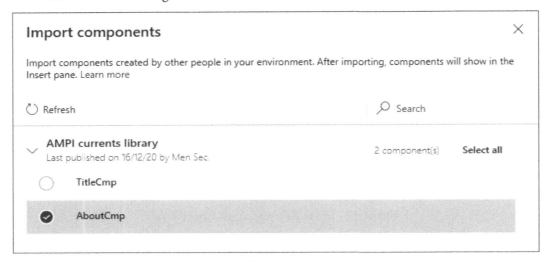

Figure 10.20 – Import components pane

Click on **Import** when done.

4. From the **Insert** panel, expand **Library components** and select **AboutCmp**. Set its properties as follows:

    Using the **Properties** pane, set **Width** to `550` and **Height** to `400`.

    Using the formula bar, set **X** to `(Parent.Width - Self.Width) / 2` and **Y** to `(Parent.Height - Self.Height) / 2`.

    The component should display the logo successfully.

How it works

If we hadn't converted the image to Base64, the imported component wouldn't be able to display the logo image. We would have to upload the logo to every application using this component.

The following screenshot shows the component imported into the app:

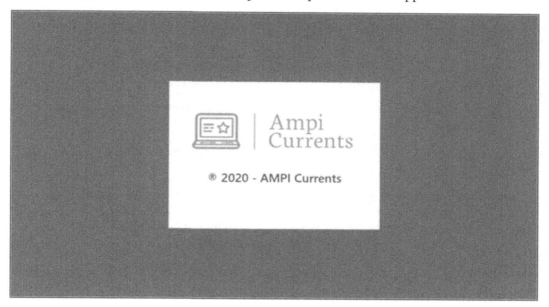

Figure 10.21 – About the component

As we mentioned before, the component packs only its definition, and that includes the code elements. As the image got transformed into code, it also gets included in the component's definition.

There's more...

Even though components isolate themselves from applications, they can access Power Apps collections when these components are created inside the app, not using component libraries. This feature can be useful in some scenarios when building components for one specific app.

Changing Azure SQL Server connections in Power Apps with ease

Building a Power App using the Azure SQL connector is a great approach when creating a complex solution to solve a business need. This data source provides many advantages, such as the following:

- Views, which can help transfer the data joining and transformation processes to the database engine
- Stored procedures, which consist of a series of code routines that execute at the database level that can help with data processing and validation tasks
- Scalability, as you can improve the database engine's performance on-demand or by setting a set of rules

These are just some examples of the instant capabilities your application gets when using this data source.

When building complex solutions, it's a good practice to use environments such as development, testing, and production. These environments help developers iterate application versions without affecting end users in their daily tasks when using your solution.

However, when using Azure SQL canvas apps, transferring apps between environments is not as straightforward as it should because the data source gets linked to each environment's database connection.

Getting ready

In this recipe, we will discover a solution to make the transfer process easier with PowerShell's help. The required script is available at our GitHub repository located at `https://github.com/PacktPublishing/Microsoft-Power-Apps-Cookbook/tree/master/Chapter10`

PowerShell

Starting with Windows 7 SP1, Windows PowerShell comes preinstalled with Windows, but there is also a newer version called PowerShell Core, which is multiplatform and is available on Windows, macOS, and Linux. For more information on how to install it, please refer to `https://docs.microsoft.com/en-us/powershell/scripting/install/installing-powershell?view=powershell-7.1`

Notice that PowerShell has an execution policy to invoke scripts. Use the following command for a quick bypass:

```
Set-ExecutionPolicy -ExecutionPolicy Bypass
```

For more information regarding these policies, please visit `https:/go.microsoft.com/fwlink/?LinkID=135170`

Azure SQL databases

For this scenario, we will need two databases: one for the development environment and another for the production environment. To help you build the required databases, you can follow this quickstart: `https://docs.microsoft.com/en-us/azure/azure-sql/database/single-database-create-quickstart?tabs=azure-portal`. Be sure to select to use sample data when creating the databases.

How to do it

To demonstrate the use of this recipe, first, provision the Azure SQL databases. For simplicity, we will assume these names: `devDatabase` and `proDatabase`.

We will also need two environments: `Development` and `Production`. If you already have these environments, you can skip to the *Building the app* section.

Creating the environments

1. Go to the Power Platform admin center by opening this URL: `https://admin.powerplatform.microsoft.com` or `https://aka.ms/ppac` for short. Once in the admin center, select **Environments** on the left panel.

2. From the toolbar, click **New** and, on the panel that opens on the right, enter `Development` for **Name**. For **Type**, choose **Sandbox** and then select a **Region** closer to your location. Leave **Purpose** as the default and leave the **Create a database for this environment?** option unchecked. Click **Save** when finished.

3. Repeat *step 2*, but set **Name** as `Production` and **Type** as **Production**.

Building the app

1. Go to the Power Apps portal, `https://make.powerapps.com/`, and make sure you are on the **Development** environment by using the **Environment** selector located near the end of the **Power Apps** toolbar.

2. On the home page, click on **SQL Server** in the **Start from data** section.

3. On the **Connections** page, click on **New connection**. Look for **SQL Server** in the list located on the left and then choose **SQL Server Authentication** from the **Authentication Type** selector on the right pane.

    Enter the configuration parameters gathered from when you created the development database, devDatabase, as seen in the following screenshot:

Figure 10.22 – SQL Server parameters

Click **Create** when finished.

4. When the new connector gets configured, a list of tables will appear on the right. Select **SalesLT.Customer** and click on **Connect**. Power Apps Studio will create the application from the table structure.

> **Bad Data Source error**
>
> If you encounter this error, remove the current connector and disable **Enhanced Microsoft SQL Connector** by going to **File | Settings | Advanced settings**. After making this change, you can re-add the Azure SQL connection to the app.

5. Click on **File | Save** and give the app a name like `Azure SQL Solution`. Click on the **Save** button and then click on **Close** on the left pane. Close the browser tab.

Exporting the app

1. Back in the Power Apps portal, click on **Apps** on the left pane and look for the **Azure SQL Solution** app we just created. Click on the ellipsis next to it and select **Export package**.

2. On the **Export package** page, enter `Azure SQL Solution` for **Name** and click on the wrench icon next to the **App** resource and select **Create as new** on the panel that opens on the right. Hit **Save** afterward.

    Click **Export** and download the application package to a folder on your device.

3. On the left panel, expand **Data** and select **Connections**. Look for the Azure SQL connection used to create the app and click on its name to open the details page. Grab the connection ID from the browser's address bar located near the end of the URL, as seen in the following screenshot:

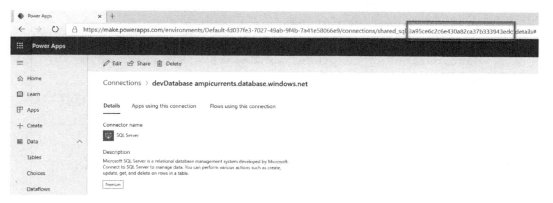

Figure 10.23 – Azure SQL connection ID

Keep this ID somewhere safe as we are going to use it for the package transformation process.

4. Using the **Environment** selector located at the Power Apps portal screen's upper right, change to the **Production** environment.

5. On the left panel, expand **Data** and select **Connections**. Click on **New connection** on the toolbar and click on **SQL Server** on the list. On the dialog that opens, choose **SQL Server Authentication** as the **Authentication Type** and enter the configuration parameters gathered from when you created the production database, `proDatabase`, and then click **Create**.

6. Click on the name of the newly created connection from the list to open its detail page. From the browser's address bar, grab the connection ID located near the URL's end, as we did in *step 3*. Keep this ID as well, to perform the package transformation.

Transforming the exported package

1. Get the PowerShell script from our GitHub repository in the same folder of the downloaded package.

   Using Windows File Explorer, go to this folder and, using the menu, click on **File | Open Windows PowerShell**.

2. Invoke the script by using the configuration properties and the connection IDs gathered from the previous steps. The following is an example of the script invocation:

```
.\SQLMigrator.ps1 `
-fileName .\AzureSQLSolution.zip `
-sourceServer devServer.database.windows.net `
-sourceDatabase devDatabase `
-sourceConnectionID 3a95ce6c2c6e430a82ca37b333943edc `
-destinationServer proServer.database.windows.net `
-destinationDatabase proDatabase `
-destinationConnectionID 1196004e99734f52ac5794eac172333f
```

> **PowerShell backtick**
> Using the backtick symbol (`) allows writing the commands using multiple lines. It improves readability on scripts that require many or too-long parameters.

Enter the corresponding parameters and then press *Enter*.

3. When the script finishes, a new file will appear with the `-migrated` suffix.

4. Go back to the Power Apps portal and make sure you are in the **Production** environment. On the left pane, click on **Apps** and then click on the toolbar's **Import canvas app** button. Click on **Upload** and browse to select the `migrated` version of the package.

5. When the **Import package** page opens, click on the wrench icon next to the **SQL Server Connection** resource and, on the pane that opens on the right, select the production connection and click on **Save**. Click on **Import** when finished.

6. When the platform completes the import, an **Open app** link will appear in the **Next steps ...** section. Click on it to open the app.

    Since this will be the first time you open the app, you will get prompted to consent to the Azure SQL connector's use.

7. Go to the **Data sources** pane on the left (represented by a database icon) and verify that the application now uses the destination database by hovering over the connection as seen in the following screenshot:

Figure 10.24 – Production database connection

8. Click on the connection's ellipsis and select **Refresh**. If it refreshes successfully, the connection transformation process was a success.

9. Click on **File | Close** to end the Power App editing.

How it works

Using the provided script, you can change the connections included in the exported package. It takes care of the package configuration properties as well as the included Power App. It replaces the source connection configuration with the destination one.

The previous example transforms a simple application with just one database connection configured. Complex solutions tend to have multiple connections for each table or view used in the app. Manually changing them when transferring the app from different environments would be a tedious task.

You can use this technique not only in different environments of the same tenant, but you can also transfer one app you've been building in your organization for an external third party. Each time you complete a milestone, export the app, execute the script on the package, and install it to your client's environment.

Renaming files in SharePoint document libraries

SharePoint is the ideal choice for document classification systems. This platform provides a standard set of metadata properties while allowing us to create custom properties to improve data categorization.

As an example, let's take a document library that will hold company contracts. We can enhance this library by adding extra columns such as the contractor's name, the contract expiration date, and the department that requested this contract. Besides using this information for ordering and classification, you can also act on this data:

- Build a Power Automate cloud flow that sends a Teams notification to a department channel warning them about an expiring contract.

- Design dashboards based on this data to gain insight into the number of contracts per contractor or which department is requesting more contracts.

- Create a Power App to request more data while on the go. This app can even gather signatures for these contracts.

Through this book, we have seen several recipes that handle SharePoint metadata in many ways using Power Automate. However, a particular metadata property is not editable by default: the filename.

Let's focus now on this example: At the end of the year, you need to send contracts to an attorney who uses a legacy platform to handle the company's legal issues. If you extract these documents from SharePoint, you might lose some metadata.

In this recipe, we will change the names of the files inside the Contracts document library to prepare them for extraction, giving them meaningful names from the stored metadata.

Getting ready

The Power Automate cloud flow created in this recipe, as well as some sample files and code, are available in our GitHub repository located at `https://github.com/PacktPublishing/Microsoft-Power-Apps-Cookbook/tree/master/Chapter10`

How to do it

Let's build this recipe by creating the SharePoint document library and then creating the Power Automate cloud flow.

Creating the SharePoint document library

1. Go to your desired SharePoint site, click on the gear icon located at the top right, and then select **Site contents**.

2. From the toolbar, click on **New | Document library**. On the pane that opens on the right, enter Contracts for **Name**, leave **Description** empty, uncheck **Show in site navigation**, and click on **Create**.

3. In the new library, click on the **Add column** indicator at the end of the column titles. From the dropdown, select the column type, fill in the required properties on the pane that opens on the right, and then click **Save**. Add each of the following columns:

Column name	Column data type
Contract number	Single line of text
Reference	Single line of text
Expiration	Date and time

Figure 10.25 – Contracts library columns

4. Reorder the columns by dragging them to get the desired order.

5. From the toolbar, click on **+ New | Folder**. On the dialog that opens, enter AMPI Currents and click **Create**. Click on the name of this folder in the document library to open it.

    Upload some sample files to this folder using the **Upload** button on the toolbar or by dragging them from the **File Explorer** to this document library. You can use the sample files provided from our GitHub repository.

6. Update the column data of these files using test data. For easier updates, click on **Edit in grid view** from the toolbar to edit data in bulk. The **AMPI Currents** folder should look similar to the following:

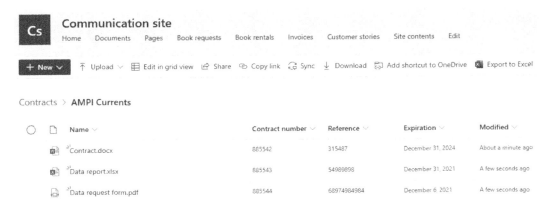

Figure 10.26 – AMPI Currents folder inside the Contracts library

Now that we have created the document library, let's build the cloud flow.

Building the cloud flow

1. Go to the Power Automate portal, `http://powerautomate.microsoft.com/`, and from the left pane, select **+ Create**. Click on **Instant cloud flow**, enter `Process Contracts` for **Flow name**, select **For a select item** under **SharePoint**, and click on **Create**.

2. On the trigger action, open the dropdown on **Site Address** and select **Enter custom value**. Enter `No data` and press *Enter*. Repeat the same procedure for **List Name**.

Disconnected flow

We are doing this so the flow does not get linked to any list and therefore anyone could execute it from a selected item.

---

3. Click on **New step** and look for **Get files (properties only)** under **SharePoint**.

    For **Site Address**, select the site where your `Contracts` document library is located and then select it from the **Libray Name** dropdown.

    For the **Limit Entries to Folder** field, select **fileName** from the **Dynamic content** pane.

4. Click on **New step** and look for **Send an HTTP request to SharePoint** under **SharePoint**.

    Choose the same site as before for **Site Address**, select **PATCH** for **Method**, and for **URI**, enter the following code:

    ```
    _api/web/lists/getbytitle('Contracts')/items()
    ```

    Put the cursor between the last parentheses and select **ID** from the previous step using the **Dynamic content** pane. This action will automatically add an **Apply to each** action so it can process all files found in this document library.

    In the **Headers** section, enter If-Match for key and * as its value.

    In the **Body** section, enter the following code:

    ```
    {
    "FileLeafRef": "@{items('Apply_to_each')?['ID']}-@
    {items('Apply_to_each')?['Contractnumber']}-@
    {items('Apply_to_each')?['Reference']}-@
    {triggerBody()?['entity']?['fileName']}"
    }
    ```

    This action should look like the following screenshot:

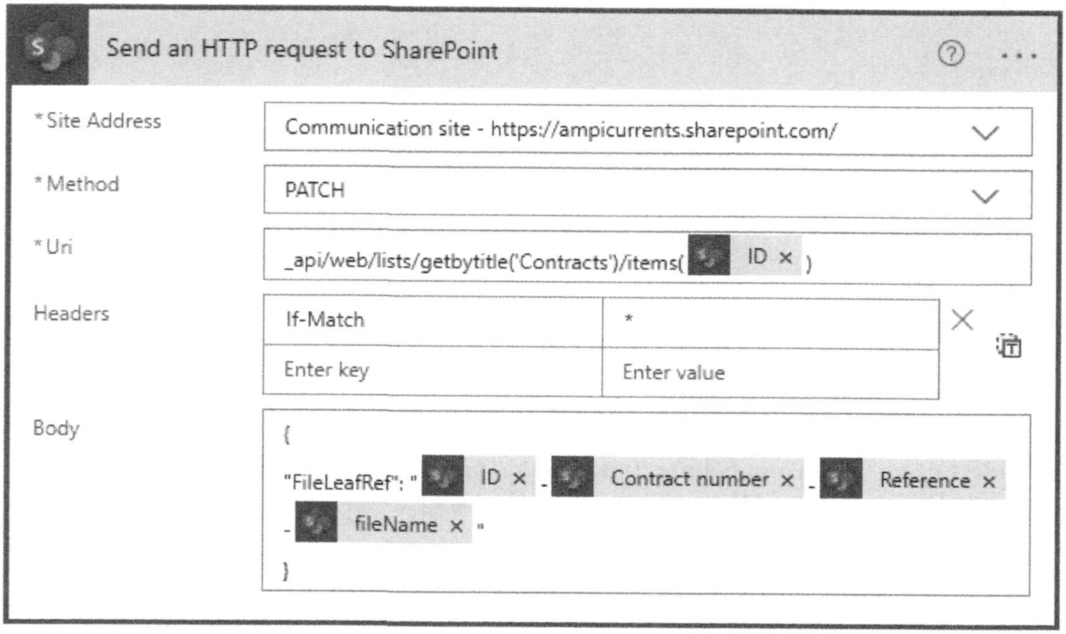

Figure 10.27 – HTTP request to SharePoint action

5. From the toolbar, click on **Save** and then click on the back arrow located on the left. Grab the cloud flow ID from the browser's address bar near the URL's end, just before the word `details`.

Configuring the document library

1. Go back to the **Contracts** document library on SharePoint. Click on the **Name** column, and select **Column settings | Format this column**.

    On the pane that opens on the right, click on the **Advanced mode** link near the bottom. Paste the contents of the `Column formatting.json` file, available from our GitHub repository. Look for the text `<FLOW_ID>` and replace it with the cloud flow ID collected in the previous step. When finished, click on **Save** and close this pane.

2. With the column format applied, the **Name** column will display a **Rename all** button next to each folder in this library, as seen in the following screenshot:

Figure 10.28 – Name column formatted

Let's discover how the complete solution works.

How it works

We have integrated a cloud flow into a document library to process all files' names inside subfolders using SharePoint column formatting. This solution will help recognize these files' metadata using their filenames whenever they get extracted from SharePoint.

Let's test this functionality by clicking on **Rename all** in the **AMPI Currents** subfolder. The first time you click on it, a right pane will ask for consent to use the SharePoint connector. Click on **Continue** to proceed to the confirmation to run the cloud flow. Click on **Run flow** to start it.

After a couple of seconds, open the **AMPI Currents** subfolder to view its contents. The filenames should have changed using the metadata gathered from the file ID, the **Contract number**, the **Reference** column, and the contractors' name as seen in the following screenshot:

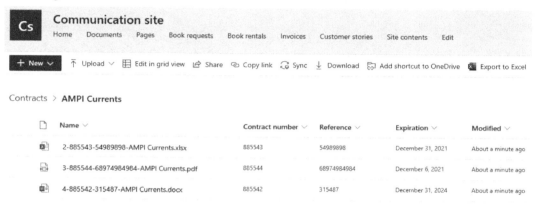

Figure 10.29 – Files' name changes

You can set the filename pattern by changing the **Body** section of **Send an HTTP request to SharePoint**.

Some things to notice:

- We used a custom **Site Address** and **List Name** for the trigger action, so you can't invoke this cloud flow from a selected item in the document library.

- The button only appears in subfolders of this document library by setting a **CSS** display property inside the JSON column formatting, like so:

```
"display": "=if([$File_x0020_Type] == ", 'inherit',
'none')"
```

SharePoint column formatting and view formatting are great tools to improve the views used in SharePoint. For more in-depth information about these features, please visit https://pnp.github.io/sp-dev-list-formatting/

11

Advanced Techniques with Power Apps Component Framework

Low-code platforms offer many possibilities for building applications focusing on easy-to-learn languages, ready-to-use solutions, and a robust backend to support almost all business requirements.

However, some specific scenarios might require a professional developer to solve a particular task. Thankfully, the Power Platform is open to these approaches as well, and that's why we can leverage the advanced techniques of professional development using the **Power Apps Component Framework (PCF)**.

This framework consists of code components that work just like regular Power Apps components. Using standard web technologies such as HTML, CSS, and TypeScript paired with an extensive set of framework APIs creates reusable components built in a single solution package. More information regarding these code components is provided here: `https://docs.microsoft.com/en-us/powerapps/developer/component-framework/custom-controls-overview`

Through a series of recipes, we will discover how to build a PCF solution that allows the use of Font Awesome resources inside your canvas apps. These recipes will work together to deliver a complete solution:

- Setting up your environments
- Configuring Font Awesome
- Creating the project
- Building the application logic
- Deploying the solution
- Testing the component on a canvas app

Technical requirements

When using PCF, the licensing requirements depend on the capabilities of the component. If it doesn't connect to external services or data sources, then it will only require a minimum license of Microsoft 365. On the other hand, connecting external services, including Dataverse for model-driven components, involves using a Power Apps license.

For more information, please refer to `https://docs.microsoft.com/en-us/powerapps/developer/component-framework/overview#licensing`

The complete code solution, as well as the canvas app using it, is available in our GitHub repository located at `https://github.com/PacktPublishing/Microsoft-Power-Apps-Cookbook/tree/master/Chapter11`

Setting up your environments

Building PCF components requires configuring your local development computer and, in the case of canvas apps, your Power Platform environments as well. These configurations involve the installation of specific tools to aid component lifecycle management.

The Power Apps **Command-Line Interface (CLI)** is the primary tool to prepare PCF's project structure, and it requires several tools to perform its tasks. This recipe will cover the detailed steps to prepare the Power Apps CLI installation by separating each tool's installation into different sections.

Getting ready

At the time of writing, the required tooling to build PCF projects is supported only on Windows 10.

When choosing a development tool to build these components, you have two options: **Visual Studio (version 2017 or later)** or **Visual Studio Code (VS Code)**. We do recommend using VS Code as it is a lightweight editor focused on web technologies.

Regarding the Power Platform environment, it needs to have a Dataverse database to be able to access the configuration settings to enable PCF use.

How to do it

Before creating the PCF component, we will dive into the detailed installation instructions to configure the complete development environment.

Node.js/npm

1. Go to the Node.js website, `https://nodejs.org/en/`, and look for the Windows download button with the **Long Term Release (LTS)** tag. As of today, the current version is **14.15.3 LTS**.

2. Once downloaded, execute the `.msi` file to begin the installation wizard.

    Click **Next** on each step, making sure that the npm package manager gets included in the installation. It gets included by default.

    Don't include **Tools for Native Modules** unless you want to, as we will not use them for our solution.

3. When the install process finishes, right-click on the **Start** menu, **Windows PowerShell | Windows PowerShell** to verify the Node.js/npm installation:

    Enter `node  -v` and press *Enter*. You should receive a message like **v14.15.3**.

    Enter `npm  -v` and press *Enter*. You should receive a message like **6.14.9**.

    These messages verify the correct installation of this tool. Keep in mind that these versions get updated over time.

.NET Framework 4.6.2

1. Navigate to `https://dotnet.microsoft.com/download/dotnet-framework/net462/` and click on the **Download .NET Framework 4.6.2 Developer Pack** button.

2. Once downloaded, execute the `.msi` file to begin the installation. Click on **Install** and when the process finishes, click on **Close**.

3. When the install process finishes, start **Windows PowerShell** to verify the .NET Framework installation:

    Enter the following sentence and press *Enter*:

    ```
    (Get-ItemProperty "HKLM:\SOFTWARE\Microsoft\NET Framework
    Setup\NDP\v4\Full").Release -ge 394802
    ```

    You should receive a **True** message validating the installation.

Editor – Visual Studio 2017 or later

If you plan to use this editor, we recommend using the 2019 edition as it is the latest version to date:

1. Navigate to `https://visualstudio.microsoft.com/downloads/` and click on the **Free download** button just below the **Community** section of the page. This action will initiate the download of the Visual Studio Installer. Once downloaded, run the executable.

2. The installer will download the required components, and then it will display the **Workloads** tab. Select **Node.js development**.

3. Go to the **Individual components** tab and, using the `Search components` field, enter `Nuget targets` and check this component to include it in the installation, as seen in the following screenshot:

Figure 11.1 – Individual components tab

4. Click on **Install** and wait for the installation process to complete.

Visual Studio will start automatically when the installation finishes.

Editor – Visual Studio Code

This editor is the preferred development tool to create PCF components:

1. Navigate to `https://dotnet.microsoft.com/download` as installing .NET Core is a requirement to use Visual Studio Code. Click on the **Download .NET Core SDK x64** button to get the installation package.

2. Once downloaded, run the executable. Click **Install** to begin the installation process. Click on **Close** when finished.

3. When the install process finishes, start **Windows PowerShell** to verify the .NET Core installation.

   Enter `dotnet --version` and press *Enter*. You should receive the **3.1.404** message.

4. Navigate to `https://code.visualstudio.com/Download` to get the Visual Studio Code installer. Click on the **Windows** button to download the installation package.

5. Once downloaded, run the executable. Click on **Next** on each screen of the installation wizard. On the **Select Additional Tasks** screen, we recommend checking all options in the **Other** section as they make VS Code easier to access from the system:

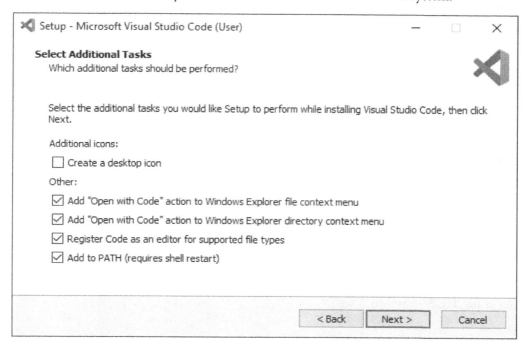

Figure 11.2 – Select Additional Tasks screen

Remember that If you choose this path, you need to install the build tasks using the Visual Studio Installer. Only follow *steps 1, 3*, and *4* from the *Editor – Visual Studio 2017 or later* section.

Power Apps CLI

1. Open the following address, `https://aka.ms/PowerAppsCLI`, to download the CLI installer.

2. Once downloaded, execute the `.msi` file to begin the installation. Click on **Install** and when the process finishes, click on **Finish.**

3. When the install process completes, start Windows PowerShell to verify the .NET Core installation.

   Enter `pac` and press *Enter*. You should be able to see the **Microsoft PowerApps CLI** usage options.

Configuring the Power Platform environment

1. Go to the Power Platform admin center by opening this URL: `https://admin.powerplatform.microsoft.com` or `https://aka.ms/ppac` for short.

2. From the list of **Environments**, click on the name of the one that will use the PCF component to open its details page.

3. From the toolbar, click on **Settings** and then expand the **Product** section to click on **Features**.

   On this page, enable the **Allow publishing of canvas apps with code components** option and click **Save.**

How it works

All the tools installed using this recipe play a different role in the PCF building process:

- npm manages the modules needed for this tooling
- .NET Framework and .NET Core help with the application building
- Visual Studio / VS Code serves as a full-fledged code editor

Keep in mind that all program versions noted in this recipe might change on updates, except for .NET Framework 4.62.

There's more

Whether you choose to work with Visual Studio or Visual Studio Code, you will always need to install the Microsoft Build Tools. Besides using the Visual Studio Community installer, there is also a lightweight version available here: `https://aka.ms/vs/16/release/vs_buildtools.exe`

These tools are only available when you invoke a **Developer Command Prompt for VS 2019** from the **Start** menu on Windows 10. To allow access through the whole system, you can add the location of these tools to the global system path by following these steps:

1. Right-click the **Start** menu icon and select **Run**. You can also use the keyboard shortcut *Win + R*.

2. Enter `sysdm.cpl` and click **OK**. When the **System Properties** dialog opens, go to the **Advanced** tab and click on **Environment Variables…**.

3. In the **System variables** section, look for **Path** and click **Edit…**.

4. On the **Edit environment variable** dialog, click on **New** and enter the following path:

   ```
   C:\Program Files (x86)\Microsoft Visual Studio\2019\
   Community\MSBuild\Current\Bin
   ```

   If you used the lightweight version installer of the build tools, then the path should be the following:

   ```
   C:\Program Files (x86)\Microsoft Visual Studio\2019\
   BuildTools\MSBuild\Current\Bin
   ```

   To be safe, you can also click on **Browse…** to navigate to the folder path. Click **OK** when finished and then click **OK** on all remaining dialogs.

You can now invoke the `msbuild` command-line tool from any console in your system. This solution is useful when using it from the integrated console in VS Code.

Configuring Font Awesome

Font Awesome is a well-known service among web developers for providing a massive variety of icons and social logos for websites around the world.

This service provides users with **Kits** to use its features. You can use different Kits for each web project as they act as a container to set different configurations on each.

Among the highlights of this service, we can find the following:

- A **content delivery network** (**CDN**) for faster delivery of assets to use in your solutions
- Domain-level security to limit which sites can use your Kits
- The ability to create icon subsets to only load the icons you need for your project

How to do it

1. Navigate to the Font Awesome website, https://fontawesome.com/, and click on the **Start for Free** button.

2. On this page, you will need to enter your email account to create your first Kit. Once entered, click on **Send Kit code** and wait for the confirmation email to arrive in your inbox.

3. When the email arrives, click on the confirmation message that will send you to the Font Awesome website to configure your password. Set it and continue until you reach the **How to Use** section of your first Kit, as seen in the following screenshot:

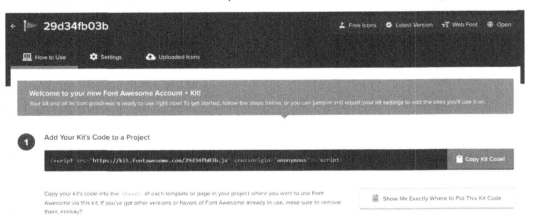

Figure 11.3 – Font Awesome Kit configuration

4. Keep the URL of this Kit in a safe place as we will need to use it as a parameter of our PCF component. In the previous screenshot, the URL inside the src is as follows:

```
https://kit.fontawesome.com/29d34fb03b.js
```

This completes the account configuration and the creation of your Kit.

How it works

The Kit provides a great solution to configure the service to the requirements of each project. Using the **Settings** tab, you can complete the Kit's configuration, such as its name, the pricing tier, and the allowed domains, among other options.

Using this approach, you can configure your solution using just the Kit's URL. Later on, you can make changes to your Kit without redeploying modifications to your project.

Creating the project

When working with PCF, the Power Apps CLI is responsible for creating your component's project structure. It also manages the project's packaging into a solution to deploy it on the Power Platform environments.

This command-line tool also performs other tasks, such as the following:

- Managing plug-in projects, which harness the event framework of Dataverse
- Handling authentication to deploy solutions to the Power Platform environments directly from the command line

Please refer to the official documentation to discover these and other functionalities: `https://docs.microsoft.com/en-us/powerapps/developer/data-platform/powerapps-cli#common-commands`

Explanation and overview

Once we have the project's structure in place, we need to configure the manifest. This file defines your component by describing its metadata with information such as the name, version, properties, or required resources.

For a detailed reference on this file, please refer to `https://docs.microsoft.com/en-us/powerapps/developer/component-framework/manifest-schema-reference/manifest`

Let's continue building the project structure for our PCF component and configure the project's manifest. Even though we will mention how to start creating the component using Visual Studio, we will continue the recipe using VS Code as it is the ideal editor for this type of project.

How to do it

1. Open the **Start** menu on Windows 10, and from the list of programs, expand **Windows System** and click on **Command Prompt**.

2. From this console, navigate to the desired path for your project. For this recipe, we will use the following path:

    *   Move to the root of the drive by entering CD \ and pressing *Enter*.

    *   Create the repos folder and the FontAwesomePCF subfolder by entering MD repos\FontAwesomePCF and pressing *Enter*.

    *   Enter the FontAwesomePCF folder by entering CD repos\FontAwesomePCF and pressing *Enter*.

3. Let's build the project structure using the Power Apps CLI using the following command:

    ```
    pac pcf init --namespace AMPICurrents --name
    FontAwesomeComponent --template field
    ```

    > **Namespace**
    > This term refers to a logical container to hold identifiers of this component.

4. Once we receive the successful project creation message, we need to install the external modules issuing the npm install command and then press *Enter*.

    You will receive a series of console messages, including warnings, which are safe to ignore.

5. When the installation completes, open the project with your editor of choice:

    Visual Studio: Open the folder by clicking on **File | Open | Folder…** and continue the code editing from there. You will need to keep the console open to issue the required commands.

    VS Code: Enter the code . command on the console to open the editor in the current folder. You can close the Command Prompt console as we will continue using Visual Studio Code's internal terminal.

    > **Development editor**
    > The rest of the chapter will continue using Visual Studio Code.

6. Using the **Explorer** pane on the left, locate `ControlManifest.Input.xml` inside the `FontAwesomeComponent` subfolder and open it.

Locate all code comments and remove them. The representation of these comments are blocks that start with <!-- and end with -->.

Locate the `control` tag and change the `description-key` attribute to Font Awesome loader.

Locate the `external-service-usage` tag and change the `enabled` attribute to false.

Find the `property` tag and change it to the following:

```
<property name="FontAwesome_KitURL" display-name-
key="FontAwesome_KitURL_Display_Key" description-
key="FontAwesome_KitURL_Desc_Key" of-type="SingleLine.
URL" usage="bound" required="true" />
```

With the preceding changes, the complete manifest should look like the following:

```
<?xml version="1.0" encoding="utf-8" ?>
<manifest>
  <control namespace="AMPICurrents"
  constructor="FontAwesomeComponent" version="0.0.1"
  display-name-key="FontAwesomeComponent" description-
  key=" Font Awesome loader" control-type="standard">
    <external-service-usage enabled="false">
    </external-service-usage>
    <property name="FontAwesome_KitURL" display-name-
    key="FontAwesome_KitURL_Display_Key" description-
    key="FontAwesome_KitURL_Desc_Key" of-
    type="SingleLine.URL" usage="bound" required="true"
    />
    <resources>
      <code path="index.ts" order="1"/>
    </resources>
  </control>
</manifest>
```

7. On the menu, click on **File | Save** or use the shortcut keys *Ctrl + S*.

How it works

As you can see, the Power Apps CLI takes care of creating the project's skeleton, leveraging the rest of the tooling to complete the body by installing all the required modules.

The manifest file acts as the control center by defining the capabilities and interaction of this component:

- Changing the `external-service-usage` tag to `false` allows the platform to acknowledge that this component will not use external services or data sources, thus labeling it as a non-premium component.

- The `property` tag indicates that we are going to receive parameters for this component. In this case, the Font Awesome's Kit URL.

- The *Resources* section specifies all resource files that the component will use, such as code, images, or CSS styles.

Building the application logic

Now that we have the project structure and manifest configuration completed, we can start building the application logic in the provided code resource file: `index.ts`.

This file will be the component's entry point and will be in charge of the control initialization, event handling, and control removal.

How to do it

1. From the menu, click on **Terminal | New terminal**. This action will open the integrated PowerShell console of Visual Studio Code.

2. From this integrated console, enter `npm run build` and press *Enter*. This command will execute the build process of the component, including the manifest configuration.

3. Using the **Explorer** pane, expand **FontAwesomeComponent** and double-click the `index.ts` file to open it.

4. Enter the following code just below the `export class` sentence:

```
private _URL: string;
```

5. Find the `init` function and enter the following code between the curly brackets:

```
this._URL = context.parameters.FontAwesome_Kit
URL.formatted ? context.parameters.FontAwesome_KitURL.
formatted : "";

// Create the request for the Font Awesome Kit
var script = document.createElement("script");
script.id = "FontAwesomeKit";
script.type = "text/javascript";
script.crossOrigin = "anonymous";

// val is the default when debugging
if (this._URL.length > 0 && this._URL != "val") {
  script.src = this._URL;
}

document.getElementsByTagName("head")[0].
appendChild(script);
```

6. Look for the `updateView` function and replace the contents between the curly brackets with this code:

```
this._URL = context.parameters.FontAwesome_Kit
URL.formatted ? context.parameters.FontAwesome_KitURL.
formatted : "";

if (this._URL.length > 0 && this._URL != "val") {
  // We get the previously created link element
  var script = <HTMLScriptElement>document.getElementById
  ("FontAwesomeKit");
  script.src = this._URL;
}
```

7. Save the file by pressing *Ctrl + S*.

8. From this integrated console, enter `npm run build` and press *Enter*. Once the code compilation process completes, enter `npm start` and press *Enter*.

    This command will invoke the PCF test environment in a browser window, as seen in the following screenshot:

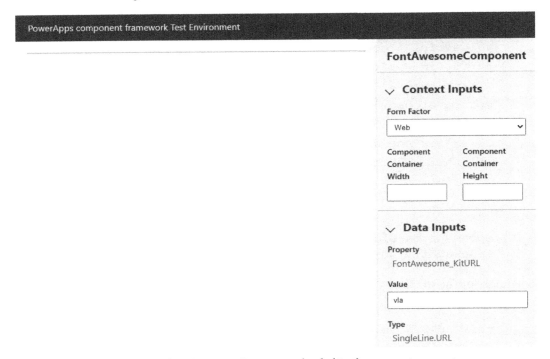

Figure 11.4 – FontAwesomeComponent loaded in the test environment

9. Go back to Visual Studio Code, and from the integrated console, press *Ctrl + C* to stop the debugging session by confirming that you want to **Terminate the batch job**. Close the browser window.

How it works

Through this recipe, we have completed the required application logic to load the Font Awesome script inside our code component.

From the `index.ts` file, we will use the following:

*   The `init` function to create the placeholder for the script embedding in the header section of the web page serving the component. As Power Apps runs on a browser, it is also considered a web app.

- The `updateView` function will trigger when the Font Awesome Kit's URL value gets entered in the `FontAwesome_KitURL` property.

This technique uses the script to load Font Awesome elements inside the app using the PCF component.

One important thing to notice is that every modification of the manifest file will require a code compilation using `npm run build` to make the elements of this configuration file available in our code. An example would be, the use of the `FontAwesome_KitURL` property in the `updateView` function as `context.parameters.FontAwesome_KitURL`.

We also discovered how to use the test environment to debug our code component. This environment allows the loading of the code components to see how they will react when deployed to a Power App using the manifest's properties.

Deploying the solution

When your project's development and testing phase is complete, you can now package it and ship it as a solution. The Power Apps CLI can help you create a solution from this project and even deploy it to the desired environment.

In this recipe, we will create the solution package using the CLI and then deploy it to our Dataverse environment.

How to do it

First, let's configure and build the solution package and then import it using the Power Apps portal.

Building the solution

1. Using the integrated console, create a subfolder to hold the solution components by entering the following command: `MD FontAwesomeSolution`. Once created, navigate to this subfolder by entering `CD FontAwesomeSolution`.

2. Execute the `pac solution init --publisher-name AMPICurrents --publisher-prefix apc` command to build the solution structure.

3. Enter the `pac solution add-reference --path ..` command to add a reference to our code component.

4. From the **Explorer** pane, navigate to **FontAwesomeSolution | src | Other** and double-click to open the `Solution.xml` file.

5. Change the `LocalizedName` of the `SolutionManifest` from `FontAwesomeSolution` to `Font Awesome Solution`. Press *Ctrl + S* to save this file.

6. Back in the integrated console, execute the `msbuild /t:restore` command to build the package and then `msbuild` to build the solution.

7. You will find the solution package in the `FontAwesomeSolution\bin\debug` subfolder.

Deploying to the environment

1. Go to the Power Apps portal, `https://make.powerapps.com/`, and from the left pane, click on **Solutions**.

2. From the toolbar, click on **Import**. On the pane that opens on the right, click on **Browse** and navigate to select the solution package deployed in the previous section. Click on **Next** and then on **Import** to start this process.

3. After a couple of seconds, **Font Awesome Solution** should appear in the list of **Solutions**.

How it works

Just as when creating a solution in the Power Apps portal, you will need to define the publisher and its prefix, and they need to be unique in your environment. The next step would be to add an existing component, and that's what the `add-reference` command is doing.

MSBuild completes this process by doing precisely what the export solution does in the portal, creating a package to deploy it to an environment.

As you can see, the Power Apps CLI is a great alternative when performing manual tasks in the portal. It can be an essential tool when automating development processes or applying **Application Lifecycle Management** (**ALM**) to our projects.

Now let's test this PCF component on a canvas app.

Testing the component on a canvas app

This is the final step of our deployment process: import the PCF component to a canvas app and verify the result. We will do this by creating an app from scratch.

How to do it

1. Go to the Power Apps portal, `https://make.powerapps.com/`, and from the home page, click on **Canvas app from blank**.

2. On the dialog that opens, enter `Font Awesome Test` for **App name** and keep the **Tablet** format.

3. Once the Studio opens, from the **Insert** toolbar at the top, click on **Custom | Import component**.

   On the pane that opens on the right, look for the **Code** tab at the top and select it. From the list of elements to import, you should see **FontAwesomeComponent** in the list, as seen in the following screenshot:

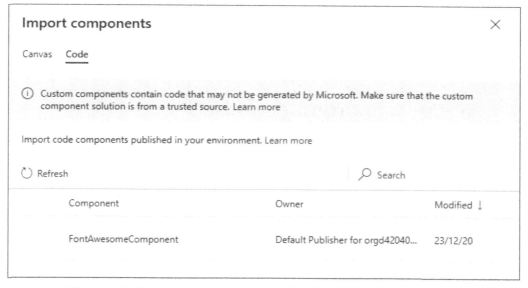

Figure 11.5 – FontAwesomeComponent under the Code Component section

   Select it and click on **Import**.

4. From the **Insert** panel on the left, you should now see a new section called **Code components**. Expand it and click on **FontAwesomeComponent**.

5. Once added to the canvas, select it and, using the formula bar, set the `FontAwesome_KitURL` property to your Kit's URL, as per our example, `"https://kit.fontawesome.com/29d34fb03b.js"`.

6. From the **Insert** panel on the left, expand **Display** and click on **HTML text**. Set its properties as follows:

    Using the **Properties** pane on the right, change **Font size** to 64, **Width** to 120, and **Height** to 140.

    Using the formula bar, set the **X** property to (App.Width - Self.Width) / 2, **Y** to (App.Height - Self.Height) / 2 - 60, **Color** to RGBA(50, 86, 160, 1), and **HTMLText** to the following:

    ```
    "<i class='fas fa-robot '></i>"
    ```

    Notice the extra space after the icon name. Name this control RobotHtml.

7. Back in the **Insert** panel, expand **Display** and click on **HTML text**. Set its properties as follows:

    Using the **Properties** pane on the right, change **Font** to **Segoe UI**, **Font size** to 24, **Width** to 390, and **Height** to 64.

    Using the formula bar, set the **X** property to (App.Width - Self.Width) / 2, **Y** to (App.Height - Self.Height) / 2 + 20, **Color** to RGBA(130, 141, 158, 1), and **HTMLText** to the following:

    ```
    "<i class='fas fa-hand-point-right '></i> Welcome to our
    app <i class='fas fa-hand-point-left '></i>"
    ```

    Name this control WelcomeHtml.

    The completed application should look like the following:

Figure 11.6 – Canvas app using Font Awesome icons

8. From the menu, click on **File | Save** and then on the **Save** button at the screen's lower right. From the left pane, click on **Close**.

How it works

The PCF component works without a user interface. It's a code-only component that helps load the script required to use Font Awesome icons in Power Apps.

As the embedding acts at the head level of the web page's document element, it becomes available to all controls using the provided classes. This is when the HTML text control becomes handy as it can handle HTML code to render its content.

For more information, please refer to the official documentation regarding the process of building a code component at `https://docs.microsoft.com/en-us/powerapps/developer/component-framework/create-custom-controls-using-pcf`

There's more

Code components are also available for model-driven apps to improve the rendering of elements in forms, dashboards, and views.

As an added resource, please visit the PCF gallery, `https://pcf.gallery/`, for a massive collection of PCF components created by the community to extend canvas and model-driven apps.

Other Books You May Enjoy

If you enjoyed this book, you may be interested in these other books by Packt:

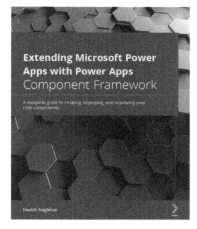

Extending Microsoft Power Apps with Power Apps Component Framework

Danish Naglekar

ISBN: 978-1-80056-491-6

- Understand the fundamentals of Power Apps Component Framework
- Explore the tools that make it easy to build code components
- Build code components for both a field and a dataset
- Debug using test harness and Fiddler
- Implement caching techniques
- Find out how to work with the Common Data Service Web API
- Get to grips with using React and Fluent UI controls
- Discover deployment strategies

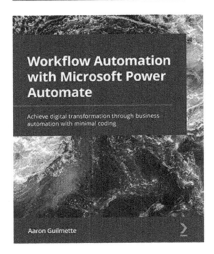

Workflow Automation with Microsoft Power Automate

Aaron Guilmette

ISBN: 978-1-83921-379-3

- Get to grips with the building blocks of Power Automate, its services, and core capabilities
- Explore connectors in Power Automate to automate email workflows
- Discover how to create a flow for copying files between two cloud services
- Understand the business process, connectors, and actions for creating approval flows
- Use flows to save responses submitted to a database through Microsoft Forms
- Find out how to integrate Power Automate with Microsoft Teams

Leave a review - let other readers know what you think

Please share your thoughts on this book with others by leaving a review on the site that you bought it from. If you purchased the book from Amazon, please leave us an honest review on this book's Amazon page. This is vital so that other potential readers can see and use your unbiased opinion to make purchasing decisions, we can understand what our customers think about our products, and our authors can see your feedback on the title that they have worked with Packt to create. It will only take a few minutes of your time, but is valuable to other potential customers, our authors, and Packt. Thank you!

Index

Made in the USA
Middletown, DE
09 June 2022